VCs of the First World War

GALLIPOLI

STEPHEN SNELLING

WRENS
PARK

A Sutton Publishing Book

This book was first published in 1995 by
Alan Sutton Publishing, an imprint of Sutton Publishing Limited
Phoenix Mill · Thrupp · Stroud · Gloucestershire GL5 2BU

This edition first published in 1999 by Wrens Park Publishing, an imprint of
W.J. Williams & Son Ltd

A catalogue record for this book is available from the British Library

ISBN 0-905-778-332

Typeset in 10/13pt Sabon.
Typesetting and origination by
Sutton Publishing Limited.
Printed in Great Britain by
Redwood Books Limited,
Trowbridge, Wiltshire.

CONTENTS

ACKNOWLEDGEMENTS

Just as it is now difficult to recall the precise beginnings of this book, so it is almost impossible to know where to start in thanking all those who made it possible. To pay tribute to all who assisted by name would be to run the risk of an appreciation of Hollywood Oscar ceremony proportions. I am indebted to all those librarians, museum curators, relatives and regimental secretaries who have helped me throughout my odyssey, and I hope they will forgive me if I single out for especial thanks the late Canon William Lummis, the doyen of VC researchers, whose enthusiasm did so much to fuel my interest.

The research for this book has spanned four years and two continents. In this country, my chief guides have included Nigel Steel, of the Department of Documents at the Imperial War Museum, who has pointed me in the right direction on countless occasions as well as acting as a most reliable sounding board, and Peter Liddle, whose outstanding collection of personal testimonies is now housed at Leeds University. Mr Liddle has been most generous in granting me access to his own research, while Dennis Pillinger, the Military Historical Society's Custodian of the Lummis VC Files, has been a tireless worker on my behalf.

My research on the Australian VCs owes much to the kind help of Anthony Staunton, whose own works on the subject are justly acclaimed by fellow military historians. H. Murray Hamilton allowed me to use extracts from the personal diaries of Fred Tubb VC which will form the basis for his own eagerly awaited biography of this gallant Australian soldier.

Closer to home, I must thank my friends Frank Gordon and Nolan Lincoln for their help and guidance, while the support of Gerald Gliddon, author of two books in this series, and Alan Sutton Publishing Limited, has been invaluable.

But my greatest debt must be to my family; my ever-supportive wife Sandra and my long-suffering daughters Katie and Holly, who, over four years, have come to accept my grand obsession with extraordinary equanimity. It is to them that I dedicate this book.

PICTURE CREDITS

ABBREVIATIONS

AA & QMG	Assistant Adjutant & Quartermaster-General
AB	Able-bodied (seaman)
ADC	Aide-de-camp
AIF	Australian Imperial Force
CB	Companion of (the Order of) the Bath
CMG	Companion of (the Order of) St Michael and St George
CMS	Church Missionary Society
CO	Commanding Officer
CRA	Officer Commanding Royal Artillery
CSM	Company Sergeant-Major
DCM	Distinguished Conduct Medal
DSC	Distinguished Service Cross
DSO	(Companion of the) Distinguished Service Order
GHQ	General Headquarters
GOC	General Officer Commanding
GSO	General Staff Officer
HE	High explosive
IWM	Imperial War Museum
KCIE	Knight Commander of the Order of the Indian Empire
KCMG	Knight Commander of the Order of St Michael and St George
KOSB	King's Own Scottish Borderers
LG	London Gazette
NCO	Non-commissioned officer
NTO	Naval Transport Officer
NZ	New Zealand
OC	Officer Commanding
OTC	Officers Training Corps
PNTO	Principal Naval Transport Officer
PO	Petty Officer
PRO	Public Record Office
QMG	Quartermaster-General
RA	Royal Artillery
RAF	Royal Air Force
RHQ	Regimental Headquarters
RM	Royal Marines

RMA	Royal Military Academy (Sandhurst)
RMC	Royal Military College
RMLI	Royal Marine Light Infantry
RNAS	Royal Naval Air Service
RND	Royal Naval Division
RNR	Royal Naval Reserve
RNVR	Royal Naval Volunteer Reserve
RSF	Royal Scots Fusiliers
SHAEF	Supreme Headquarters Allied Expeditionary Force
TA	Territorial Army
TBD	Torpedo boat/destroyers
VC	Victoria Cross

INTRODUCTION

In the 137 years since the Victoria Cross (VC) was instituted as the nation's premier reward for valour, 1,353 men have been awarded the distinction. Almost half that number were earned during the First World War, and of the 633 men so honoured 39 were presented for deeds of gallantry performed during the operations designed to wrest control of the Dardanelles from the Turks. Although small by comparison to the number of Crosses awarded for acts of bravery on the Western Front, this total represents the highest number of VCs won in a 'sideshow' theatre during the First World War.

What began, in February 1915, as a purely naval enterprise became, after 18 March, a full-scale, Anglo-French invasion. The landings on the Gallipoli Peninsula on 25 April 1915 represented the greatest amphibious operation carried out by any of the belligerents during the course of the war. The campaign, which promised so much and which was filled with countless examples of squandered heroism, ultimately became a tragedy of lost opportunities. With the benefit of hindsight, the operations can be divided into a number of distinct phases: the naval operations (February–March), the battle for the beaches (April), the consolidation (April–May), the first major offensive (June), the new landings at Suvla (August), the last great offensive (August), stagnation (September–December), the evacuation (December–January, 1916). The eight-month campaign on the peninsula would eventually swallow up 410,000 British Empire troops. Of this number, 43,000 were killed, died from wounds or disease, or were posted missing. By January 1916, when the last men were taken off the peninsula, the casualty list, including the sick, totalled 205,000. By any reckoning, the campaign had proved a costly failure. Yet it was a failure relieved, in part, by the stoicism displayed by the front-line soldiers. At Anzac that fortitude became enshrined in Australian folklore. But no less remarkable were the fighting records of their New Zealand comrades and the men of the 29th Division who came through one trial after another with their numbers depleted but their spirit undaunted.

To the 'incomparable 29th' fell the honour of winning more VCs than any other division on the peninsula. Thirteen VCs went to the division which was charged with the critical task of carrying out the main landing on 25 April. Six were won by a single battalion. The 'Six VCs before breakfast' won by the men of the 1st Lancashire Fusiliers was only one fewer than the record seven given to the 2/24th Foot (South Wales Borderers) for their heroic defence of the mission station at Rorke's Drift during the Zulu War of 1879.

The Gallipoli operations threw up a number of records of their own. The four VCs won by crew members of the *River Clyde* on 25 April was the highest number given to a single ship's company for one action. During the course of the First World War no other unit exceeded the six VCs won in a single day by the 1st Lancashire Fusiliers. The closest any unit came to beating it was when the 7th Battalion, Australian Imperial Force, won four during the bitter fighting at Lone Pine, Gallipoli, on 8–9 August 1915. Among the 'VC firsts' the campaign can lay claim to are the war's first Australian VC, first New Zealand VC and first Royal Marine VC.

Of the thirty-nine Victoria Crosses, eleven went to the Royal Navy (including two to submariners, two to the Royal Naval Division and one to a Royal Naval Air Service pilot) and twenty-eight to the Army. The latter consisted of eighteen awards to units of the British Army, nine to Australians and one to a New Zealander. Eleven of the VCs were posthumous awards, although only seven of this number were awarded to men who were killed or died from wounds received in the actions for which the Cross was earned. And of the twenty-eight who survived the campaign, a further three did not survive the war.

The most distinguished VC winner of the campaign was Lt. Col. C.H.M. Doughty-Wylie, CB, CMG, a 46-year-old soldier-diplomat attached to Sir Ian Hamilton's Staff as an intelligence officer. There were two instances of VC winners receiving a second gallantry award for their services on the peninsula: A.J. Shout (1st Bn, AIF) and P.H. Hansen (6th Bn, Lincolnshire Regt.) both won Military Crosses. The campaign's oldest recipient of the VC was Cdr. E. Unwin, captain of the *River Clyde*, who was 51 at the time of his exploits on V Beach, Cape Helles. He became the second-oldest naval VC of the First World War. The youngest VC winner of the campaign was Midshipman W. Malleson, who was 18 years old when he won his award. 2nd Lt. G.R.D. Moor was only a month older when he won his six weeks later during the Third Battle of Krithia.

In keeping with the democratic traditions of the VC, the recipients ranged in rank from humble privates to a lieutenant colonel. Of the thirty-nine awards, twenty-two were given to officers, ten to NCOs, and seven to privates or naval ratings.

The impact of the awards on the recipients themselves varied markedly. Albert Jacka became a national hero in his native Australia and the exploits of 'Dick' Doughty-Wylie and the submariner Martin Nasmith acquired legendary status in the hands of the popular Press. For some, such as William Dunstan and Herbert James, the sudden elevation from private obscurity to public adulation was almost as painful as the VC actions themselves. The mere presence of the letters VC after their names, however, ensured that none of the recipients could ever entirely escape public attention.

That the VC was not necessarily a passport to success in the post-war world was reflected in the lives of the Gallipoli Campaign's surviving recipients. Of the professional servicemen among their ranks, five reached high rank in their respective services. Sqn. Cdr. Richard Bell Davies became the first rear-admiral of Naval Air Stations, Lt. Cdr. Martin Nasmith became an admiral and C.-in-C. Plymouth and Western Approaches, Lt. Cdr. Edward Boyle achieved the rank of rear-admiral, Lt. Cdr. Eric Robinson was promoted rear-admiral on the Navy's Retired List and Capt. Percy Hansen, who was to add a Distinguished Service Order to the VC and MC won on the peninsula, served as a brigadier during the Second World War. Of the remainder, probably the most successful was William Dunstan, a man of immense modesty who never talked about his VC. He rose from office clerk to become one of the top-ranking executives in the Murdoch newspaper empire.

In stark contrast were the fortunes of William Forshaw, Albert Jacka and Hugo Throssell, who all endured business failure. Saddest of all was the case of Throssell, who committed suicide in the hope that it would result in a pension to his family. Jacka, arguably the most celebrated of all the Gallipoli VCs, became mayor of St Kilda, in Victoria, but died aged 39, not long after the collapse of his business. Richard Willis, one of the six Lancashire Fusiliers to win the VC, was another to suffer financial hardship. In old age, he was reduced to writing a begging letter to the Press appealing for £100 because of his 'desperate need'. For others, it could fairly be said that the suffering endured on the peninsula did not cease with the end of the war. When William Cosgrove died, aged 47, in 1936, it was discovered that splinters of shrapnel which had not been removed following his VC action at Gallipoli had been slowly poisoning him. Similarly, Walter Parker, the Royal Marine VC, never fully recovered from the injuries he sustained in winning his award at Anzac. He died four months after Cosgrove, fighting in vain for a disability pension.

To the majority of the thirty-nine VC winners, the acts of valour performed on the battlefields of the Gallipoli Peninsula or in the waters of the Dardanelles marked the zenith of their military careers and, for some, their whole lives.

Their experience was probably best summed up by Leonard Keysor, the London-born Australian bomb-thrower of Lone Pine fame, who once confessed: 'The war was the only adventure I ever had'.

E.G. ROBINSON

Near Yeni Shehr, 26 February 1915

Lt. Cdr. E.G. Robinson

It was a beautiful spring day in the Dardanelles on 19 February 1915. The wintry storms of the past two weeks had subsided, giving way to clear skies and calm seas. To Vice-Admiral Sir Sackville Carden, commanding the Royal Navy's Eastern Mediterranean Squadron, the break in the weather could scarcely have been more opportune. After weeks of careful planning, his ships' crews were ready and waiting for the order to begin a naval offensive designed to force a way through the heavily-defended straits separating Europe from Asia. The objective, the fulfilment of the First Lord of the Admiralty Winston Churchill's grand ambition, was to open up a vital new supply route to Russia and isolate Germany and Austria-Hungary by driving Turkey out of the war.

Now, at last, the moment had arrived. At 7.30 a.m. advance units of the fleet, consisting of two destroyers and a seaplane, headed for the mouth of the Dardanelles. The reaction of the Turkish defences was swift and uncompromising. At precisely 7.58 a.m. one of two 9.4-in guns sited in No. 4 Orkanieh battery, dug in along the Asiatic shore less than five miles from the ruins of ancient Troy, opened fire. The first shot of the Dardanelles campaign fell harmlessly between the two destroyers. However, it set in train a series of events which would culminate in the first Victoria Cross action of the operations. By mid-morning Carden was ready to begin the task of destroying the outer forts guarding the entrance of the straits. The 12-in. guns of the pre-Dreadnaught HMS *Cornwallis* heralded the Allied offensive. She was followed, in turn, by HMS *Vengeance*, flying the flag of Carden's second-in-command, Rear-Admiral Sir John de Robeck. Their fire was directed on to the Orkanieh battery, sited between the strategically important fortifications at Kum Kale and Yeni Shehr, a village dominated by a ridge crowned with a line of distinctive white windmills.

The bombardment continued fitfully until sunset, with disappointing results. A fire was seen to break out behind the battery and one direct hit on the

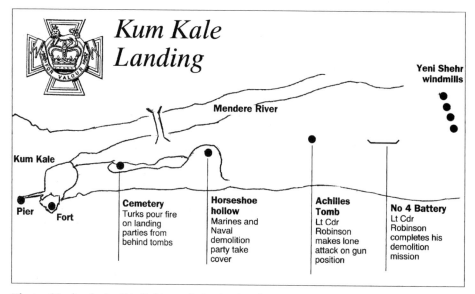

The course taken by Lt. Cdr. Robinson during his demolition operation on 26 February 1915

emplacements made the Turkish gun crews 'run like blazes'. Yet, when the *Vengeance* turned her attentions to the Helles batteries, on the European shore, she came under renewed fire from the guns at Orkanieh, leaving her masts and decks peppered with splinters.

Bad weather returned to delay the resumption of the assault, but when Carden's battleships reappeared on 25 February they came fully armed with the experience gained from the first day's ineffectual action. Anchoring out of range of the shore defences, they began the task of pounding the forts at Helles, Kum Kale and Orkanieh into submission. The Orkanieh battery was silenced by a succession of crushing salvoes delivered by the battleships *Irresistible*, *Cornwallis* and *Vengeance*. One gun was dislodged from its mountings, while the other was thought to have been seriously damaged.

The following day, while returning from an unsuccessful foray against the intermediate forts, inside the Dardanelles, de Robeck decided to complete the destruction of the guns in the ruined forts by landing a naval demolition party with a covering force of Royal Marines. The operation was launched shortly after 2.00 p.m. on 26 February. In command of the demolition party was Lt. Cdr. Eric Gascoigne Robinson, *Vengeance*'s torpedo officer and explosives expert. A highly experienced officer, unaccountably known to his friends as 'Kipper' Robinson, he was a veteran of the Naval Relief Expedition in China during the Boxer Rising of 1900.

His orders were to destroy any serviceable guns in the vicinity of Kum Kale and Orkanieh, a dangerous mission, rendered even more hazardous, by the lack of information concerning the strength or dispositions of the Turks. Robinson's force consisted of fifty seamen, the majority of whom were needed to carry the gun-cotton charges, and a protection party of fifty Royal Marines, commanded by Maj. Granville Heriot, DSO. They landed unopposed and, by 2.30 p.m., under the watchful eyes of senior officers on the bridge of HMS *Vengeance*, had set about their allotted task. From Kum Kale, they followed the line of the Mendere River as it flowed past a cemetery and then took the road south-west towards a rise known as Achilles Mound. Beyond it lay the Orkanieh battery and Yeni Shehr. Between the cemetery, with its sun-bleached tombs, and the mound, the ground fell away sharply into a horseshoe-shaped depression. The movements of the raiding parties were clearly visible to the men aboard the ships. One of the *Vengeance*'s officers later recalled:

> We saw them go past the cemetery, up to the semi-circular hollow, and they then signalled that they were attacked: so *Dublin* fired a salvo at Yeni Shehr mills, which downed three mills and stopped the enemy's fire from there. We also gave Yeni Shehr a few rounds: however, the Marines still remained in the hollow firing fairly hard. It appears they were attacked from Mendere on their left flank, and from hidden snipers in the cemetery; also, till the guns stopped them, by a large force from Yeni Shehr . . .

With his line of retreat threatened by an unknown number of Turks and the way forward hotly contested, Robinson could justifiably have abandoned the operation there and then and attempted to extricate his small party. Instead, he pressed on towards Achilles Mound. An eyewitness from the *Vengeance* recorded:

> When halfway up the slope (under fire all the time from Yeni Shehr) Robinson's party stopped and took cover, with the exception of one who went up to Achilles Mound, where the *Vengeance*'s shells had earlier disclosed two Turkish anti-aircraft guns nearby, got inside the sort of crater at the top, walked calmly down again and, when he was just clear, we saw an explosion, and up went both anti-aircraft guns.

The lone figure, whose actions were plainly visible to friend and foe alike, was Eric Robinson. With resistance stiffening and not knowing whether or not the gun sites were manned, he had decided to put only his own life at risk. Leaving his party under the command of his young aide, Midshipman John B. Woolley, he advanced over the lip of the Achilles position. Fortuitously, it was unoccupied.

Robinson in action

He coolly placed a gun-cotton charge on the guns and lit a slow match fuse allowing himself just sufficient time to escape the blast.

Not content with this success, or perhaps heartened by it, he decided to capitalize on the crushing impact of the *Dublin's* salvo directed at Yeni Shehr by leading a small portion of his force against the left-hand 9.4-in gun which remained in the Orkanieh battery. Once more Robinson sought to minimize the danger to his men, but on this occasion his attempt to repeat his single-handed exploit was made impossible by the weight of the charge needed to complete the gun's destruction. With a small party, he led a dash into the battery site which was also unoccupied and they were able to destroy the weapon.

Robinson's superiors, including Admiral Carden's young Chief of Staff, Cdre. Roger Keyes, watched his actions in awe. The *Vengeance's* commander, Capt. Bertram Smith, later recalled:

We had been watching Eric Robinson . . . strolling around by himself . . . under heavy rifle fire from the neighbouring rise, like a sparrow enjoying a bath from a garden hose, until the *Dublin* turned the hose off with some nicely placed salvoes. He and his party and escort were returning to the boats, while the Admiral and I were happily arranging our recommend [sic] for his VC when a fresh turmoil started all around them.

They had now passed out of sight in the trees of Kum Kale cemetery and none of us could see what was happening.

At length, they got a signal through to say they were held up with the main body of the enemy in a large domed tomb. The control could see the tomb and I could just distinguish its top when they put me on. It was invisible at the guns, but I was able to note its whereabouts in the treetops, and went down to let off a 6-inch lyddite. The range was short and the range-finder laid it exactly, so the first round sent the tomb and fragments of its inmates, both ancient and modern, flying heavenwards. Using the burst as a starting point there was no difficulty in taking the guns on to any other target to get our people clear.

The Marines, however, did not escape unscathed. During the fire fight, Sgt. Ernest Turnbull was killed and three men, Cpl. Harold Charlwood, Pte. Frank Toms and Pte. George Mardle, wounded.

In the words of the future Lord Keyes, it had been 'a very pretty little fight'. Assessed alongside a similar operation mounted against the Helles guns, Robinson's commando-style raid achieved, in the opinion of the Official Historian, 'a flattering measure of success'. The results of the mission on the Asiatic shore, however, remain difficult to accurately gauge. The Official Historian credited Robinson with the destruction of the remaining gun in the Orkanieh battery and two anti-aircraft guns on Achilles Mound. Yet Keyes, in recommending Robinson for his VC, referred only to his 'most gallant act in pushing in alone [sic] into Fort IV [Orkanieh] and destroying a 9.4 inch gun, which he found loaded and undamaged'. Whatever the true tally, there was no disputing the great courage displayed by Robinson. In a footnote to Keyes' recommendation, Admiral Carden wrote: 'This was a specially brave act, giving most valuable practical results'. As the naval operations in the straits gathered momentum, Robinson added to his growing reputation as one of the most daring officers in the fleet. A naval colleague, Lt. Cdr. Charles Brodie, described his 'imperturbable' friend as 'the foremost of Keyes' thrusters'.

During the dangerous minesweeping operations carried out in the build-up to the main naval assault, Robinson earned more praise for his coolness and skill in command of one of the converted trawlers. His 'press on regardless' spirit was displayed most notably on the night of 13/14 March when his unarmoured vessel was struck no fewer than eighty-four times by the Turkish shore batteries. A month later his consistent valour was crowned by a spectacular exploit which ranks alongside the Royal Navy's most gallant enterprises.

The mission, to destroy the British submarine E15 which had run aground under the very noses of the Turkish guns at Fort Dardanus, took place on the night of 18–19 April. Disabled by shore batteries, the stranded submarine was viewed as a great propaganda prize by the Turks. Battleships, destroyers and submarines were all sent in vain to attempt her destruction. Finally, Admiral de Robeck, apparently on the advice of Keyes, sanctioned an attack by two steam picket boats, manned by volunteer crews from the battleships *Majestic* and *Triumph*. Such was Robinson's reputation and experience gained in this narrow stretch of water, he was personally chosen by the admiral to lead what many considered a 'forlorn hope'. Indeed, following the failure of an attempt by the destroyer, HMS *Scorpion*, the risks involved were thought sufficiently grave for an appeal to be made to abandon the operation.

Brodie, who was Keyes' assistant, was convinced that a further submarine attack offered the best chance of getting through to torpedo the E15. He later wrote:

> I felt equally certain the picket boats would never see her, and lacking the speed, to say nothing of the luck, of the *Scorpion* would be sitting targets. 'Robbie' was an old friend of myself and many other submarine officers, and I was sick at heart at the thought of him being sacrificed so unnecessarily. I wanted the Rear Admiral to stop, at least to postpone the operation, but he naturally thought Keyes' opinion might be better than mine, and would not cancel movements already initiated . . . The picket boat attack bore out Roger Keyes' belief that sailors could achieve the impossible if well enough led.

In the face of terrible fire and dazzling searchlights, Robinson led the torpedo attack aboard the *Triumph*'s boat. Steering straight for Kephez, he held his course until, blinded by a searchlight at close range, he was compelled to take a chance. He fired his first torpedo, and turned away. At that moment the searchlights momentarily lifted, leaving the E15 clearly silhouetted. The midshipman commander of the *Majestic*'s boat immediately fired both of his torpedoes. At least one ran true and hit the crippled submarine, but the shore batteries bracketed his boat, scoring a mortal blow. Despite the heavy fire, Robinson brought his boat alongside and, in the full glare of the Turkish searchlights, rescued all the survivors. There was a tense moment during the rescue when Robinson's second torpedo was accidentally half-released. But eventually the sole-surviving picket boat was able to pull out of range of the guns. Robinson, uncertain of his mission's success, reported 'one possible hit'. Subsequently, however, it was learned that the operation had achieved its objective. An ecstatic Keyes wrote:

> They simply blew E15 onto her beam quite destroying her – they were only a few hundred yards from Fort 8 [Dardanus] – and any number of guns opened

fire. They were only 300 to 500 yards from the beach. We have asked for Robinson's promotion at once – he ought to get a VC for the 26th Feb.

The attack on the E15 was so courageously executed that it is sometimes cited as one of the actions for which Robinson was awarded the Victoria Cross. It was not, however, as Keyes' letter underlines, though Brodie was not alone in believing his friend merited another VC for his leadership that night. Keyes' recommendation, based on Robinson's exploits at the Orkanieh battery and in the minefields off Kephez Point the following month, was sent off on 1 April. For his courage in leading the picket boats on the night of 18/9 April, an operation that many felt dwarfed even his earlier exploits, Robinson would have to be satisfied with promotion to the rank of commander. Every other member of the picket boats' crews was decorated, including Robinson's faithful midshipman from the Orkanieh episode. John Woolley, who accompanied him aboard the *Triumph*'s boat, received a Distinguished Service Cross. Six days after the destruction of the E15, Keyes wrote: 'I am honestly lost in admiration for Robinson, he has done splendidly & I honestly am surprised. I did not think much of him as a First Lieutenant. But that evidently does not prevent him being an exceedingly brave man.'

When the naval assault gave way to land operations on the peninsula, Robinson spent some time at Kephalo, on the island of Imbros, one of the main bases for the Gallipoli operations. He was hurriedly sent by Keyes to take over the post of Naval Transport Officer at the Anzac beach head on 5 August. 'I wanted the man to be gallant and stout-hearted so I sent Commander Robinson', wrote Keyes. His appointment, however, proved a short one, barely twenty-four hours long. Keyes explained the sudden move back to Kephalo: 'Robinson was wanted for an important job in the new landing and I was anxious to get him and his midshipman he always takes about with him back.' Any hopes of adding to his exploits were, however, curtailed the following morning, 7 August, when Robinson was, in Keyes' words, 'badly wounded, not dangerously', during the landings at Suvla Bay.

Nine days later, the *London Gazette* announced the award of his Victoria Cross. The citation stated:

Lieut Commander Robinson on the 26th February advanced alone, under heavy fire, into an enemy's gun position, which might well have been occupied, and, destroying a four-inch gun, returned to his party for another charge with which the second gun was destroyed. Lieut Commander Robinson would not allow members of his demolition party to accompany him, as their white uniforms rendered them very conspicuous. Lieut Commander Robinson took part in four attacks on the minefields always under heavy fire.

Cdr. Robinson, his promotion having been confirmed, received his Victoria Cross from George V at Buckingham Palace on 5 October. He did not return to the Dardanelles and while his career continued to flourish he was presented with fewer opportunities to display his distinctive brand of inspiring leadership.

Eric Gascoigne Robinson, a Britannia term-mate of two future Admirals of the Fleet, Cunningham and Somerville, was born on 16 May 1882, into a naval family – his father John Lovell Robinson MA, was Chaplain of the Royal Naval College, Greenwich. He went to sea in 1898 and two years later received his baptism of fire, and his first wound, in China when as a midshipman he marched in Admiral Seymour's Peking Relief Expedition.

Promoted lieutenant on 15 August 1903, he became a torpedo specialist and served with the submarine depot ship *Thames* before joining HMS *Vengeance*. Shortly before the outbreak of war, Robinson married Edith Gladys Cordeux.

After his work in the Dardanelles, Robinson served in the Eastern Mediterranean in command of the monitor M21, operating along the Palestine coast. His services were recognized by the award of the Order of the Nile in 1917 and a mention in dispatches.

During the Allies' war of intervention against the Bolsheviks, Robinson achieved further distinction. As the commander of a small force of Coastal Motor Boats, he helped the Royal Navy gain mastery of the Caspian Sea. On one occasion, during a reconnaisance of Fort Alexandrovsk in May 1919, Robinson led his CMBs into the Bolshevik-held harbour and sank a barge before a hastily raised white flag signalled the port's surrender. His post-war adventures earned him the Russian Order of St Anne and he was also made an officer of the recently created Order of the British Empire. On 31 December 1920 his distinguished war services culminated in promotion to the rank of captain.

Between the wars Robinson held a number of sea- and land-based appointments. His last post, before retirement in 1933 with the rank of rear-admiral on the Retired List, was as captain of Devonport Dockyard. Recalled to active service in 1939, he served as a convoy commodore until ill-health forced his second retirement in 1941. He lived out the last twenty-five years of his life in Langrish, near Petersfield, Hampshire, where his public services continued as a church warden, member of the parochial church council and an elected member of Petersfield Rural Council.

Admiral Eric Gascoigne Robinson died at Haslar Naval Hospital on 20 August 1965, and was buried in St John's churchyard, Langrish. Today, an altar frontal in the village church commemorates the man whose name became a byword for courage among the crews of the East Mediterranean Squadron during the dark days of 1915.

F.E. STUBBS, W. KENEALLY,
C. BROMLEY, A. RICHARDS,
R.R. WILLIS AND J.E. GRIMSHAW
W Beach, Cape Helles, 25 April 1915

W Beach, a small sandy cove flanked by steep cliffs lying between Tekke Burnu and Cape Helles, was one of three beaches which formed the main landing zone for the 29th Division on 25 April 1915. It represented a formidable obstacle to the covering force, the 86th Fusilier Brigade spearheaded by the 1st Battalion, Lancashire Fusiliers, whose orders were to seize the beach and link up with the units landing at X Beach to the north and V Beach to the east.

In the five weeks following the abortive naval assault of 18 March, Turkish engineers toiled to turn the beach at Tekke Burnu into a mini-fortress. A belt of wire, three rows deep, stretched almost the entire length of the 350-yd strip of sand. Submerged trip wires were laid just beyond the water's edge and crude, but effective, land mines were sown on the shoreline. The beach, which varied in depth from 15 to 40 yd, was covered by three short trenches; one on each cliff and a third on the sandy rise which lay in the gully between them. This low ridge was in turn commanded by more Turkish positions to the north and south. According to British reports, the defences also included two machine-gun posts burrowed into the cliff faces ready to enfilade the main wire entanglements. Further inland, two wired-in redoubts were sited to halt any breakthrough in the direction of Hill 138, a Turkish position between W and V Beaches.

'So strong were the defences,' the Official Historian stated, 'that even though the garrison was but one company (3rd/26th Regt.) of infantry, the Turks may well have considered them impregnable to an attack from open boats.'

The 1st Lancashire Fusiliers, commanded by Maj. H.O. Bishop, were under no illusions about the immensity of the task confronting them. Reconnaissances had clearly revealed the Turkish state of readiness. Furthermore, they knew that the element of surprise, so critical in such a hazardous operation as an opposed amphibious landing, would not be on their side.

At about 6.00 a.m. on 25 April 1915, following a 45-minute-long naval bombardment, the landing operations began at W and X Beaches. Off Tekke Burnu, six groups, each consisting of four ship's cutters towed by a picket boat, drew away from HMS *Euryalus* and headed for the shore in line abreast at 50-yd

Cpl. J.E. Grimshaw, Sgt. F.E. Stubbs and Capt. C. Bromley

Capt. R.R. Willis

Sgt. A. Richards in 1915 with his VC

Pte. W. Keneally

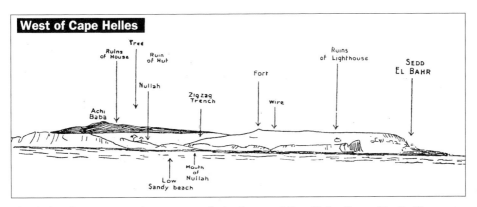

Sketch plan showing W Beach, approximately 1 mile west of Cape Helles (Lancashire Fusiliers Annual)

intervals. Crammed in the boats were 672 soldiers. They had been there for ninety minutes, watching the sun rise above the cliffs and waiting for the order to go. All were heavily laden with full kits, including three days' rations and 200 rounds of ammunition. On the right, A and B Companies, commanded by captains Richard Haworth and Harold Shaw, together with the battalion's machine-gun section, were to rush the cliff-top trenches and drive inland towards Hill 138 which they had orders to capture. C Company, commanded by Capt. Richard Willis, on their left, was faced with the task of piercing the barbed wire entanglements and capturing the Turkish trenches guarding the centre and left-hand sectors of the beach. They were then to advance towards Hill 114, where they were to link up with units from X Beach. Two platoons from D Company were to accompany Willis' company as reserves and they would be joined by two tows, from HMS *Implacable*, carrying the remainder of D Company together with Headquarters Company, including Maj. Bishop and the adjutant, Capt. Cuthbert Bromley.

At first all appeared to go smoothly. Capt. Willis later recalled:

The sea was like glass, but as the picket boats drew off to get into formation our boats heeled over dangerously, and one of the men remarked to the cox, 'I 'listed to get killed, not to get drowned . . .'

As the tows got to a safe distance from the ships the shelling began again, the guns lifting their fire as we approached the shore. When the water began to get shallow the picket boats called out 'Slip', for the tow ropes to be cast off, and we began to approach the shore under the oars of the naval ratings. There were five to each boat.

Not a sign of life was to be seen on the Peninsula in front of us. It might have been a deserted land we were nearing in our little boats. Then crack! The stroke oar of my boat fell forward, to the angry astonishment of his mates. The signal for the massacre had been given: rapid fire, machine guns and deadly accurate sniping opened from the cliffs above, and soon the casualties included the rest of the crew and many men.

Years later, a former member of C Company who had been in the boat next to Capt. Willis, recorded:

I saw him stand up and everyone in the boats heard him, above the noise of the bullets and the guns, shout 'Come on, C Company! Remember Minden!' That was it. Whenever we were in trouble, whenever we looked like going under, the cry 'Remember Minden!' brought us back to our senses. Captain Willis could not have timed it better.

According to Willis:

The timing of the ambush was perfect; we were completely exposed and helpless in our slow-moving boats, just target practice for the concealed Turks, and within a few minutes only half of the thirty men in my boat were left alive. We were now 100 yards from the shore, and I gave the order 'Overboard'. We scrambled out into some four feet of water, and some of the boats with their cargo of dead and wounded floated away on the currents still under fire from the snipers. With this unpromising start the advance began. Many were hit in the sea, and no response was possible, for the enemy was in trenches well above our heads.

We toiled through the water towards the sandy beach, but here another trap was awaiting us, for the Turks had cunningly concealed a trip wire just below the surface of the water, and on the beach itself were a number of land mines, and a deep belt of rusty wire extended across the landing place. Machine-guns, hidden in caves at the end of the amphitheatre of cliffs enfiladed this.

Our wretched men were ordered to wait behind this wire for the wire-cutters to cut a pathway through. They were shot in helpless batches while they waited, and could not even use their rifles in retaliation since the sand and the sea had clogged their action. One Turkish sniper in particular took a heavy toll at very close range until I forced open the bolt of a rifle with the heel of my boot and closed his career with the first shot, but the heap of empty cartridges round him testified to the damage he had done.

Safety lay in movement, and isolated parties scrambled through the wire to cover. Among them was Sgt. Richards with a leg horribly twisted, but he managed somehow to get through.

'Six VCs Before Breakfast'. An artist's impression of W Beach landing, showing Capt. Willis, centre, with his walking stick

An astonishing sight was now seen: soldiers on the beach under close fire of the enemy getting out brushes and oil to clean their rifles, a job which would not have been necessary if the company commander's request for rifle covers had been listened to.

The troops on our left had landed at a more suitable spot, and suffered but little compared with us on the beach, and at length they made it possible for us to advance. Small parties pushed on, scrambled up the cliffs, and gained the heights known as Hill 114, but at the cost of many casualties, for the Turks were stubborn fighters.

They were remarkably good shots, and their grey uniform was hard to distinguish, especially as the water and sand made our glasses useless for about two hours.

My company, what was left of it, reached its first objective, but when I looked back I saw that a lot of men were still lying down below, behind the wire on the beach, apparently waiting for the word to advance. I ordered one of my company to signal down 'No enemy in sight', to bring them on, but he evidently thought I was mad, and signalled 'Enemy in sight' instead, whereupon L/Cpl. Grimshaw, who was near, laughingly threatened him with extra drill, and he gave the correct signal. But right or wrong, signals did not matter, for I suddenly realised those men would never advance again. They were all dead – four officers and seventy-five men fallen in one line as they came under the fire of the machine guns . . .

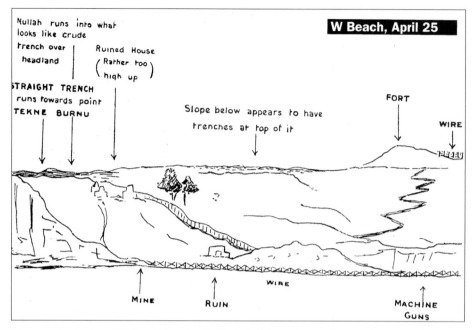

Close-up sketch plan of W Beach showing the Turkish defences (Lancashire Fusiliers Annual)

As Willis reported, disaster was only averted by the success of the northernmost landing parties. With the tows bearing down upon the beach strewn with dead, Brig. Steuart Hare and his brigade major, Capt. Thomas Frankland, stood up and, by hand signals and shouting, managed to divert a number of boats towards the left, where the beach was sheltered by the cliff. On landing, Brig. Hare and Capt. Frankland led a small party of men up the cliff. The men, weighed down by their 80-lb packs and ammunition, struggled to climb the final steeper section and for a few moments the leading group of officers and their orderlies were left to face a line of Turks 30 yd away, dug in on the clifftop. Taking a rifle from one of his men, Capt. Frankland shot three Turks in quick succession before the rest of the Lancashire Fusiliers scrambled to the top. The Turks fell back and Frankland made his way to the right-hand company to urge them to link up with the brigadier's party. He found there a willing accomplice in the adjutant, Capt. Bromley, a supremely powerful man who had once been a physical training instructor. Bromley appeared to be everywhere that morning; leading small leaderless parties forward, encouraging men to extra exertions and always he appeared oblivious to the enemy's fire.

At about 7.15 a.m. Brig. Hare was severely wounded while leading a reconnaissance in the direction of X Beach. By then the beach was being subjected to sporadic fire and Capt. Frankland, having assumed temporary command of the brigade, set about securing the right flank and pushing inland towards V Beach, from where there was no word. He found Capt. Haworth reorganizing the remnants of his double company.

Haworth's attempt to storm the right-hand cliff had been swept away by the explosion of what was initially thought to have been a Turkish mine, but was in fact a naval shell. Now with only fifty men, he was joined by twelve survivors from B Company's first wave and Capt. Thomas Cunliffe who, having been unable to land his machine guns, had swum ashore under a hail of bullets. Together with Frankland and Capt. Mynors Farmar, the brigade staff captain, this force set off under cover of the cliffs to attempt to take Hill 138 from the south. The attack, hindered by faulty maps, was halted by a belt of unbroken wire and it was here, at about 8.30 a.m., that the gallant Frankland was killed. As the party sheltered behind a low bank, any forward movement appeared doomed to failure.

It was then that Pte. William Keneally took matters into his own hands. He had already distinguished himself as a runner, delivering messages under heavy fire, and now he decided to risk almost certain death in an attempt to cut a way through the wire. Knowing that anyone raising their heads above the bank would attract a hail of fire, he crawled forward towards the wire. His efforts were all in vain, but the attempt was no less brave for that. Still more remarkably, Keneally returned unscathed.

Capt. Haworth and the survivors remained in their precarious position together with Capt. Farmar and the remnants of the brigade's headquarters staff until reinforcements arrived during the late afternoon, when the two redoubts were carried.

Elsewhere, all of the Lancashires' objectives had been gained, although at a terrible cost. The following morning the battalion mustered only 16 officers and 304 men out of a total of 27 officers and 1,002 men who embarked for Gallipoli. Capt. Willis' C Company had endured some of the heaviest fighting on the beach and during the capture of Hill 114. His company was reduced to four officers and 83 men. Among the survivors was L/Cpl. Grimshaw, a company signaller. His pack and water bottle were riddled by bullets and another shot had smashed his cap badge, but miraculously he was unharmed. Throughout the day he had remained cheerful and calm, frequently braving intense, close-range fire to send vital and coherent messages.

There were many similar examples of great courage. Sgt. Alfred Richards, mentioned in Willis' account of the landing, had scarcely reached the beach when a burst of fire almost severed his right leg. Realising that to remain behind the barbed wire was to court annihilation, he called on his men to follow him forward. Dragging his mutilated leg, he crawled through the wire and, despite the terrible pain, continued to shout encouragement as they advanced to assault the Turkish positions beyond. Another C Company NCO, Sgt. Frank Stubbs, displayed great leadership in urging men through the wire and on up the cliff. He was killed later in the morning as he led the way towards the crest of Hill 114, his company's final objective.

Of the officers, captains Willis, Bromley and Haworth had all shown outstanding gallantry and leadership. Bromley, who landed with Headquarters Company, perhaps did more than anyone to get the men through the wire and up the cliffs. L/Cpl. Grimshaw, who witnessed Bromley's tireless endeavours on W Beach, later stated: 'His personal example was unequalled by anyone. His bravery was superb, and he was admired by the whole battalion . . . He was one of the first men to reach the top of the cliff.'

On 15 May Maj.-Gen. Sir Aylmer Hunter-Weston (29th Div., GOC) wrote to GHQ: 'The landing is a deed of heroism that has seldom been equalled and I strongly recommend that the gallantry of the deed may be recognized by the bestowal of six VCs on the two most distinguished officers and the four most distinguished NCOs and men', namely captains C. Bromley and R.R. Willis, sergeants A. Richards and F.E. Stubbs, Cpl. J. Grimshaw and Pte. W. Keneally. The six had been nominated by the battalion's commanding officer, Maj. Bishop, after consulting 'the officers who happened to be with him at the time and who did not include either of the officers awarded the Cross'. Hunter-Weston stated:

> Their deeds of heroism took place under my own eyes . . . Where all did so marvellously it is difficult to discriminate, but the opinion of the battalion is that Bromley and Willis are the officers. and Stubbs, Richards, Grimshaw and Keneally are the NCOs and men to whom perhaps the greatest credit is due. As the representatives, therefore of the battalion, as well as for the deeds of great gallantry performed by themselves under my own eyes, I strongly recommend these officers, NCOs and men for the VC.

The recommendation was endorsed by the GOC, Sir Ian Hamilton, but it foundered amid War Office bureaucracy and the rules governing the award of the Victoria Cross. Not until August was the matter resolved, when a second recommendation was dispatched under Article 13 of the Victoria Cross warrant which allowed for the balloting of units for the award of up to four VCs. According to Hunter-Weston, a vote had been held among the surviving members of the battalion which resulted in Willis being selected by the officers, Richards by the NCOs and Keneally by the other ranks. The latter had wished to nominate Grimshaw in place of a second private, but this was not allowed and only three names went forward.

On 23 August 1915 the *London Gazette* announced:

The King has been pleased to award the Victoria Cross to the undermentioned officers, non-commissioned officers, and men in recognition of their most conspicuous bravery and devotion to duty in the field:

Captain Richard Raymond Willis,

No 1293, Sergeant Alfred Richards,

No 1809, Private William Keneally, all of the 1st Battalion Lancashire Fusiliers.

Their joint citation read:

On 25th April, 1915, three Companies and the Headquarters of the 1st Battalion Lancashire Fusiliers in effecting a landing on the Gallipoli Peninsula to the west of Cape Helles were met by a very deadly fire from hidden machine guns, which caused a great number of casualties. The survivors, however, rushed up to and cut the wire entanglements, notwithstanding a terrific fire from the enemy, and, after overcoming supreme difficulties, the cliffs were gained and position maintained. Amongst many very gallant officers and men engaged in this most hazardous enterprise, Captain Willis, Sergeant Richards and Private Keneally have been selected by their comrades as having performed most signal acts of bravery and devotion to duty.

Captain Haworth received a Distinguished Service Order and, in November, the *London Gazette* belatedly announced the award of a Distinguished Conduct Medal to L/Cpl. Grimshaw. However, matters did not rest there. Troubled by what he considered to be an injustice done to Bromley, Stubbs and Grimshaw, Brig. Owen Wolley-Dod, himself a Lancashire Fusilier who as Hunter-Weston's general staff officer had landed at W Beach shortly after noon on 25 April, continued to press for the case to be re-examined. His efforts were eventually crowned with success. On 15 March 1917 the *London Gazette* announced the award of VCs to all three men. The citation accompanying their awards was the same as that published for Willis, Richards and Keneally.

By this time Bromley was dead and Grimshaw, by then a sergeant, could scarcely believe the reports cancelling his DCM for a VC. He told a journalist: 'I thought you were joking . . . I remember at the time that a vote was taken but never expected to get the VC, especially as the DCM was given me.'

The heroes of Lancashire Landing, as W Beach became known, soon entered the war's popular mythology and have since become enshrined in British Army folklore as the 'Six VCs before breakfast'. As with so many sayings, it is not strictly accurate. For while the landing was indeed carried out at 'breakfast time', regimental records clearly state that the men ate their breakfast before disembarking from the *Euryalus*. Still less attention has been paid to the men who actually won the six VCs.

Frank Edward Stubbs was the only member of that gallant band to be killed during the battle for W Beach. A Londoner, he was born in Walworth, near the Kennington Oval, on 12 March 1888.

He enlisted as a boy soldier in London and served with the Lancashire Fusiliers in India. Sgt. Stubbs has no known grave and is commemorated on the Helles Memorial, one of 20,752 names carved on the tall, honey-coloured obelisk which overlooks the entrance to the Straits.

Stubbs never married and his mother received his Cross at a Buckingham Palace investiture in May 1917. Many years later, his elderly spinster sister sold the medal to the Regimental Museum at Bury for £300.

William Keneally was born at 38 Parnell Street, Wexford, in Ireland, on Boxing Day, 1886. He was one of five sons born to John Keneally, a colour sergeant in the Royal Irish Regiment. The family moved to Wigan, Lancashire, at the end of his father's military service. The journey proved an eventful one. The SS *Slavonia*

Keneally's grave, Gallipoli

18

was wrecked but the Keneally family, including four-year-old William, were all saved.

Educated at St John's School, Wigan, and St Oswald's School, Ashton-in-Makerfield, William joined the Low Green Collieries as a pit boy, aged thirteen. A prominent member of the local football team, he spent ten years in the mines before deciding to pursue a military career, like his father before him. In September 1909 he enlisted for seven years. All his service was spent with the 1st Battalion, Lancashire Fusiliers. Returning from India after the outbreak of war, he re-enlisted and spent four days leave at his parents' home in Stubshaw Cross.

Like the majority of men in his battalion, the landing at W Beach on 25 April 1915 represented his baptism of fire. Promoted lance corporal, Keneally survived the three battles of Krithia which decimated his unit. He was mortally wounded in the Battle for Gully Ravine on 28 June, when the battalion was commanded by Maj. Bromley, and died the following day. His grave is located in the Lancashire Landing Cemetery where his rank is given as lance sergeant, although there is no record of this promotion.

News of his death did not reach his family until October 1915, long after they had celebrated his Victoria Cross award and after plans had been made by the local council to honour him.

Cuthbert Bromley, the adjutant and later temporary commanding officer of the 1st Battalion, was widely recognized as one of the unit's most outstanding personalities.

He was born on 19 September 1878 at Sutton Corner, Seaford, in Sussex, the second son of Sir John and Lady Bromley. He entered St Paul's School, Barnes, in September 1890 and earned a reputation as an enthusiastic athlete and rower. School reports reveal his intended occupation to have been the 'medical or civil service'. However, his last report, in July 1895, was scarcely that of an outstanding scholar: 'Science: weak; fair worker. French: very moderate . . . General Remarks: good in Divinity and English, only moderate in other subjects.' Not surprisingly, Cuthbert Bromley, one of four brothers to be educated at St Paul's, decided against a medical or civil service career. Instead he chose the Army, gaining a commission in the Lancashire Fusiliers in May 1898, after serving a spell in a militia unit, the 3rd King's Liverpool Regiment.

Promoted lieutenant the same year, he was gazetted captain and volunteered for the West African Frontier Force in 1901. He saw a good deal of active service in Eastern Nigeria and qualified for the Aro Expedition clasp to his African General Service Medal. Bromley returned to the Lancashire Fusiliers, then stationed in India, and served as transport officer, before being appointed superintendent of Gymnasia in Ireland in 1906.

A man of immense physical strength – on one occasion he performed the notable feat of swimming from Malta to Gozo – he seemed well-suited to his new role, but he chose to rejoin the 1st Lancashire Fusiliers before his appointment expired. The Gymnasia's loss was evidently the Fusiliers' gain. According to Regimental records:

> His influence for vigorous endeavour in every form of competition work, sport or play, was extraordinary. Under his energy, skill, tact and powers of management the 1st Battalion became famous throughout India as the champions of Army football, boxing and cross-country running.

Bromley also made his mark in the social life of the battalion, where he was noted for writing comic verse.

Barely three months before the outbreak of war in August 1914 he was made adjutant of the battalion which had become his life. And such were his organizational abilities, that he was appointed ship's adjutant on the SS *Arcadian* during the 29th Division's passage to the Dardanelles.

Injured in the back during the landing at W Beach, Bromley refused to leave the unit until a bullet through his knee, sustained during the first advance on Krithia on 28 April, necessitated hospitalization. He returned to the battalion on 17 May, as soon as he was able to hobble, and his quiet, indomitable spirit helped lift the men to meet each new challenge. After the battalion had suffered heavy losses in the ill-fated Third Battle of Krithia on 4 June, he made a gallant attempt to save the wounded lying in no man's land. A truce was turned down, but permission was given for a party to go out under a Red Cross flag. On the morning of 6 June it was raised above the fusiliers' trench, but before the stretcher parties could move, shots were fired from a British battery. The Turks immediately replied. However, when the firing ceased, the flag was hoisted aloft again and the shooting stopped. The regimental annual stated:

> Captain Bromley bravely mounted the parapet and stood fully exposed in front of it. This action drew a spatter of bullets from the enemy's trenches which struck the parapet on either side of him, so he returned into the trenches. At 80 yards the Turks could hardly have missed him, but Bromley of his own initiative took the risk.

Promoted major, he took command of the battalion on 13 June when the CO fell ill, and he led the unit in his last action on the peninsula, the Battle of Gully Ravine, on 28 June.

Bromley delivered a stirring speech to his men before leading them over the top. Wounded in the heel early in the advance, he refused to leave. For a time, he struggled forward using two Turkish rifles as makeshift crutches. Later, he

C. Bromley, Seaford War Memorial

ordered two stretcher bearers to carry him. Eventually he was persuaded to go to hospital, but only after working through the night to consolidate his battalion's hard-won gains.

Evacuated to Egypt, he made a full recovery and as soon as he was able to walk begged his way aboard the troopship *Royal Edward* which was returning to the peninsula. But the 1,117-ton vessel never arrived. On 13 August, while crossing the Mediterranean, she was torpedoed and sunk by the German submarine UB-14 with the loss of 866 lives. Cuthbert Bromley was seen in the water but, according to eye-witnesses, was drowned when a boat rescuing survivors collided with him.

The Revd Oswin Creighton, chaplain of the 86th Brigade, wrote of him: 'He had an absolutely cool head and never seemed in the least perturbed or worried . . . In my opinion, he was one of the finest soldiers in the Division.'

Alfred Joseph Richards' part in the Gallipoli Campaign was as short-lived as it was distinguished. Wounded in the first rush, he was evacuated as soon as the beach was secured and did not return.

21

He was born on 21 June 1879 in Plymouth, Devon, one of six children, to Charles and Bridget Richards. It could almost be said that he was born into the Lancashire Fusiliers; his father had served twenty-one years with the 2nd Battalion, rising to the rank of colour sergeant.

A Catholic, Alfred Richards was educated at St Dominic's Priory School, near Byker Bridge, Newcastle. On 6 July 1895 he followed his father into the Lancashire Fusiliers as a bandboy, giving as his trade musician. He served with the 1st Battalion in Ireland and was appointed a full drummer. In 1899 the battalion embarked for Crete, where Richards undertook training as a mounted infantryman in the hope of being accepted for service in South Africa, where the conflict with the Boers was raging. He passed the course, but did not reach South Africa as he later noted: 'The Adjutant . . . kept me for my musical abilities, and made me Lance Corporal, my first step.'

The battalion's Mediterranean service continued, with spells at Malta, Gibraltar, and Alexandria in Egypt. During these years Richards gained a reputation as one of the battalion's best footballers and helped his team win the Gibraltar Garrison Cup in 1904. When the battalion returned to England in 1907, Richards, at the end of his period of engagement, took his discharge. He was still a lance corporal and his Army record referred to him as being 'of sober habits, intelligent, honest and hard-working'. Civilian life, however, did not appeal, and two months later, on 26 July 1907, he re-enlisted and was sent with a draft back to his old battalion which was then stationed in India. He remained there, serving at a variety of Army stations, until the outbreak of war. He later noted: 'We were very joyful at the news, and chance of at last seeing the real thing.' By then he was a sergeant serving in C Company, and it was with this company that he disembarked into HMS *Euryalus'* cutters for the landing at W Beach.

A month after sustaining his terrible wounds on the peninsula, surgeons in Egypt amputated his right leg above the knee. Evacuated to England, he was discharged from the Army on 31 July 1915, as 'being no longer fit for war service (but fit for civil employment)'. He had served twenty years and six days with the Colours, all of that time with the Lancashire Fusiliers, and had been awarded the Long Service and Good Conduct Medal.

He was living at the Princess Christian Soldiers' and Sailors' Home in Woking when news reached him of his VC award. He told journalists that he could remember little about the landing. Of his award, he said: 'I am proud to learn that my comrades chose me as one of three of the bravest, but we all did our duty even though luck may have helped some to more noticeable acts. I don't know how the vote was taken, but had it been a comrade selected instead of myself I should feel just as proud.' He ended on an optimistic note: 'I am going to fit myself for a new occupation. I have come here to learn carpentry.'

Newspapers referred to him as the 'Lonely VC'. His parents had emigrated to

Australia and two of his brothers were serving with the Anzacs. One newspaper account stated: 'Outside the regimental circle he has no friends in the world, no relatives to welcome him home, no townsmen to do him honour, though any city might be proud of him.'

In fact, he did not remain alone for long. A year after he received his Cross at Buckingham Palace 'looking very ill', he married Miss Dora Coombs at Weybridge on 30 September 1916. They had met while he was recovering from his wounds at a nearby hospital.

Throughout the remainder of his life he maintained strong ties with his old regiment. A leading member of the Southern Branch, Old Comrades

Sgt. A. Richards in later life

Association, he was also connected for many years with the Lord Roberts memorial scheme for the employment of disabled soldiers.

During the Second World War he joined the Home Guard and served as provost sergeant of the 28th County of London Battalion at Wandsworth. His son, Harold, saw service with the Queen's Royal West Surrey Regiment in Northern Europe and the Middle East.

Alfred Richards died at his home, 69 Astonville Street, Southfields, London, on 21 May 1953, after a short illness. He was seventy-three. At his funeral were survivors of the Gallipoli landings. He was buried in Putney Vale Cemetery and fourteen years later, when it was reported that his grave was in a neglected state, the trustees of the Lancashire Fusiliers paid for a new headstone carrying the regimental crest and inscription. His medals, consisting of the VC, 1914–15 Star, British War Medal, Victory Medal, Defence Medal (1939–45), Coronation Medal (1937) and Long Service and Good Conduct Medal, have appeared at auction on at least two occasions in recent years. They are now privately owned.

A correspondent, writing in the *Regimental Gazette*, said of Richards:

Everyone who met him was impressed by his sympathetic and kind nature and his true modesty. He was indeed a great Regimental character, and few people realised the continual pain and discomfort which he bore silently throughout his life as the result of his amputation.

Like Richards, **Richard Raymond Willis** had spent his entire service career in the Lancashire Fusiliers.

He was born on 13 October 1876 at Woking in Surrey, the son of R.A. Willis, and was educated at Harrow and the RMC Sandhurst. Gazetted to the Lancashire Fusiliers on 20 February 1897, he joined the 2nd Battalion at Quetta in India and accompanied it to Egypt in January 1898, where it formed part of Kitchener's Army for the reconquest of the Sudan.

Promoted lieutenant on 20 July, he was engaged in a number of patrols, on one occasion being accompanied by the famous Slatin Pasha, who had been a prisoner in the hands of the dervishes. Willis took part in the campaign's climactic battle at Omdurman, after which he transferred to the 1st Battalion, serving with them in Crete, Malta, Gibraltar and Egypt. During those years he played an active part in the life of the battalion, representing the unit at polo and hockey. For several years he held the title of champion revolver shot. He was also an excellent linguist and a gifted musician. In 1907 Willis, by then a captain, married Maude Temple, the daughter of Col. J.A. Temple.

At the time of the Gallipoli landings, Willis held the unique distinction of having commanded C Company for fifteen consecutive years. Three days after going ashore at W Beach, he led a small force which seized a fir wood on the outskirts of Krithia. It appeared momentarily as if his advance would compel the Turks to withdraw, but no support arrived and his party was forced to pull back. On 2 May, when the Turks launched a major attack on the beach-head, Willis figured prominently in the defence. During a night of bitter fighting, four men were killed beside him, a bullet passed through his cap, and another smashed his periscope without harming him.

Willis appeared to bear a charmed life. Twice over the next fortnight he escaped unhurt when men were killed within feet of him. His luck, however, deserted him on 4 June when, after a brief spell of sick leave, he returned to command D Company for the attack designed to break through the Turkish lines in front of Krithia. During what the unit's historian described as 'this lamentable day', the 1st Battalion suffered more than 500 casualties. Willis, wounded by a bullet beneath the heart, was evacuated to Egypt and then England.

When his Victoria Cross was announced, he urged journalists to 'Please, keep me out of it'. However, he did later assist an *Illustrated London News* artist with his impression of the W Beach landing. It depicted the rush for the shore and had Willis as its central figure, one hand cupped to his mouth, shouting encouragement to his men and the other waving a walking stick in the air. It was this enduring image which gave rise to the nickname 'Walking-stick Willis'.

Once asked how it felt to return to action after having been seriously wounded, the VC winner admitted: 'It's not pleasant, but by far the worst of it in my case is that all my brother officers and most of my men are gone.' In fact, he did not rejoin the 1st Battalion. Promoted major on 1 September 1915, Willis, by then having made a full recovery, received his Cross from the king at Buckingham Palace on 21 September and was posted to France with a draft for the 2nd Battalion.

He saw service on the Somme and in the Ypres Salient with the 1st Royal Inniskilling Fusiliers, the 8th West Ridings and the 6th York and Lancasters. While commanding the 1st Inniskillings, acting Lt. Col. Willis was congratulated by the commander-in-chief, Corps and Divisional commanders, for his battalion's distinguished service at Transloy and Beaumont Hamel. The battalion was mentioned in dispatches for its good work. Later, Willis was commandant of a reinforcement camp where he won further praise for his work in marshalling men following the German breakthrough on the Lys in April 1918.

Maj. Willis returned to his regiment at the end of the war and was appointed second-in-command of the 2nd Battalion. He temporarily commanded the unit in India before his retirement from the Army on 26 November 1920.

He became a teacher, serving with the RAF Education Branch for six years and then working in a succession of private schools, notably as a tutor at Carlisle and Gregsons. He and his wife had two sons and a daughter, and both boys pursued careers in the Army, one of them winning a Military Cross. The two sons later emigrated, one to South Africa and the other to Southern Rhodesia.

The last twenty years of Willis' life were marked by a steady decline in his health and finances. He received a number of grants from the regiment's Compassionate Fund and Officers' Association and then, in 1957, he appealed in the Press for a loan of £100, claiming himself to be 'in desperate need'. His 'begging letter' provoked a public outcry with Questions raised in the House of Commons. Five years later, Willis, by then a widower living in Faithful House, a Cheltenham Nursing Home, wrote to an old friend: 'I am so nearly blind now that I can hardly read at all . . . I did 37 years teaching, from royalty to ploughboys, till my sight failed, and I enjoyed it even though the pay was a third of today's, AND I had four languages . . .'

'Walking-stick Willis' died on 9 February 1966 at Faithful House. Mourners at his funeral six days later included the acting colonel of the Lancashire Fusiliers and one of the survivors of the W Beach landing.

In an obituary published in the *Regimental Gazette*, the then Lt. Col. Grimshaw VC, who had served under Willis at Gallipoli, wrote: 'I shall always remember him as my old Company Commander and the excellent example of courage and leadership that he always displayed which made one feel proud to serve under him. He was a great man who we will always remember.'

J.E. Grimshaw after being commissioned

Willis' death left Grimshaw as the last-surviving member of the 'Six VCs Before Breakfast'. Only twenty-two years of age when he set foot on W Beach, he lived to the grand old age of eighty-seven.

John Elisha Grimshaw was born on 23 January 1893 at Abram, near Wigan, in Lancashire, the son of carpenter John Grimshaw. Educated at St John's School, Abram, he worked, like his father, as a carpenter at Messrs Cross, Tetley and Company's collieries in the Wigan coalfields until enlisting in the Lancashire Fusiliers in 1912 at the age of nineteen. The following year he joined the 1st Battalion in India and returned to England with his unit after the outbreak of war. By the time of the landing at W Beach, he was a lance corporal signaller in C Company, and his role throughout the operation was to maintain contact with the headquarters aboard HMS *Euryalus* and neighbouring units. He did this and more, showing marked leadership in the crisis which threatened to overwhelm his battalion.

Writing to his parents on 10 June 1915, he gave a graphic account of the unremitting strain of life on the peninsula:

As I write this letter our trenches are being shelled by the Turks, and they are dropping rather close. In fact, one has dropped about six yards in front of us, covering us with loose earth. But we are used to it now. We are taking it easy for a few days after having been through some more heavy fighting, in which we drove the Turks back, taking two lines of trenches. No doubt you will be pleased to see that I have been promoted to Sergeant so I am not doing badly and if God spares me I shall get higher still.

It's terrible, though, is war, and I think it's worse here in Gallipoli than anywhere, for it is simply hell, and you don't know but that the next minute will be your last. But we have to go some time, and we might as well go fighting for our country.

Whether Grimshaw was aware of his name featuring among his CO's nominations and the subsequent ballot for the VC is uncertain. However, he was aware that his name had been put forward for a DCM, the recommendation presumably being made after Hunter-Weston failed to have him included in place of a second private soldier. After the DCM was confirmed, he wrote to his parents:

It came as a bit of a surprise to me, for I had forgotten all about it. I heard I was getting it when the General sent me a card, but I thought nothing of it at the time. I only hope I have the luck to come back after the war, and have the honour of wearing it. It will give you all a bit of satisfaction to know that if anything happens to me you will know I did a bit of good.

Grimshaw, who counted himself 'very lucky to escape wounds' at what he called 'that terrible landing', survived the fighting only to fall victim to frostbite. Evacuated from the peninsula, he spent five weeks in hospital before being sent home to England to recuperate. While convalescing, he was invited back to his home town for the presentation of his DCM which the burghers of Abram had persuaded the War Office to send to them. It was pinned on his chest at Abram Parish Church School by the district council chairman, who also presented him with a gold watch bearing the inscription: 'Presented to Sergeant J.E. Grimshaw from the public of Abram and district as a mark of appreciation on his securing the DCM for conspicuous bravery at Cape Helles, on April 25th, 1915.' The packed hall then rose as one and delivered a rousing rendition of 'For he's a jolly good fellow'.

Following his convalescence, Sgt. Grimshaw was posted to Hull, as an instructor, and it was there that he met his future wife, Maggie Stout. The couple were married on 26 August 1916. News of his belated VC was broken to Grimshaw by a journalist at an army camp on Humberside. By his own account, he was dumbfounded. 'I know nothing of the matter except what you have just told me', he said. 'The DCM was given me for the landing at Gallipoli on 25th April, 1915. I don't believe there's another decoration for me.' The account carried in the *Hull Times* continued: 'His chums crowded round with inquiries as to what was the trouble. The "trouble" was explained to the sergeant's comrades, who asked if any official intimation had been received. On being told there was no doubt about the news being correct, Sergeant Grimshaw was congratulated all round.' Nine days after his award was gazetted, Grimshaw received his Cross from the king at Buckingham Palace.

Later that year, Grimshaw, who was described as an 'excellent soldier on active service', went to France and was commissioned in the field. In 1918 he was posted to India where he served with the 1/75th Carnatic Infantry on the Sub-Continent and in Arabia. In 1921 he rejoined the Lancashire Fusiliers. His last posting with the regiment was to Ireland where the troubles were approaching their climax. A few months later he retired to take up the post of army recruiting officer in Cardiff. After eleven years in the job he was promoted lieutenant colonel and served as chief recruiting officer in Northumberland until 1944, and then in East Anglia. Lt. Col. Grimshaw retired from the Army in 1953 aged sixty, after completing forty-one years' service. He lived in Warrington and Lymm in Cheshire, before settling in Twickenham, London, where he died on 20 July 1980. He left a widow, two daughters, eight grandchildren, and eleven great grandchildren. His son, who served as a squadron leader in the Royal Air Force, had died some years earlier.

His VC award made him a regimental celebrity and throughout his life he carried the responsibility that accompanied the honour with quiet dignity. He regularly attended the annual Gallipoli Sunday parades in Bury, the home of the Lancashire Fusiliers. As the number of survivors dwindled, he continued to march at their head, providing a proud echo of one of the British Army's most celebrated actions.

E. UNWIN, W.C. WILLIAMS
G.L. DREWRY, G. MCK. SAMSON
W. ST A. MALLESON AND
A.W. ST C. TISDALL

V Beach, Cape Helles, 25 April 1915

In the early hours of 25 April 1915 a vast fleet closed in on the darkened shore of Gallipoli. They ranged from destroyers to dreadnaughts, yet the vessel destined to play the leading role in the landing operations that morning was not a man-of-war at all, but a converted collier. The SS *River Clyde*, her hull painted a dun brown colour, presented an incongruous sight as she steamed towards Cape Helles. From holes cut in her side ran gangways of wooden planks strung along her bows. In tow she had a 150-ft long steam hopper and three large lighters. Together, this unlikely invasion taskforce represented the linchpin of Sir Ian Hamilton's V Beach plan and was destined to provide the enduring image of the landings and, indeed, the campaign.

At the appointed hour the *River Clyde*, known throughout the expeditionary force as the 'wreck ship', would be run ashore, the hopper and lighters providing a jetty across which her cargo of 2,000 troops, mainly from the Royal Dublin and Munster Fusiliers, were to dash ashore. Bold and imaginative in its conception, the V Beach plan with its reliance on a hastily converted cargo vessel appeared to owe more to Heath Robinson than any staff college. Provided everything went according to plan, however, the *River Clyde* scheme did possess one notable virtue, the opportunity of swiftly reinforcing the first wave of assault troops in greater numbers than would have been possible by any other means.

The man responsible for this piece of improvisation was Cdr. Edward Unwin, a 51-year-old former Merchant Navy officer with a reputation for brusqueness, bluff good humour and forceful leadership. Brought out of retirement in August 1914, Unwin's war had thus far been an unspectacular one. He had served as coaling officer to the Grand Fleet before being given command of HMS *Hussar*, a 20-year-old torpedo boat converted to the role of communications yacht for the C.-in-C., Mediterranean Fleet.

By late February 1915, however, Unwin found himself part of the huge British naval force concentrating at Mudros. His 'energy, ability and cheerfulness' made

Capt. E. Unwin

Able Seaman W.C. Williams

Midshipman G.L. Drewry

Seaman G. Samson

Midshipman W. Malleson

Sub-Lt. A. Tisdall

a swift impression on Rear-Adm. R.E. Wemyss, the newly appointed governor of Lemnos. Recruited on to the governor's staff, Unwin busied himself with the task of helping transform the harbour at Mudros into a naval base. It seems likely he would have remained a key member of the base staff, but for an appearance at a meeting of the joint staffs in early April. The plan for the landings was already well advanced, yet one difficulty remained. How could the initial wave of 2,200 troops be rapidly reinforced? The size of the beach at Cape Helles coupled with a shortage of boats for ferrying in the troops meant the second wave would be delayed by at least forty-five minutes.

Unwin's solution was to run a harmless-looking collier, crowded with a further 2,000 troops, on to the beach. Within minutes, he argued, the number of men ashore would be doubled. Furthermore, he felt his plan afforded the assault troops not only greater protection than a landing from open boats, but also provided them with an element of surprise, rather in the manner of the wooden horse of Troy. Despite staff scepticism, the scheme was eventually accepted, due largely to the enthusiastic advocacy of Rear-Adm. Wemyss. Unwin was promoted to the rank of acting captain and given command of the operation. Under Wemyss' direction, Unwin chartered the 4,000-ton SS *River Clyde*, a 10-year-old Glasgow-built collier which had been used to transport mules from North Africa. Work on converting the vessel began on 12 April. Four doors, known as sallyports, were cut in each side of the hull, and from the rearmost a wooden gangway led to the bows. There, they were designed to meet the stern of a flat-bottomed steam hopper, the *Argyll*. This vessel, to be towed towards Cape Helles by the *River Clyde*, was intended to be released shortly before beaching to form a link between ship and shore. If the gap, however, proved too great, Unwin had devised a plan for using specially decked lighters, three of which were also to be towed by the *River Clyde*, to bridge any gaps. Lastly, in order to provide covering fire for the troops, three armoured and sandbagged casemates were constructed on the foredeck to house machine-guns manned by a unit of the RNAS Armoured Car Squadron under the command of Lt. Cdr. Josiah Wedgewood.

To assist him in the enterprise, Unwin chose one of his junior officers aboard the *Hussar*, Midshipman George Drewry, a boyish looking 20-year-old, whose tender years belied an adventurous pre-war career in the Merchant Navy. The rest of the 24-man crew was made up of volunteers. They included six seamen, six engine-room ratings and the carpenter from his former ship's crew. In addition, Unwin took Leading Seaman William Williams, a 34-year-old reservist and Boer War veteran, who literally talked himself on board the *River Clyde*. Unwin later recounted:

Williams came up to me and asked if he could not come. I told him I was full up and that I did not want any more petty officers, to which he replied, 'I'll chuck my hook [give up his rating] if you will let me come', and I did, to his cost but everlasting glory.

Drewry, as Unwin's number one, was ordered to take command of the steam hopper during the landing operation. The vessel was to be manned by six Greek seamen, who although non-combatants had volunteered, and one member of the *Hussar*'s crew, Seaman George Samson.

At 5.00 a.m. on 25 April Drewry and his crew clambered aboard the hopper. The mist-shrouded shore was barely two miles distant as the *River Clyde* and her assorted tows steered for her landing place. The coastline appeared to quake under a rain of shells from the assembled fleet. The Turkish reply was muted by comparison. Among the senior army officers alongside Unwin on the bridge of the *River Clyde* was Lt. Col. Weir de Lancy Williams. He recorded the ship's final run-in to the shore in his diary:

> 6.10 a.m. Within ½ mile of the shore. We are far ahead of the tows. No OC Troops on board. It must cause a mix-up, if we, 2nd line, arrive before the 1st line. With difficulty I get Unwin to swerve off and await the tows.
>
> 6.22 a.m. Ran smoothly ashore without a tremor. No opposition. We shall land unopposed.

Such optimism, however, proved shortlived. At 6.30 a.m. the boats carrying the first wave were met by a hurricane of fire. In a matter of a few minutes, the 700-strong landing party from the Royal Dublin Fusiliers were reduced to barely 300 men, many of them wounded and incapable of further action. It was a

SS River Clyde

massacre. Trapped in their boats, weighed down by their equipment, they were sitting targets for the Turkish machine-gunners and riflemen lining the hills above V Beach. Meanwhile, amid the confusion, Unwin's plan had also gone awry. A loss of speed caused by the late turning manoeuvre to avoid arriving before the first wave meant the *River Clyde* had run ashore further out than intended. To add to his difficulties, Unwin saw the steam hopper lying grounded on his port side, broadside on to the beach some 10 to 15 yd from the bow of the *River Clyde*.

The cause of this fiasco remains a mystery. The strength of the current undoubtedly played a part. Perhaps the Greek crew panicked at the vital moment. Whatever the reasons, Drewry was left a helpless spectator to the destruction wrought among the first wave. In a desperate attempt to rescue the operation, Drewry and Samson began hauling the lighters, connected by a rope to the stern of the hopper, towards the bow of the *River Clyde*. Unwin, however, had made up his mind to use the lighters to link the *River Clyde* to a spit of rocks on the starboard side of the ship. He made his way down on to the lighters with Leading Seaman Williams and, with the help of a steam pinnace which had been used to tow the troop-carrying boats in the first wave, he manoeuvred them as close to the rocks as possible. Then, with the pinnace unable to go any closer to the shore for fear of grounding, Unwin and Williams dived into the sea and began hauling the lighters into position. Ordering Samson to take cover from the hail of fire, Drewry leapt overboard and waded ashore, where he met a wounded soldier. He later wrote:

> I and another soldier from a boat tried to carry him ashore but he was again shot in our arms, his neck in two pieces nearly, so we left him and I ran along the beach towards the spit. I threw away my revolver, coat and hat and waded out to the captain. He was in the water with a man named Williams, wading and towing the lighters towards the spit. I gave a pull for a few minutes and then climbed aboard the lighters and got the brows lowered onto the lighter. The captain sang out for more rope, so I went on board and brought a rope down with the help of a man called Ellard. As we reached the end of the lighters the captain was wading towards us carrying Williams. We pulled him onto the lighters and Ellard carried him on board the ship on his shoulders ... Williams was dead however.

The previous night Unwin had told Williams to stick close to him throughout the landing. Thus, when Unwin made his way on to the lighters, Williams had accompanied him. Together, they threw a gangplank across two of the lighters, and together they half-swam, half-waded ashore, pulling the lighters behind them. Within a matter of minutes they succeeded in dragging the first lighter to

An artist's impression of Unwin and Williams' VC action

within a few yards of the beach. There they remained, waist-deep in water, holding the lighters in place under a murderous fire from the Turkish defenders dug in along the heights. It was at this moment, with the 'bridge' precariously linking ship to shore, that Unwin called for the disembarkation to begin.

Two companies of the 1st Royal Munster Fusiliers rushed out from the sallyports to be met by a withering fire that decimated their ranks. No sooner had the survivors reached the beach, than the bridge was broken. While holding the rope alongside his captain, Williams had been mortally wounded by a shell fragment, and, as he let go his grip, Unwin dropped the line in an attempt to support him. The result was that the lighter nearest the shore drifted away from the beach and was carried by the current into deeper water.

For more than an hour, in the face of a concentrated fire, Williams had carried out his orders to the last letter. He died in Unwin's arms, and his captain later wrote of him: 'Williams was the man above all others who deserved the VC at the landing.'

With the surviving Munsters stranded ashore, the disembarkation was halted until the bridge could be restored, a prospect which, in the circumstances, seemed improbable if not impossible. However, Midshipman Drewry had not given up hope. He succeeded in taking a rope from the lighter nearest to the

River Clyde to the spit of rocks, and then 'with difficulty' hauled the exhausted Unwin onto the lighter. The captain, by then suffering from cold brought on by prolonged immersion in the water, was taken aboard the *River Clyde*, leaving Drewry alone on the lighter. He later recorded:

> All the time shells were falling all around us and into the ship, one hitting the case of one boiler but doing no further damage. Several men were killed in No 4 hold. I stayed on the lighters and tried to keep the men going ashore but it was murder and soon the first lighter was covered with dead and wounded and the spit was awful, the sea around it for some yards was red. When they got ashore they were little better off for they were picked off many of them before they could dig themselves in.
>
> They stopped coming and I ran on board into No 1 hold and saw an awful sight, dead and dying lay around the ports where their curiosity had led them. I went up to the saloon and saw the captain being rubbed down. He murmured something about the third lighter so I went down again and in a few minutes a picket boat came along the starboard side and gave the reserve lighter a push that sent it as far as the hopper . . .

Drewry had gone aboard the third lighter together with Lt. Tony Morse, who had arrived with the third tow of boats carrying troops towards V Beach from the fleet waiting offshore. Morse was the senior member of a 38-strong party from HMS *Cornwallis*, whose task was to ferry reinforcements ashore. They were divided among four boats, towed in shore by a steam pinnace from HMS *Albion*. Having helped unload the dead and wounded from the boats which succeeded in making the return trip from the first and second waves, they were under no illusions about the strength of the Turkish defences. To follow their progress, and the next stage of the gallant attempt to restore the bridge crucial to the landing operation, we must turn to the account of 18-year-old Midshipman Wilfrid St Aubyn Malleson. One of the *Cornwallis*' party, he was in the second of the four boats as it approached V Beach around 7.00 a.m. He later wrote:

> We arrived starboard side of the *River Clyde*. In coming in we only sustained about 4 or 6 casualties all due to stray rifle fire. Even in getting out of the boat we got off very lightly. It was in the act of getting out of the boat that Mid Hardiman was fatally wounded. This was about the nearest escape I had, as I was standing about 2 ft away from him. Sub Lieut Waller and Mr Spillane (Bosun) stayed in the boat with the crew and took her round to the stern of the *River Clyde*. We lost sight of them.
>
> Our remnant of the Beach Party was now on its face in the lighter. Nothing very much was possible as bullets were whistling over our heads and the

Midshipman G. Drewry, right, shortly after the landing

lighters were all isolated and swaying backwards and forwards on account of the current. After about an hour of inaction, during which time occupants of the lighter sustained about one casualty every ten minutes, I observed a lighter on the starboard side, manned by Lieut Morse and Mid Drewry, being pushed from behind by our 2nd picket boat (Mid Voelcher). This lighter was pushed into place between my lighter and the next, a very skilful performance, owing to the numerous shoals, constant rifle fire and general unwieldiness of the lighter.

The fore end of the new lighter was secured, but the near end began to drift away owing to the current.

Just as the lighter reached the steam hopper, still lying broadside on to the beach, Drewry, who had borne a charmed life until now, was felled by a shrapnel wound to the head. Within seconds, however, the young officer was back on his feet. With blood streaming down his face, he helped secure the lighter to the hopper. Then, while he went below in the hopper's engine-room to have his wound bandaged, Lt. Morse attempted to make the lighter fast with the help of Midshipman Lloyd, another member of the *Cornwallis'* party who had been forced to seek shelter aboard the steam hopper. They eventually succeeded, but at the cost of a third wound to Lloyd.

Drewry, his wound dressed, returned and set about the job of joining together the remaining lighters. Scorning cover himself, he urged one young midshipman who was lying on the bullet-riddled hopper to go below as he was in a 'somewhat dangerous place', and then dived over the side with a rope with the intention of linking the lighters. Malleson, who was able to see Drewry from his prone position on the lighter, recorded that 'Owing to the fact that he had to swim against the current, and his rope was too short, he got into difficulties. I therefore got together some rope and, getting a soldier [Munster, name not known] to pay it out, managed to get it across.' What the young midshipman

An artist's impression of Malleson's VC action

neglected to mention was that the only rope he could find was the one which had originally kept the bridge of lighters connected to the spit of rocks on the starboard side. To retrieve it, he had to stand up, in full view of the Turkish positions, and haul it in. By the time he had finished, Drewry, his strength ebbing away, had drifted away on the current. It was left to Malleson to make the connection, swimming across the gap churned by Turkish fire. His account continues:

> I was a bit done, so Lieut Morse made it fast. The new lighter had by now drifted to seaward of the hopper. I therefore swam to the hopper and managed to get a rope from it and started to tow one end back. However [the] rope was too short, and feeling exhausted, I scrambled aboard the lighter again. Lieut Morse told me to get a dry change so I crawled into the *River Clyde* where I remained till the evening.

By 9.00 a.m. a new bridge, linking the *River Clyde* to the stranded steam hopper, had been established. Drewry, like Malleson, had succeeded in returning to the *River Clyde*, where Surgeon Paul Burrowes Kelly treated his wound and rubbed him down. 'I was awfully cold', Drewry recounted. 'He would not let me get up and I had to lay down and listen to the din.' What he heard was almost

Capt. E. Unwin

certainly the renewed attempt to get men ashore from the *River Clyde*. So heavy were the losses among a third company of the Munsters that the disembarkation was once again suspended. Orders were issued to the troops to 'hold on and wait'. In truth, there was little else they could do.

Unwin, however, refused to admit defeat. Ignoring his doctor's protestations, he made his way back to the lighters, which by then were strewn with dead and wounded. From his bed aboard the *River Clyde*, Drewry heard a cheer go up, and, looking from a porthole, he 'saw the captain standing on the hopper in white clothes. A line had carried away and, by himself, he had fixed it.' Apparently, Unwin, still barely recovered from his previous exertions, was assisted in his latest endeavours by a seaman and a boy of about eighteen, possibly a midshipman from the *Cornwallis'* beach party. The steam hopper was a shambles, its decks littered with dead and wounded. While on board her, Unwin was hit in the face and neck by fragments from a bullet richochet. Struggling back to the *River Clyde*, the tireless captain was treated for cuts to his cheek, chin and wrist. At approximately 9.30 a.m., under direct orders from Maj.-Gen. Aylmer Hunter Weston (GOC, 29th Division), a third effort was made to land the troops. One company of the 2nd Hampshires rushed out from the sallyports to the same fate as the Munsters. The attempt was quickly abandoned.

An impasse had been reached which was to be broken shortly after 10.00 a.m. by the arrival of Brig. Gen. H.E. Napier, commanding the 88th Brigade. Realizing the futility of a further landing from open boats, the senior officer aboard the *River Clyde* hailed the brigadier's tows to come alongside. But as the troops filed aboard the collier, Napier leapt onto the nearest lighter in an apparent effort to renew the landing. Perhaps he had mistaken the bodies choking the lighters for men sheltering from the Turkish fire. His intentions must remain a matter of conjecture. For after rushing across the lighters towards the steam hopper he was shot dead, along with his brigade major.

The landing having been halted, Unwin now turned his attentions to the wounded men, who could be heard calling out from the shore. Quite what drove him to risk his life a third time is unclear. Perhaps, as the man chiefly responsible for the landing plan, he felt a personal obligation towards the men he had delivered on to the peninsula. One officer recalled seeing Unwin 'maddened by the failure of his landing plan'. Whatever the cause of his actions that morning, it is clear from the numerous eyewitness accounts that at about 11.00 a.m. Unwin made his way down on to a steam pinnace, alongside the *River Clyde*. He then proceeded to punt himself to the spit of rocks off the starboard bow, which was, in itself, no mean feat given his state of near exhaustion. From there he crawled along the rocks, covered by Turkish fire, searching for the living among the dead.

According to one account, Unwin recovered seven wounded men, placing each one in the pinnace. He was assisted in his work by Petty Officer John Russell, a member of the RNAS Armoured Car Squadron acting as machine-gunners aboard the *River Clyde*, who swam out to him. Russell was seriously wounded in the stomach as he helped Unwin lift a soldier into the boat. Both men lay in the water, as if pretending to be dead, and then, during a lull in the fighting, they clambered aboard the pinnace and were pulled back to the *River Clyde* by a rope. Unwin, his shirt torn where he had ripped a piece off to bind Russell's wound, was on the point of collapse.

The rescue work he had started, however, was taken up by others. Most prominent among them was a young officer from the Royal Naval Division detachment aboard the *River Clyde* who had witnessed Unwin's selfless acts of gallantry. Hearing the cries of the wounded, he was heard to say, 'I can't stand it. I'm going over'. And thus began the self-ordained mission which would earn him, in due course, a richly deserved Victoria Cross.

Sub-Lt. Arthur Tisdall, a 24-year-old Cambridge scholar and poet, was the only RND officer aboard the *River Clyde*, a fact which would lead to considerable problems in recognizing his acts of gallantry. His unit, 13 Platoon, D Company, Anson Battalion, was assigned to the landing force as a beach-carrying party. They had lost three men killed, when a shell burst in No. 4 hold. At some point during the morning Tisdall made his way up on deck. There, he was seen by Lt. Cdr. Wedgewood setting off in a boat for the shore, accompanied by two men, one of them a member of the RNAS Armoured Car Squadron. Petty Officer William Perring, of 13 Platoon, recalled seeing Tisdall 'out in the water assisting Commander Unwin [*sic*] and a few ratings to get the wounded men out of the water into the boats'.

Perring made a call for volunteers among the Anson men below decks to help their officer. It was answered by Leading Seaman Fred Curtis, Leading Seaman James Malia and Leading Seaman James Parkinson. Together with Petty Officer Mechanic Geoffrey Rumming, of Wedgewood's Armoured Car Squadron, they joined Tisdall in numerous journeys to and from the spit of rocks. In all, it would appear that Tisdall made four or five trips, pushing and towing a lifeboat filled with wounded. Each of his companions took part in at least two of these hazardous journeys.

Rumming, who at the time did not know the officer's identity, later recalled:

An artist's impression of Tisdall's VC action

There were four men in the boat, the late Sub-Lt. A.W. St Clair Tisdall, a black bearded 1st class Petty Officer [*sic*], a seaman with no badges or stripes on his sleeves whatever, and myself . . . We got three wounded in the boat the first trip and four men the second trip.

Beyond getting a few bullet holes in the boat above the waterline, the first trip was quite successful. On the second trip Sub-Lt. Tisdall and myself clambered over a spit of rock, to get the men lying higher up. We got shot at, lay down for a time. As we were lifting the last wounded man into the boat I got hit again in the back.

We had taken the boat a little further ashore, and when we went to push off again, we found her grounded. When we did eventually succeed in getting off Lt. Tisdall and myself were unable to climb into the boat and so we hung on to the side as the two men, keeping as low as possible, rowed us back to the *River Clyde*.

Unfortunately, on the way back Lt. Tisdall got some wooden splinters off the boat driven into his wrist by a bullet, and the black bearded PO got hit just between the fingers.

The latter may well have been Leading Seaman Malia, the first of the Anson platoon to join Tisdall. He recorded that while 'going out for another boat of wounded the oar was broken between my hands with a bullet and I had to jump into the water for shelter from the exceedingly heavy fire to which I was exposed'.

Not all of the wounded recovered from the shore survived the return journey. Leading Seaman James Parkinson, who had a narrow escape when a bullet passed through his cap, recounted the story of his second trip, when they brought off three wounded men:

The boat was leaking very badly and one of the last three was drowned in the boat bottom. We were then called back by one of the ship's officers who stated that it was sheer madness to go on, and if we did not return on board and under cover, anything we did would not be recognised. And if we did carry on we should probably be dead men because the Turks had by now got a machine-gun trained on us.

We had no alternative than to obey orders and the boat was getting full of water. So we were able to grasp the holes in the side of the *River Clyde* and pull ourselves in board.

It is unclear precisely when Tisdall was compelled to stop his rescue work. An officer, from the 2nd Hampshires, aboard the *River Clyde* saw him helping wounded off the rocks around midday. For more than an hour Tisdall and his gallant party had toiled to save lives in the face of what one eyewitness described as 'murderous' Turkish fire. Tisdall's inspirational leadership made a deep impression on Lt. Cdr. Wedgewood, who had also been greatly impressed by the gallantry displayed by petty officers Rumming and Russell, from his own unit. On 26 April he wrote to his friend Winston Churchill, informing him of the efforts of 'Lieut Tidsdale (?) RND' [sic], and added that he had recommended Rumming and Russell for the VC.

Throughout the long day at V Beach, there were countless more acts of heroism, many of which went unseen and unrecognized. One man whose repeated acts of bravery were destined to be rewarded was Seaman George

Samson, who we last encountered aboard the steam hopper *Argyll* with Midshipman Drewry. After the failure of the original plan, Samson had helped Unwin, Drewry and Malleson to establish a bridge to the shore. Then, when each in their turn was forced by wounds or exhaustion to give up their work, Samson remained on the hopper and lighters, tending the wounded.

According to Drewry, 'Samson . . . did very well in the afternoon, two or three times he took wounded from the beach to the hopper'. Samson later insisted he had been inspired by the example of Unwin and Drewry who, he said, had gone about their work 'just as if they were aboard the *Hussar* in peacetime'. Hearing the 'calls of help' which, he said, 'came from all around', Samson felt compelled to act. He later recounted:

> The hail of bullets from the Turkish rifles was beginning to take its terrible toll, and I soon found fresh duties to perform – that of carrying the wounded from the shore to the hopper, from which they were, as soon as it was possible, transferred to the *River Clyde* . . . I cannot say that I felt quite as cool as I may have looked. I am not a very excitable sort when there is serious trouble about. It takes a good deal to disturb me, but I can say without hesitation that this was the 'goods' for excitement.
>
> During these first dark hours on the Gallipoli Peninsula I had many narrow escapes, just the same, of course, as my companions . . . Bullets were whizzing about our heads every few minutes, and we were soon aware of the fact that machine guns were in operation now that our forces were beginning to land in big numbers. Men were falling down like ninepins quite near us, and perhaps it was only the thought that we must give them a helping hand that made us forget our own danger . . . Really I feel I cannot say too much in praise of my officers – their work was absolutely an inspiration to me . . .

Samson's numerous acts of gallantry were probably of a longer duration than any of those performed by the heroes of V Beach. There is no record of him quitting his work during a day-long struggle in which any movement was certain of drawing heavy fire. He was still making his dangerous journeys, bringing much-needed succour to the wounded, well into the evening. Midshipman H. Weblin, one of the midshipmen from the *Cornwallis* who had spent much of the day sheltering from the Turkish fire aboard the steam hopper, recorded:

> We tried in vain to get medical assistance from the *Clyde* and in the evening Samson, AB, got a launch and we got everyone except one man who was too bad to move into the launch and went to the *Clyde*, which was by then, of course, joined to the hopper by lighters.

Samson's luck, however, ran out the following day. While giving covering fire from the decks of the *River Clyde*, he was badly wounded by shrapnel. He had been in action without a break for almost thirty hours. Carried below, he was found to have suffered more than a dozen separate wounds. So serious were his injuries that two doctors gave him no chance of survival.

Surgeon Burrowes Kelly, who had treated more than 200 men aboard the *River Clyde* despite being wounded himself, later wrote:

> At the request of Captain Unwin I hobbled down to see him (not knowing that he was hit), and I remember how he asked me if there was any chance for him. I answered 'Yes', and I felt 'Yes', because he was possessed of such wonderful physique and strength. He was in great agony when I last saw him, and whether he lived or died I knew he had won the VC.

In the days following the landings, a degree of confusion arose over the awards for gallantry at V Beach. On 5 May, with V Beach firmly in British hands, Rear Admiral Wemyss submitted VC recommendations for the four heroes from the *River Clyde*. 'It has been a great pleasure doing so', he noted in his diary, 'but very difficult to find suitable language without being gushing'.

As the weeks passed without word of honours for the naval heroes, the Army took a hand. On 6 June Lt. Gen. Hunter-Weston, who had commanded the 29th Division during the landing operations, broke with tradition and recommended two naval officers – Unwin and Drewry – for the Victoria Cross. 'These names', he noted, 'were not submitted with my list of recommendations as I was under the impression that the Admiral was going to forward them'. The general had long been aware of the great gallantry displayed by Unwin and his faithful midshipman. Cdre. Roger Keyes later recorded that. 'The general told me at least half a dozen dirty scraps of paper reached him from comparatively junior officers which bore testimony to Unwin's devoted heroism, some written in the heat of action by officers who did not survive it.' Among them was a note written by Capt. G.W. Geddes, who led one of the first parties of Munsters onto the beach. He wrote: 'I saw Commander Unwin [*sic*] 3 or 4 times going out to the rocky spit . . . though wounded and under fire, picking up wounded men, putting them in a boat and bringing them back to the *River Clyde*.' Another officer, Capt. R. Neave, of the 1st Essex, saw Unwin 'standing in the water with a wounded man on his shoulders lifting him out of the water, into a boat . . .'. According to Capt. A. Sinclair Thomson, Unwin and Drewry had been 'under a very heavy close-range rifle and machine-gun fire and both . . . knew that it was almost certain death to cross the area between the *River Clyde* and the beach'.

On 16 August, almost two months after the first Army VCs of the campaign, the *London Gazette* announced the award of Victoria Crosses to Unwin, Drewry, Malleson, Williams and Samson. But slow as their official recognition was in coming, it was swift by comparison with the award of Tisdall's VC. After a lengthy investigation, the award was eventually gazetted on 31 March 1916 – some three weeks after the announcement of the campaign's last VC!

Unwin's citation read:

While in *River Clyde*, observing the lighters which were to form the bridge to the shore had broken adrift, Commander Unwin left the ship, and under a murderous fire attempted to get the lighters in position. He worked on until, suffering from the effects of cold and immersion, he was obliged to return to the ship, where he was wrapped up in blankets. Having in some degree recovered, he returned to his work against the doctor's orders and completed it. He was later again attended by the doctor for three abrasions caused by bullets, after which he once more left the ship, this time in a lifeboat, to save some wounded men who were lying in shallow water near the beach. He continued at this heroic labour under continuous fire, until forced to stop through pure physical exhaustion.

The four other VCs announced on 16 August received only short citations. They read as follows. Drewry:

Assisted Commander Unwin at the work of securing the lighters under heavy rifle and maxim fire. He was wounded in the head, but continued his work, and twice subsequently attempted to swim from lighter to lighter with a line.

Malleson:

Also assisted Commander Unwin, and after Midshipman Drewry had failed from exhaustion to get a line from lighter to lighter, he swam with it himself and succeeded. The line subsequently broke, and he afterwards made two further but unsuccessful attempts at his self-imposed task.

Williams:

Held on to a line in the water for over an hour under heavy fire, until killed.

Samson:

Worked on a lighter all day under fire, attending wounded and getting out lines; he was eventually dangerously wounded by Maxim fire.

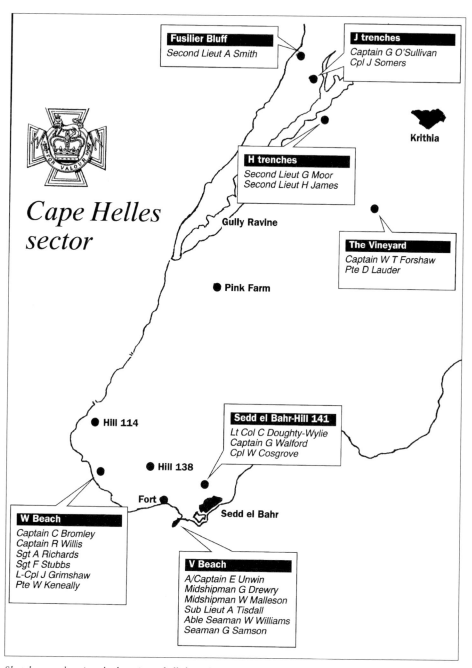

Fusilier Bluff
Second Lieut A Smith

J trenches
Captain G O'Sullivan
Cpl J Somers

Krithia

H trenches
Second Lieut G Moor
Second Lieut H James

Cape Helles sector

Gully Ravine

The Vineyard
Captain W T Forshaw
Pte D Lauder

Pink Farm

Hill 114

Sedd el Bahr-Hill 141
Lt Col C Doughty-Wylie
Captain G Walford
Cpl W Cosgrove

Hill 138

Fort

Sedd el Bahr

W Beach
Captain C Bromley
Captain R Willis
Sgt A Richards
Sgt F Stubbs
L-Cpl J Grimshaw
Pte W Keneally

V Beach
A/Captain E Unwin
Midshipman G Drewry
Midshipman W Malleson
Sub Lieut A Tisdall
Able Seaman W Williams
Seaman G Samson

Sketch map showing the location of all the VCs won in the Helles sector

As the architect of the *River Clyde* plan, **Edward Unwin** ranks among the outstanding personalities of the Gallipoli Campaign. In the space of a few weeks, this middle-aged naval officer emerged from relative obscurity to command the single-most important vessel in the landing operations.

Born on 17 March 1864, at Forest Lodge, Fawley in Hampshire, the son of Edward Wilberforce Unwin MA, JP, and Henrietta Jane (née Carnac), Unwin was privately educated at Cheltenham, Malvern Wells, and Clavering in Essex.

At the age of fourteen, he joined the *Conway* training ship in the River Mersey, where a stormy two years culminated in him receiving two dozen strokes of the birch. His disciplinary record, however, did not blight his sea-going career. He served fifteen years in the Merchant Navy, first aboard a clipper owned by Donald Currie and then with P. & O., before transferring to the Royal Navy with the rank of lieutenant on 31 October 1895.

Unwin married Evelyn Agnes Carew, daughter of Maj.-Gen. W. Dobree Carew, in 1897, and shortly afterwards embarked on his first military operation, a punitive mission against the West African kingdom of Benin, where a British trading party had been murdered. During the subsequent land operations, Unwin became embroiled in the fighting when hostile Edo tribesmen launched an attack on the supply camp which he commanded. The assault was repulsed and Unwin came through his first test unscathed. The expedition ended with the execution of the chiefs held responsible for the massacre. Unwin, for his part, received his first campaign medal.

After a spell on the port guard ship HMS *Thunderer*, Unwin saw service in the second Boer War, for which he received the Queen's South Africa Medal. In 1903 Unwin was promoted lieutenant commander and he retired from the Royal Navy six years later with the rank of commander. Recalled to active service shortly before the outbreak of war in the summer of 1914, Unwin was appointed fleet coaling officer on Admiral Jellicoe's staff aboard HMS *Iron Duke*. The following February he was given command of HMS *Hussar*, part of the Mediterranean Fleet.

Unwin's subsequent involvement in the Gallipoli campaign was interrupted by a brief spell in England, where he was evacuated to recuperate from his exertions at V Beach. He underwent an operation at the Royal Naval Hospital, Haslar, but by early July he was back in Mudros, in command of the cruiser HMS *Endymion*.

Plans were already well advanced for a new landing to the north of Anzac at Suvla Bay in an effort to break the deadlock. Unwin, probably as a result of his experience gained at V Beach, was given command of a fleet of motor-lighters, designed to ferry the men of two New Army divisions ashore at night. Nicknamed 'Beetles' on account of their black hulls and antennae-like raised ramp arms, the bullet-proof lighters could carry 500 men on to the beaches.

Unwin set about his new task with all his customary vigour, assisted by his former first lieutenant, George Drewry, who had volunteered to join him. Between 6 August, when Unwin directed the approach of the motor-lighters to the Suvla beaches, and 11 August the two *River Clyde* shipmates toiled tirelessly, ferrying men and equipment from ship to shore.

On one occasion, Unwin's determination to lead from the front evidently got the better of him. Drewry recorded:

> The beach was a narrow cove just room for three lighters and I had to wait about 20 mins. As I went in Unwin boarded me cursing the other people for not going in hard enough and getting their brows dry on the beach.
>
> He would show them the way. We went in at a fine speed and certainly got our brow dry, however, when we wanted to back out we found we would not budge. To make matters worse another lighter barged into our quarter and sent us up another three feet. A trawler hooked on but could not manage it so we remained on the beach all night and until the next 11.00 a.m.

Drewry returned to HMS *Hussar* on 11 August. Unwin, however, remained at Suvla, serving there first as beachmaster and then, during the evacuation, as naval transport officer. In the days before the final withdrawal from Suvla, Unwin was to be found night and day on the beach piers superintending the removal of men, animals and stores. As at the V Beach and Suvla Bay landings, Unwin led by example. An army officer noted:

> Commander Unwin . . . stands over 6 feet and is broad in proportion, with the typical clean-shaven face of a sailor, and with a voice that roars orders through a megaphone, causing those who are ordered to jump about a good deal quicker on their jobs than they probably would do otherwise.

Fittingly, Unwin was the last man to leave Suvla, in the early hours of 20 December. Flames from a blazing mountain of stores lit the sky as a picket boat ferried him to a waiting ship. Unwin's extraordinary Gallipoli service, however, was eventful to the last. As a lighter crowded with soldiers neared one of the troop transports one man was seen to fall overboard. Unwin immediately dived into the sea and swam to his rescue, prompting Rear Admiral Wemyss to recommend him for a Royal Humane Society medal. In his final list of recommendations for services during the Gallipoli operations, Wemyss wrote of Unwin:

> His conduct during the intervening time [25 April–20 December] has been such as to call for the admiration and respect of all with whom he has been

brought in contact and I would respectfully ask that his acting rank of Captain may be confirmed.

In March 1916 Unwin was created a Commander of St Michael and St George (CMG) for his part in the successful evacuation. Two months earlier, on 15 January, Unwin had an appointment at Buckingham Palace to receive his Victoria Cross from George V.

Not surprisingly, perhaps, the remainder of Unwin's war services appear as something of an anticlimax. Given command of the light cruiser HMS *Amethyst*, serving on the remote South-East America Station, Unwin later returned to administrative staff duties, first as principal naval transport officer in Egypt (for which he later received the Order of the Nile) and then as PNTO in the Eastern Mediterranean. Promoted commodore in 1919, he was created a Companion of the Bath (CB) for his war services and went back into retirement the following year with the rank of captain, his seniority back-dated to 11 November 1918 as a reward for his distinguished record.

In the years that followed, Unwin maintained close links with the men who shared with him the unfulfilled hopes of a campaign rich in gallantry and missed opportunities. Two years after retiring from the navy, he unveiled a memorial to Seaman Williams in Chepstow. Unwin, who regularly attended the annual memorial service for the veterans of the 29th Division at Eltham in Kent, remained a fierce critic of those he felt responsible for the failure of the Gallipoli operations. At one such service, he declared:

If the campaign had been properly managed, Constantinople would have been taken, for no nation has sent forth to battle braver troops . . . At great sacrifice we landed, but we had not enough guns . . . A few more guns and the men would have got there.

Unwin enjoyed an active retirement, combining numerous civic duties with sporting pursuits. A glittering array of trophies testified to his prowess as a yachtsman, and he was also a keen tennis and croquet player. After the war he lived at Cheltenham, before moving to the family seat, Wootton Lodge, Ashbourne, in Derbyshire, a splendid Elizabethan mansion. When Unwin left for Hindhead in Surrey in 1936, he brought to a close a 200-year family association.

From 1929 until 1939 Unwin was deputy lieutenant of Staffordshire and, while living at Ashbourne, he was president of the Ellastone branch of the Royal British Legion.

Capt. Unwin, who described the Gallipoli Campaign as a 'heaven-sent idea of Mr Winston Churchill's', died on 19 April 1950. The former Merchant Navy officer, who achieved a measure of fame as captain of a converted collier on the beach of Sedd el Bahr, collapsed as he stepped from his wheel-chair on his way for his customary early morning shave in Grayshott. Carried into the barber's shop, he died shortly afterwards. His wife had died the previous year, eighteen months after their golden wedding anniversary. They were survived by their two sons and two daughters. Thirty-five years to the day after the *River Clyde* had sailed out of Tenedos bound for V Beach and a place in naval history, the body of her renowned captain was laid to rest in Grayshott cemetery.

William Charles Williams was the first member of the Royal Navy to be awarded a posthumous Victoria Cross. Described by Capt. Unwin as the bravest sailor he ever knew, Williams was born on 15 September 1880, at Stanton Lacy, Shropshire, to William Williams and his wife Elizabeth.

When Williams was still a boy, the family moved to Chepstow, where his father worked as a gardener at Pillinger's Nurseries. One of a large family living at 11 Nelson Street, he had six sisters and, when his father later remarried, he gained a number of step brothers and step sisters.

Educated at Chepstow Grammar School, he enlisted for Boy's Service in the Royal Navy at Portsmouth on 17 December 1895. On his eighteenth birthday, after three years' service, he signed on for twelve years. Little is known about his life. His naval record is merely a factual account of his services. It does, however, offer some physical description of the man. He had black hair, a fair complexion and grey eyes and was 5 ft 8½ in tall.

Williams underwent his baptism of fire as a member of Percy Scott's celebrated Naval Brigade during the Boer War operations culminating in the relief of Ladysmith. In April 1900, during the Boxer Rising, he was part of the naval detachment landed in China with the mission to relieve the besieged embassies. Williams was commended for his gallantry during both campaigns.

Peace-time service offered little opportunity for advancement, however, and he was still an able seaman when his regular service ended a day short of his thirtieth birthday. Williams joined HMS *Vernon*, as part of the Royal Fleet Special Reserve, on 19 September 1910. Returning to the Welsh border country, Williams lived with a married sister at 12 Victoria Crescent, Newport, and found work with Messrs Lysaghts Orb Works. Later he served as a policeman in the Monmouthshire Constabulary, being stationed at St Mellions and Tredegar. The lure of the sea, however, proved too strong. Williams joined the Merchant Navy and when war broke out in August 1914 he was at sea, serving aboard a steamer. His family had not seen him for nearly a year, and they were never to see him alive again.

As a member of the Fleet Reserve, Williams was recalled to active service on 28 August, and within a month he was serving on HMS *Hussar*. His family had no inkling of his final mission on the shores of the Gallipoli Peninsula until the announcement of his Victoria Cross in August 1915. His last letter home, shortly after the outbreak of war, had merely requested his family send on his naval pension papers and other documents.

Williams' VC was presented to his father by George V at Buckingham Palace on 16 November 1916. Six years later, the people of Chepstow paid their own tribute to Williams' great courage. On 8 January 1922 a gun from a German submarine, given to the town by the king, was unveiled by his sister, Mrs Frances Smith, and dedicated in his honour. On the same day, in St Mary's Parish Church, Chepstow, Charles Dixon's painting of the V Beach landing was unveiled by Capt. Unwin. It had been purchased by public subscription as a memorial to the town's Gallipoli VC. Both memorials survive to this day, although the gun was moved closer to the town's war memorial because of redevelopment work in the 1960s. Williams' decorations, his VC, 1914–15 Star, British War Medal, Victory Medal, Queen's South Africa Medal with clasps for Relief Of Ladysmith and Tugela Heights, and China Medal, 1900, were held by his family for many years, but are now in a private collection.

Williams has no known grave. He is commemorated on the Portsmouth Naval Memorial.

George Leslie Drewry, the first officer of the Royal Naval Reserve to be awarded the Victoria Cross, was only twenty years of age when he won the nation's premier award for valour. Yet in a short life, dogged by misadventure, he had already experienced more incidents of high drama than most men manage in a lifetime.

Born at Forest Gate, Essex, on 3 November 1894, the third of four sons to Thomas Drewry and Mary (née Kendall), he appears to have been destined for a sea-going career. His father was works manager for the P. & O. Steam Navigation Company, a prestigious enough post for the family to live in the comfort of a detached house in Claremont Road, Forest Gate. Drewry was educated at Merchant Taylor's School, Blackheath, and at fourteen joined the Merchant Navy as an apprentice.

By then he had already survived two narrow brushes with death. Once, while playing with his younger brother Ralph in Wanstead Park, they had fallen into a bog. Disappearing up to their necks, their cries were heard by a passer-by who hauled them to safety. On another occasion, Drewry had been knocked over by a car. The catalogue of accidents followed the high-spirited youngster to sea. During his early training aboard the sailing vessel *Indian Empire*, he fell from the mast into the sea and was only rescued by the gallant efforts of the ship's mate who dived overboard. On a subsequent voyage, the ship ran into a storm as it rounded Cape Horn and was wrecked on the remote, uninhabited Hermit Island. Drewry and the crew survived for fourteen days as castaways, living on roots and shellfish, until discovered by a Chilean gunboat.

In 1912 he joined the P. & O. Line, serving as an officer on the Australia and Japan routes. The following year he joined the Royal Naval Reserve. On 3 August 1914, while at Port Said, he was called up and posted as a midshipman to HMS *Hussar*. The months prior to the Dardanelles expedition were filled with the monotonous routine of ferrying the Mediterranean Fleet's mail and officers from ship to ship. All of that, however, ended on 12 April 1915 when he joined Unwin in preparing the *River Clyde* for her important role in the V Beach landings.

Surgeon Burrowes Kelly, who accompanied Drewry aboard the *River Clyde*, described the young midshipman as being 'of medium height but powerfully built . . . He was a very good-looking, modest and charming young man. He was devoted to his captain, and was considered by all the naval officers who knew him to have been an exceedingly brave fellow.' It would appear, from his own account of the landings written as a letter to his father, that he was remarkably unaffected by the bloodbath at V Beach. Yet, when he toured the ruined village of Sedd el Bahr, three days after the landings, he fainted at the sight of so many Turkish and British bodies. 'Never afterwards would he photograph anywhere near Sedd el Bahr', recorded Surgeon Burrowes Kelly.

Drewry's courageous exploits coupled with his tender years briefly made him a newspaper celebrity back home in Britain. By then, however, he had embarked on his second Gallipoli landing, alongside Unwin at Suvla Bay. The operation on the night of 6 August was in stark contrast to his experiences at V Beach. To his father, he wrote describing the scene at Suvla:

I stayed on various lighters until ashore and had a run on the beach but it was uncanny, the troops got ashore in record time and then came batteries and mules and munitions. I could not understand it, I stood on the beach and saw guns being landed and horses, and behind us a few yards away was the dark bush, containing what? There was little firing, now and then a sharp rattle quite close and then silence, I thought of Helles and then wondered if we had landed by mistake at Lemnos or if we were ambushed and the maxims were just going to clear the beach of living in one sweep . . .

During the next five days, Drewry worked ceaselessly, together with his former captain, ferrying men and stores from ship to shore. On one occasion he was compelled to make the dangerous journey across to Anzac beach before any link-up had been made with the forces at Suvla. Recalling the night run, he later wrote:

About half a mile out feeling our way in, bullets began to hit us and became thick as we got closer, overs from the trenches, almost spent that make a nasty sighing sound as they come. There was only the coxs'un [*sic*] and myself on deck and I had to go right forward to see where we were going. I had no cover and felt most funky, the beach itself was not so bad only a few bullets falling here and there.

Drewry returned to HMS *Hussar* on 11 August. He was prevented from staying on with his former captain by an order forbidding midshipmen from going ashore unless they were inoculated.

In October Drewry applied for promotion, and was confident of being made acting sub-lieutenant by November. The following September, he was promoted acting lieutenant and appointed to HMS *Conqueror*. Two months later, on 22 November, he was invested with his VC by George V at Buckingham Palace. As the first RNR officer to be so decorated, he was presented with a Sword of Honour by the Imperial Merchant Service Guild.

By the summer of 1918 Drewry had his own command, HMT *William Jackson*, a decoy trawler. It was while serving aboard this vessel in the bleak waters of Scapa Flow that the final, tragic misfortune befell the 'Midshipman VC'. On the evening of 2 August a block fell from a derrick and struck him, fracturing his skull and breaking his left arm. He died the following day. His fellow officers in the Northern Patrol commissioned a memorial window in his honour in All Saint's Church, Forest Gate. Drewry's VC was later placed on display at his old school, beside a painting of the *River Clyde*. Today, his gallantry is recalled by a dramatic diorama of the V Beach landing in the Imperial War Museum.

During the two years that followed his VC award, the popular, accident-prone war hero remained totally unaffected by his many honours. Years later his brother Ralph recalled: 'He said he was only doing his duty and had never expected the VC. When I showed him all the newspaper cuttings about him that we had kept he told me to put them in the toilet.'

George McKenzie Samson was born on 7 January 1889, at Carnoustie, in Fife, Scotland, the second son of Mr David Samson, a shoemaker. The family lived at 63 Dundee Street, Carnoustie and Samson was educated in the town's school, where his fellow pupils included Charles Alfred Jarvis, another future Victoria Cross winner.

Details of Samson's short but colourful life are at best sketchy. After leaving school, he enlisted in the Army, but bought himself out and went to sea in the Merchant Navy, travelling far and wide. Wartime newspaper articles tell of him ranching in Argentina and working aboard whalers in the Arctic Ocean. When war broke out, Samson, who had joined the Royal Naval Reserve, was working, ironically, in Turkey, on a railroad at Smyrna. He immediately left his job, driving the mail train, sailed by steamer to Malta and there joined the crew of HMS *Hussar*.

The next few months were uneventful as the Mediterranean Fleet guarded against the possible break-out of the cruisers *Goeben* and *Breslau*. The only drama was provided by the elements. Writing home in early 1915, Samson said:

> We are having awful weather here, and the ship has been trying to stand on her head for the last fortnight, but has not managed it yet. The cold is far worse than the Germans, the only difference being that you can feel the cold and not see it, and see the Germans not feel them. We are all very anxious to have another go at them and get it finished.

He closed on a humorous note:

> Do you remember that lovely old song, 'Roaming in the gloaming on the bonnie banks of Clyde'? Well, here is what we sing to the same air, as well as the outside air and sea:
>
> > Coaling and patrolling outside the Dardanelles,
> > Waiting for the *Goeben* to come and taste our shells;
> > She came down to Schanac [*sic*], but she very soon went back;
> > Oh, it's lovely coaling and patrolling!

It was not long afterwards that the Mediterranean Fleet, including HMS *Hussar*, turned its attentions towards breaking through the Dardanelles instead of guarding against a Turkish break-out. And Samson, as one of the *Hussar*'s volunteers aboard the *River Clyde*, found excitement aplenty to make up for the months of inactivity.

The most seriously injured of the V Beach heroes who lived to receive the Victoria Cross, Samson was said to have suffered seventeen separate wounds. Evacuated to Port Said and then on to England, where he was treated at the Haslar Naval Hospital, he still had thirteen pieces of shrapnel lodged in his body when his VC was announced. At the time he was recuperating near Aboyne, in Scotland, and the following day he attended a civic reception in his home town of Carnoustie. Flags and bunting decorated the town's railway station as he arrived to be greeted by the provost, town councillors and burgh band. Crowds pursued Samson everywhere during the next few days. His appearance at a recruiting rally in Aberdeen resulted in more than a hundred men enlisting.

On 5 October Samson went to Buckingham Palace to receive his VC from George V. Promoted chief petty officer, he figured in the 110th anniversary

Samson being greeted on his return to Carnoustie

celebrations marking Nelson's victory at Trafalgar. The hero-worshipping continued when he returned to Carnoustie, together with his school contemporary and fellow VC winner Charles Jarvis, who had won his award for gallantry at Mons during the first month of the war. Samson was given a smoker's cabinet and a solid silver rose bowl. The VC winner, who was travelling out of uniform, also received an unexpected gift – a white feather!

On the last day of 1915, Samson married Catherine Glass, a farmer's daughter, at the Huntly Arms Hotel, Aboyne. The couple were to have one son. The following June, Samson was discharged from the Navy for a year on account of his wounds. He returned to Aboyne, where his wife was living. A newspaper report described him as looking 'bright and cheery', despite his painful injuries. There is no record, however, of Samson returning to active service.

After the war, he rejoined the Merchant Navy and in early 1922 he sailed from Dundee aboard the SS *Docina*. Taken seriously ill in the Gulf of Mexico, Samson was transferred to another vessel and taken to Bermuda for urgent medical treatment. He was found to be suffering from pneumonia and nothing could save him. He died on 23 February 1923, and was buried with full military honours in the island's military cemetery.

Wilfrid St Aubyn Malleson was the youngest recipient of the Victoria Cross during the Gallipoli operations. He was born at Kirkee, in India, on 17 September 1896, the eldest son of Maj.-Gen. Wilfrid Malleson (later Sir Wilfrid Malleson, KCIE, CB), of the Indian Army.

His early years were spent in India with his parents, but he came to England with his grandmother to attend Edgeborough prep school near Guildford. In due course his younger brothers, Rupert and Hugh, followed him, the school becoming almost a second home. Holidays were spent either with relatives or the headmaster and his wife.

In 1908, Wilfrid Malleson went to Marlborough and four years later joined the Royal Naval College, Dartmouth, as a cadet. He was promoted midshipman three days after the outbreak of war, and posted to HMS *Cornwallis*, a pre-dreadnaught battleship. The *Cornwallis* sailed from Britain to join the Mediterranean Fleet in January 1915, and to her fell the honour of firing the first British shot in the naval attempt to force a passage through the Dardanelles. Having survived the ill-starred naval assault of 18 March, the *Cornwallis* was assigned to cover the landings at S Beach, east of Cape Helles, on 25 April.

W. Malleson (back row far left) at Edgeborough School, 1908

Members of her crew, however, were detailed as beach parties with the task of ferrying troops ashore at V Beach, after the initial waves had, in theory, secured the shoreline.

Malleson was one of thirty-eight officers and men from the *Cornwallis* who were to operate the third tow of six lifeboats. Transported to the fleet sweeper *Newmarket*, lying off Tenedos, Malleson slept until 3.30 a.m. on 25 April, when he awoke to find the vessel within five miles of the straits.

During the action which followed, Malleson was the only one of the six V Beach landing VCs to survive entirely unscathed. Given the length of time he was exposed to the Turkish fire, that in itself was little short of miraculous. He returned to the *Cornwallis* on the evening of 25 April to fetch some 'fresh gear', having spent a long period sheltering on the *River Clyde*. In his account of the landings, which was written eleven months later, he recounted:

> The next boat ashore was not until about 3.00 p.m. on the 26th. Accordingly, I returned ashore then with Mr Forbes [a midshipman from the *Cornwallis*] who had volunteered for the now somewhat thinned-out beach party. We spent all the afternoon unloading water and ammunition lighters, interrupted slightly by 4.7-in or 5-in common [sic] from Asia. The Zion Mule Corps had just arrived and proved very useful. That night the beach party and beach guard [two companies of Anson Batt. RND] entrenched themselves on the beach. We heard scattered rifle shots, probably from snipers. About 12.30 a.m., I was sent out in the whaler to direct tows to the landing place. These were the French from Kum Kali [sic], due at 1.00 a.m. At dawn, I returned to the beach. For the next 5 days the French landing went on uninterruptedly. On the 3rd day, we had a French NTO and beach party, who were a great help. After the 5th day the pace slackened off a little and we were given some French steam and motor boats which slackened off the pace also. On the 6th day I was transferred to a steamboat and so left the beach.

The strain of those arduous days, following immediately after his exertions at the landings, took their toll. Malleson was evacuated to Malta's Bighi Naval Hospital suffering from rheumatic fever. According to his brother Rupert, then serving as a 15-year-old midshipman aboard the *Lord Nelson* in support of the operations at Gallipoli, it was the direct result of Wilfrid's 'long immersion and physical exhaustion off V Beach'. He made a full recovery and was promoted acting sub-lieutenant on 15 May 1916, joining his brother aboard the *Lord Nelson* in October. His rank of sub-lieutenant was confirmed on 30 December and in the following October he left to undergo submarine training.

On 2 January 1918 Malleson went to Buckingham Palace to receive his VC from George V. Two months later he was promoted lieutenant and he saw out

the war aboard the submarine depot ship *Lucia*, commanded by another
Dardanelles VC, Martin Nasmith.

After the war Malleson served in the submarines L7 and L19, the latter as first
lieutenant, before gaining his first command, H50, in 1923. His submarine
service was interrupted by a two-year spell on battleship duties. He returned,
however, to take command of L69 in August 1927.

Six months earlier he had married Cecil Mary Collinson at St Mark's,
Hamilton Terrace, St Marylebone, London. They had met and become engaged
while he was serving in Malta. The couple had a daughter, Jane, born in 1928.
Malleson was based at the time in Gosport and they settled near Plymouth.

After a short spell on the staff at Devonport, Malleson was posted to the
cruiser HMS *Berwick*, on the China Station. By then in his mid-thirties, he had
acquired, according to a fellow officer, a fierce reputation. Cdr. J.P. Macintyre
(retd.) remembered:

> He had rather definite views, though he didn't talk much. He used to look like
> a pirate. He had a slightly hooked nose which appeared more hooked in those
> days than when he grew older . . . He was known as 'Mad Malleson', that is
> not meant to be pejorative mad, but a chap who is a bit unpredictable. He was
> fiercely forgetful, abnormally so.

His career apparently becalmed, promotion came slowly during the 1930s. At
the outbreak of the Second World War he was a commander serving at
Devonport. In 1941 he joined the Retired List. However, his career was not quite
over. Brought out of retirement, he was appointed assistant captain of Malta
Dockyard and at the end of the war he was joined on the island by his wife and
daughter. Promoted captain of the dockyard and later King's Harbour Master, he
continued to serve on Malta until his second and final retirement from the Navy
in 1948, with the rank of captain. Malleson was not yet fifty, and the next twelve
years were spent in a nomadic existence as he attempted to launch a second
career on dry land. Settling first at Lifton, in Devon, the Mallesons moved to
Washaway, near Bodmin, in Cornwall, before relocating to Galloway, where they
ran an hotel. Eventually they returned to Cornwall, where, between 1950 and
1960, the retired naval captain and his wife ran Pentewan Sands caravan and
camping site near St Austell.

They retired and moved, in the early 1960s, to St Clement, a small village near
Truro. They bought a plot of land, with an adjoining orchard, and had a
bungalow built. Pendrae was the first home they had owned and it was to be
Malleson's home for the last twelve years of his life.

He had taken to wearing a monocle and became a noted village character,
although few residents knew anything of his distinguished war record. His

W. Malleson with his wife and daughter in Malta, shortly after the Second World War

daughter, Mrs Jane McWilliam, recalled that a family friend had done a painting of his VC exploit and presented it to him. 'I think my father found it a slight embarrassment as it was always hung well tucked away from the gaze of visitors.' He held a number of posts in the local community, serving as chairman of the parish hall committee and chairman of the sea cadets unit. He refused, however, to take part in any reunions of VC holders and declined to join the Victoria Cross and George Cross Association.

Captain Malleson VC, the last-surviving member of the V Beach heroes, died on 21 July 1975. His body was cremated and, in keeping with his wishes, his ashes were scattered at sea off Falmouth by his old colleague from China days, Cdr. Macintyre. His Victoria Cross, together with his other medals, was left to Edgeborough School, a place which held so many fond memories for him.

During his lifetime, Malleson had rarely spoken of his part in the landings. His report, on which a large part of this chapter is based, is believed to be the only full account he ever wrote and has never been published before. It was given to his daughter by a relative 'for safe-keeping with the injunction not to let my father know we had it or he would be sure to want his account destroyed!' In a letter to the author, Malleson's brother Hugh (a retired commander) stated:

The modesty was very real. He reckoned that he and his companions trying to replace the landing barges at V Beach . . . were available for any odd jobs, and this was an emergency. Of course, he was frightened, as were the others, but like truly modest men, he seemed to prefer keeping his reflections on the action to himself.

The hours spent in the water trying to get lighters back into position, under heavy fire was one thing, but the visible execution of hundreds of our soldiers before slipping into the water might well have un-nerved others. On this subject, therefore, Wilfrid's reluctance to talk or join in celebrations about VCs was initiated by his illness at Bighi Hospital and prolonged by the curious.

The award of the Victoria Cross to Sub-Lt. Tisdall, the first to a member of the Royal Naval Division, came only after an exhaustive investigation. The delay was chiefly caused by the absence of any senior officer witnesses from Tisdall's own battalion. Lt. Cdr. Wedgewood, who had observed his gallant conduct, had restricted his recommendations to men from his own unit, and while other officers aboard the *River Clyde* certainly knew of Tisdall's actions, they did not know his identity.

Following the landings, Tisdall's unit supplied beach parties for work in clearing up the shoreline. Two days after the landing, he wrote to his family: 'Have been under fire and are now ashore; all day spent in burying soldiers. Some of my men are killed. We are all happy and fit. Plenty of hard work and enemy shells, and a smell of dead men . . .' On that day Tisdall made his first visit to the firing line, in charge of a volunteer party carrying ammunition. His calm authority and cool courage were evident once more on 28 April, when a shell burst near a French gun team, wounding a horse and sending the gunners scurrying for cover. Tisdall went out, got the horse back on its feet, removed its harness and made the gunners return. When he went back a doctor called out in warning: 'We can get more horses, but we can't get another Tisdall.'

On 30 April the Anson Battalion joined its sister unit, the Howe Battalion, in bolstering the French sector of the Helles front. Tisdall and his platoon remained in their forward positions for five days while preparations were made for the advance on Achi Baba. On 6 May the Second Battle of Krithia, as it was officially called, began with the Anson Battalion, part of the 2nd Royal Naval Brigade, in reserve to the French. At about midday, the Anson and Hood Battalions, with a portion of the Howe Battalion, were ordered to plug a gap between the French and the British near the Kanli Dere. Tisdall led his platoon into an abandoned Turkish trench on the extreme right of his battalion. They sheltered from the heavy fire being directed at them and it was while looking over the parapet, at approximately 3.00 p.m., that Tisdall was mortally wounded by a bullet in the chest. He died a few minutes later without regaining consciousness. A member of Tisdall's platoon later wrote: 'He was one of England's bravest men. All his men cried when he went because all the boys thought the world of him.'

Tisdall died without knowing that his courageous exploits at V Beach would be recognized. Indeed, had it not been for the persistence of his father, it is highly probable that his gallantry would have gone unrewarded. Fortunately, however, he found a strong ally in Lt. Cdr. Wedgewood, who had commanded the machine-gun battery on the *River Clyde*. On 21 December 1915 Wedgewood wrote to Maj.-Gen. A. Paris (GOC RN Division), concerning Tisdall's gallant conduct. He stated:

> Commander Moorhouse [CO of the Anson Battalion] recommended him for some distinction which his death prevented. But he did not see his heroism. I did. Owing to his anomalous position, I believe he missed the VC, and now however later I should like to bear my testimony . . .

Paris agreed, and an official inquiry into the case was set up with evidence being collected from all the surviving participants. The result was a recommendation for the Victoria Cross supported by Paris, Rear Admiral Wemyss and Lt. Cdr. Wedgewood. Eleven months after the landings, on 31 March 1916, the *London Gazette* carried the announcement of Tisdall's posthumous VC. The citation read:

During the landing from the SS *River Clyde* at V Beach, in the Gallipoli Peninsula on the 25th April, 1915, Sub-Lieutenant Tisdall, hearing wounded men on the beach calling for assistance jumped into the water and, pushing a boat in front of him, went to their rescue. He was, however, obliged to obtain help, and took with him on two trips Leading Seaman Malia and on other trips Chief Petty Officer Perring and Leading Seaman Curtiss and Parkinson. In all, Sub-Lieutenant Tisdall made four or five trips between the ship and the shore, and was thus responsible for rescuing several wounded men under heavy and accurate fire.

Owing to the fact that Sub-Lieutenant Tisdall and the platoon under his orders were on detached service at the time, and that this officer was killed in action on the 6th May, it has only now been possible to obtain complete information as to the individuals who took part in this gallant act. Of these, Leading Seaman Fred Curtiss, ON Dev 1899, has been missing since 4th June, 1915.

Later, it was confirmed that Curtiss had been killed in action during the Third Battle of Krithia. Perring, Malia and Parkinson were all wounded during the campaign. Their brave work at V Beach was recognized by the award of Conspicuous Gallantry Medals to each of them. Russell and Rumming, from Wedgewood's RNAS unit, had already received the same decoration.

Arthur Walderne St Clair Tisdall was born in Bombay on 21 July 1890, the second son of the Revd Dr William St Clair Tisdall and his wife Marian (née Gray). His father, an acknowledged expert on comparative Eastern religions, was in charge of the Church Missionary Society's Mahommedan Mission.

In 1892, after a short stay in England, the Tisdall family embarked for Ispahan, in Persia, where Dr Tisdall was to head the CMS Persia–Baghdad Mission. For the next eight years of Arthur Tisdall's life, this was to be his home. 'Pog', as he was nicknamed by the rest of his family, was educated by an English governess and his father, who taught him to speak conversational Latin by the age of ten.

The family returned to England, via the Dardanelles, in 1900. Arthur Tisdall enrolled as a pupil at Bedford School, where he acquired a new nickname, 'Pussy', because of his time spent in Persia, and a reputation for high academic ability. His scholarly progress towards Trinity College, Cambridge, was paved with prizes. By the time he embarked on his university education in 1909, 'Wally' Tisdall, as he was known, was already a highly popular and impressive personality. To his academic achievement, he added sporting prowess and an infectious sense of humour. He also displayed some mildly eccentric behaviour, such as walking at night from Bedford to Cambridge. One contemporary described him as being 'over six feet high, broad-chested, strong-limbed, a broad forehead crowned with dark brown wavy hair, deep grey eyes faintly flecked with brown, a finely poised head – one felt there were such enormous possibilities in him'.

At Cambridge, Tisdall rowed for his college and amassed a plethora of academic prizes, culminating in a Double First BA Honours degree and the Chancellor's Gold Medal for Classics. Among his great enthusiasms were the growth of socialism, women's suffrage, economics, to which he devoted his final two years at Cambridge, and literature. He had started writing verse before entering Trinity and his love of poetry grew throughout his days at university. He was noted by fellow students for his comic verses; nonsense rhymes which reflected both his intellect and his sense of humour. There is little doubt, however, that he took his writing extremely seriously. His poems which have survived from this period point to the first stirrings of a talent that would go

Tisdall in his rooms at Trinity College, Cambridge

tragically unrealized. At one time he contemplated trying to make his living as a writer, but in the end opted to pursue a more orthodox career as a civil servant. In 1913, his final year at Cambridge, he passed the combined Indian and Home Civil Service examination and took up an appointment in London. The highest echelons of the Civil Service beckoned. Then war broke out.

In May 1914 Tisdall, whose only previous military experience consisted of serving in the ranks of the OTC at Bedford and Cambridge, had joined the Royal Naval Volunteer Reserve. When the RNVR was mobilized in August 1914, Tisdall cut short a camping holiday in Sussex to join his unit as an able seaman. After undergoing training at Walmer Camp, Tisdall found himself two months later in Belgium as part of the Royal Naval Division hastily despatched to help defend Antwerp from the advancing German Army. Although still a humble naval rating, he was appointed interpreter to the local Belgian commandant. On 7 October he wrote home, describing his first experience of war:

> The singing of shells is indescribably weird when first you hear it. All our kits lost by fire. The burning city of Antwerp is a terrible but magnificent sight against the blackness of the night, and lights up the whole country round. The sight of the poor women and children driven from their homes makes one's blood boil. It's horrid to feel so useless.

When the Germans broke through, the Royal Naval Division were compelled to beat a hasty retreat along the rapidly narrowing coastal corridor. More than 1000 men were forced to seek internment in Holland to avoid capture. Tisdall was among those fortunate enough to escape to England, where he was promptly commissioned into the Anson Battalion, his rank of sub-lieutenant being backdated eleven days to 1 October.

After a few weeks spent at Crystal Palace, Sheerness and Chatham, Tisdall was posted to Blandford Camp, in Dorset, where the Royal Naval Division exchanged their naval blue uniforms for khaki. A winter of discontent followed with the depression lifted only by the news, in February 1915, of impending action. Tisdall cheerily noted: 'We have been promised a six-week or two-month campaign, probably fairly exciting.' Following an inspection by Winston Churchill, the division left Blandford for Bristol on 27 February. A few days later their destination was confirmed as the Dardanelles. During a short stay on the island of Lemnos, Tisdall busied himself drawing maps, touring villages and attempting to learn the local Greek dialect. In common with many of his fellow officers, he was filled with optimism for the coming campaign. On 9 March he wrote:

> Life is so pleasant here and there's something to look forward to; to turn the Turks out of Constantinople, etc, would be a thing well worth doing, and give

me a feeling that I had really done one satisfactory piece of work. Here one really feels that we are fighting on the side of civilization.

The Royal Naval Division was shipped to Egypt while final preparations for the landings were made. They then returned to Lemnos, where Tisdall learned of his platoon's detached role aboard the *River Clyde*. Of the landings, and his heroic part in it, he left no record. His diaries were never found and his last postcard home, undated but sent the day after his death, stated:

We are in the firing line now, and spend the night being sniped at and missed. For nearly a week we had to unload barges for other people under heavy fire, which made a lot of dirt, and frightened our Allies and mules . . . When not working we sleep and eat . . .

On 7 May Tisdall was buried just a few yards from where he died. Three days later news of his death reached his father, who was then serving as vicar of St George's Church, Deal. A memorial service was held on 13 May, and later an engraved tablet was placed in the church. Fifty-five years afterwards, on 28 April 1970, Tisdall's brother and sister, F.R. St Clair Tisdall and Mrs A. Alcock, attended a ceremony at HMS *President*, where they presented his Victoria Cross and other medals to the headquarters of the London Division, RNVR.

Like his famous comrade-in-arms, Rupert Brooke, Tisdall was cut down in the prime of a life which promised greatness. Nearly eighty years after his death, he still appears to embody that intoxicating brand of romantic idealism which carried so many of his generation's best and brightest to destruction on the shores of Gallipoli.

C.H.M. DOUGHTY-WYLIE AND
G.N. WALFORD

Sedd el Bahr, 26 April 1915

Lt. Col. C. Doughty-Wylie

Capt. G. Walford

By mid-afternoon on 25 April the main landing at V Beach had been brought to a bloody standstill. Three companies of Turks, in well-sited positions overlooking the shore, had reduced the invasion to a shambles. Groups of survivors from the spearhead units of the 86th Brigade sheltered beneath a sandy ledge only a few feet from the gently lapping sea. From the ruins of Fort No. 1 on the left, across the rising ground to Hill 141 and down through the narrow streets of Sedd el Bahr to the battered Old Fort on the right, the Turks commanded every avenue of advance. To move forward towards the thick belts of barbed wire was to court almost certain death. To retreat through waters swept by machine-gun fire involved nearly as great a risk. And so they stayed where they were, a bewildered confusion of Dublins, Munsters and Hampshires, clinging to their precarious toehold, scarcely daring to move.

In the face of the rapidly disintegrating landing plan, their commanders aboard the beached *River Clyde* reached the same conclusion. As hope of an out-flanking movement from W Beach faded, Lt. Col. H.E. Tizard, CO of the 1st Royal Munster Fusiliers and senior surviving officer, ordered a halt to further landings until after nightfall. Then, with the sky lit by the flames from the burning village of Sedd el Bahr, the troops, who had been crowded aboard the *River Clyde* all day, were eventually led ashore. By 12.30 a.m. they were on the peninsula. The problem of breaking out of the tiny beachhead, however, remained unresolved. V Beach, in the early hours of 26 April, was the scene of considerable confusion. Units were hopelessly mixed. Many were officerless and badly shaken by the slaughter of the first day.

Frustrated by the chaos and loss of momentum, two of the expeditionary force's most senior staff officers went ashore on their own initiative. Lt. Col. Charles Doughty-Wylie, more familiarly known as 'Dick' Doughty-Wylie, and Lt. Col. Weir de Lancy Williams were both members of Sir Ian Hamilton's Staff. They had been aboard the *River Clyde*, together with an interpreter, as liaison officers for GHQ. Now under Tizard's command, they resolved to make a reconnaissance of the beach with a view to the speediest possible resumption of the advance.

For Doughty-Wylie in particular, the short walk from the *River Clyde* to the Turkish shore represented a moment heavy with irony. Two years before, the Sultan of Turkey had bestowed upon him the Imperial Ottoman Order of Medjidieh, 2nd Class, for his work in command of the Red Cross units serving with the Turks during the Balkan Wars of 1912–13. Earlier still, he had been fêted by the Turkish authorities, the British Government and the international community for his courageous efforts to halt the massacre of Armenian Christians in the Turkish town of Adana in April 1909. More than 2,000 people were killed in an outbreak of fratricidal violence which shocked western Europe, and there was little doubt the death toll would have been higher but for the intervention of Doughty-Wylie, then

serving as military vice-consul in the Turkish province of Konia. Donning army uniform, he rode at the head of fifty Turkish soldiers through the Christian quarter, restoring order. Shot in the right arm by an Armenian who mistook him for a Turkish officer, Doughty-Wylie returned to face the mobs. By virtually taking command of the town, he succeeded in quelling the marauding gangs and spared Adana's Christian population further bloodshed. He was made a CMG for his bravery and cool leadership.

On 26 April 1915 he would employ those same qualities against the nation which had so recently hailed him a hero. Doughty-Wylie's presence on Sir Ian Hamilton's Staff was entirely due to his pre-war experience in Turkey. It was considered that his vast knowledge, and

Doughty-Wylie with Sir Ian Hamilton aboard the Arcadian *shortly before the landings*

understanding of the Turks, would prove immensely valuable to the expedition. Promoted lieutenant colonel, he was employed in the Intelligence Section. He was not, however, among the list of staff officers originally assigned to the *River Clyde*. According to Williams, who was serving in the Operations Section, Doughty-Wylie intended to accompany the Australian and New Zealand Corps, but was persuaded by him to join the main landing party. Ever eager to be in the forefront of the action, Doughty-Wylie 'did not', in Williams' words, 'want much inducing'.

During their brief time together, Doughty-Wylie made a deep impression on his fellow staff officer; most notably by his conduct on 25 April. Writing of him, a month after the landing, Williams declared: 'He was a very splendid soldier of the very best type; he had been hit on more than one previous occasion and knew no fear; the previous day the *Clyde* was fired on throughout the day and Doughty-Wylie seemed positively to enjoy it'. However, Williams also detected in his colleague a darker side. 'He was', he wrote 'rather a fatalist . . . I am firmly of the opinion that poor Doughty-Wylie realized he would be killed in this war'.

It is clear from Doughty-Wylie's correspondence immediately prior to the landings that he was preoccupied with thoughts of his own death. In normal circumstances, such concerns might be considered a soldier's attempt to come to terms with the real possibility of being killed. However, there is considerable evidence to suggest that Doughty-Wylie's apparent fatalism on the eve of the expedition was rooted more in a personal crisis. By the spring of 1915 his tangled private life was giving him cause for growing concern. His wife, Lilian, who was working as a nursing officer in France, had spoken of committing suicide if he were to die. And there was the added complication of another woman in his life, the distinguished Middle Eastern explorer and writer, Gertrude Bell, with whom he had maintained a secret liaison. In an extraordinary echo of Lilian's suicidal urges, she too had threatened to take her own life rather than live without him.

As he prepared to set out on his final mission aboard the *River Clyde*, he wrote pleadingly to Gertrude: 'When I asked for this ship, my joy in it was half strangled by that thing you said, I can't even name it or talk about it. As

Doughty-Wylie with his wife Lilian in Turkey, 1908, photograph taken by Gertrude Bell

we go steaming in under the port guns in our rotten old collier, shall I think of it
. . . Don't do it. Time is nothing, we join up again, but to hurry the pace is
unworthy of us all.' Meanwhile, in a letter to his wife's mother, he wrote:

> I am going to embark tomorrow on what is certainly an extremely dangerous
> job, namely the wreck ship of which you will see in the papers. If the thing
> went wrong, Lily would feel intolerably lonely and hopeless after her long
> hours of work, which tell surely on anybody's spirits . . . She talks about
> overdoses of morphia and such things. I think that in reality she is too brave
> and strong minded for such things but the saying weighs on my spirits . . .

The two letters were written twenty-four hours apart, within four days of the
landing at V Beach. It seems reasonable to surmise, therefore, that for all his
outward display of calm, Doughty-Wylie was in a state of emotional turmoil,
torn, as he was, between concern for his loved ones and his sense of professional
duty. In one of his last letters to Gertrude, he had referred to the 'wreck ship, or
wooden horse of Troy' as 'an ingenious arrangement', adding prophetically: 'If I
can get ashore, I can help a good deal in the difficult job of landing enough
troops to storm the trenches on the beach – and to see the most dashing military
exploit that has been performed for a very long time . . .'

What thoughts ran through his mind as he ventured out from the *River Clyde*
on to the beach of Sedd el Bahr will never be known. For the last hours of
Doughty-Wylie's life we must rely on the observations of his fellow officers.
What is clear is that after a terrible day during which they had, in the words of
Williams, 'sat and suffered until sunset', the senior officers aboard the *River
Clyde* were determined to regain the initiative. According to Williams:

> Next day, we ought to have been able to seize the crest quite early but the men
> were sticky and lack of officers very apparent; they wanted a good leader. I
> talked it over with Wylie and decided that I should land and try to get the men
> together for an attack; he was to watch progress and bring up the reserve of
> such stragglers as would be left behind.

Williams duly departed for the left of the beach, where he organized a mixed
force of some 150 men from the Dublins and Munsters. Doughty-Wylie appears
to have followed him ashore, to reconnoitre the beach on the right, beneath the
walls of the Old Fort. The time of his first journey on to the beach is unclear.
Some accounts have him exploring ashore after nightfall and reporting back to
the *River Clyde* before midnight. Williams, however, insisted that 'neither I nor
Wylie landed that day'. Whatever the precise timing, Doughty-Wylie met Maj.
A.T. Beckwith, of the 2nd Hampshires, on the darkened shore and discussed the

possibility of renewing the attack. Beckwith had gone ashore to lead an assault on the right, but, with the men exhausted, he reported that an immediate attack was out of the question. Doughty-Wylie agreed, and asked for a naval bombardment to precede the early morning assault.

Around midnight, fresh orders from Gen. Hunter-Weston, GOC of the 29th Division, reached the *River Clyde*, calling for the advance to be resumed. They were delivered by Capt. Garth Walford, brigade major of the 29th Divisional Artillery, who had seen a considerable amount of action in France before joining the expeditionary force. Walford remained on board the *River Clyde* until Doughty-Wylie returned to report his findings to Col. Tizard. It would appear that Walford then went ashore to join Beckwith's force, apparently determined to carry out his chief's orders personally.

The hastily arranged plan for the morning attack involved a three-pronged assault. Maj. Beckwith was to lead the fresher troops, mainly consisting of the 2nd Hampshires, on the right to capture the Old Fort and village, while a mixed force of Dublins and Munsters was to link up with the troops advancing from W Beach on the left. In the centre, an assault would be made through the broad belts of barbed wire to seize Hill 141. After a short delay caused by confusion over the naval bombardment, Beckwith quickly cleared the Old Fort. From his vantage point on the *River Clyde*, Col. Tizard observed:

At about 6.30 a.m. a small party of men about six or seven with an officer leading them, I believe now that this was Major Walford [*sic*], moved from under the fort wall on the right towards the path that ran up into the village between the end of the low wire entanglements and the fort wall. When about half way up this path and opposite an abuttment of the fort that had two windows in it a machine gun opened up on them from the nearest window. None of them were hit and they jumped over a low wall on their left and took cover.

Tizard called for naval support and the guns of HMS *Albion* promptly silenced the opposition in this quarter. His account continued:

This party then advanced and got behind some buildings on the left where they were held up by snipers. A support of eight men now went up to them from the men under the bank on the right and after a bit, they got a little further into the village on the left side of it. About 7.30 a.m., or soon after, I saw this party coming back, taking cover under the compound walls and the houses, and returning the fire of the snipers who were in the houses.

Another party now started off and reinforced them and, after a bit of skirmishing behind walls etc, they pushed on into the village and I did not see them again.

What Tizard was witnessing was the start of one of the fiercest struggles of the beach-head battle; the savage, close-quarter fighting for control of Sedd el Bahr. The force on the right, having taken the Old Fort with relative ease, ran into a hail of fire as they attempted to enter the village through a small postern gate on the eastern side of the fort, which was later found to be covered by a small Turkish trench on the edge of the cliff. Anyone emerging from the gate was an easy target and the advance was briefly checked. Realizing the importance of maintaining momentum, Capt. Walford placed himself at the head of the troops who were pinned down and led them forward. Surging through the gate, they burst into the maze of streets. With Capt. A.C. Addison, of the 2nd Hampshires, alongside him, Walford led Y Company forward. The Hampshires' historian recorded:

In the village they met desperate resistance. The Turks contested every house and had to be ousted with the bayonet from one after another. Some lay quiet, concealed in cellars or ruins, till our men had passed by and then fired into their backs.

It was a brutal, costly action with no quarter given. At 8.45 a.m. Capt. Walford reported: 'Advance through Sedd el Bahr is very slow. Am receiving no support on my left.' According to Capt. G.B. Stoney, the V Beach landing officer, who was on board the *River Clyde*, it was shortly after receipt of this message that Doughty-Wylie 'asked me to come ashore with him as there was nothing doing on the boat and we might find something useful to do there'.

Once again, the exact timing of events is uncertain. In his diary, the *River Clyde*'s surgeon, Burrowes Kelly, stated that Doughty-Wylie 'returned and drank a cup of tea' at about 11.00 a.m. He noted: 'I had a chat of about a quarter of an hour with him, and he seemed depressed about the whole affair. Several times he remarked that something must be done. He then left us, and I recall vividly his walking stick . . .' In a letter home, Stoney wrote:

He [Doughty-Wylie] walked about quite regardless of the snipers, but who as a matter of fact did not fire at us. After talking to lots of people lining fences, he told me to go along and whip up any effectives and advance up the front of the hill commanding the beach and get in touch with a company of a Regt that had worked up through a village on the right.

By this time Williams' attack on the left had stalled and the centre force, under the command of Capt. Stoney, had yet to move. The hopes of the landing force, therefore, rested largely on the success of the troops assaulting on the right, and it was in that direction that Doughty-Wylie headed. The fighting to clear the village was still going on. Capt. Walford, the life and soul of the advance during its early stages, had been killed leading another party through the postern gate. Capt. Addison, his chief lieutenant in the street fighting, had also fallen, a victim of a Turkish grenade.

Doughty-Wylie had a narrow escape as he approached the village from the Old Fort. Lt. Guy Nightingale, of the Munsters, wrote:

> He was passing some distance in rear of the gateway when a bullet knocked the staff cap off his head. I happened to be quite close at the moment, and remember being struck by the calm way in which he treated the incident. He was carrying no weapon of any description at the time, only a small cane.

Some time afterwards, Nightingale saw the colonel leading a rush, armed with rifle and bayonet, but he noted that the weapon was quickly discarded. Throughout the rest of the morning, Doughty-Wylie put fresh heart into the attacking force. Nightingale later recalled:

> I saw him on several occasions that morning walk into houses, which might or might not contain a Turk ready to fire on the first person who came in, as unconcernedly as if he were walking into a shop. Naturally, this confidence of manner had a great effect on the men.

Even so, it was not until three hours after Walford had led the first parties of men into the village that Doughty-Wylie was able to report the capture of Sedd el Bahr. His men were then in position to attack Hill 141. Having reached the outer limits of the village, he arranged for a naval bombardment as a prelude to an assault on the Turkish positions by his own men in conjunction with Capt. Stoney's disparate force in the centre. Together with Capt. Nightingale, Doughty-Wylie watched the bombardment from one of the corner turrets in the Old Fort. As they observed the fall of shells, he explained how they would storm the hill. Nightingale later wrote:

> There was a strong redoubt on the top, but he decided that the remnants of the three battalions should assault simultaneously, immediately after the bombardment. He was extraordinarily confident that everything would go well, and the hill be won by sunset, and I think it was due much to his spirit of confidence that he had been able to overcome the enormous difficulties with only such exhausted and disorganised troops as he had to deal with.
>
> His sole idea and determination was that the hill should be taken that day at all costs; for he realised that it was impossible for us to hold any position between the high ground and the edge of the cliff where we had spent the previous night.

As the time was getting near for the bombardment to cease, the colonel gave his final orders to the few remaining officers before the assault. Major C.T.W. Grimshaw was to lead the Dublins. Simultaneously, the Hampshires were to assault from the far end of the village and come up on the far shoulder of the hill, while the Munster Fusiliers were to advance on the left of the Dublins, and at the same time.

When the order came to fix bayonets, however, the men scarcely waited for any orders, but all joined up together in one mass, and swept cheering up through an orchard and over a cemetery, Hampshires, Munsters and Dublins, to the first line of wire entanglements, through which was the way out leading past the deserted Turkish trenches to the summit of the hill. On the top was a flat space surrounded by a moat 20 feet deep with only one entrance leading up over it, through which the assaulting troops were led by Colonel Doughty-Wylie and Major Grimshaw.

The men lined the top edge of the moat, firing down on the retreating Turks, who were retiring down their communication trenches in the direction of Achi Baba. It was at this moment that Colonel Doughty-Wylie, who had led his men to the last moment, was killed by a shot in the head, dying almost immediately on the summit of the hill he had so ably captured.

The successful attack had taken little more than thirty minutes. By 3.00 p.m., V Beach was at last secure and the disaster which threatened to overwhelm the entire operation had been averted.

Tragically, many of those largely responsible for the reversal of fortunes were not alive to witness the fulfillment of their self-ordained mission. Walford and Addison had been killed in the battle for Sedd el Bahr, Grimshaw died on the summit of Hill 141 and Doughty-Wylie, by common consent the chief architect of the V Beach victory, had fallen at the moment of his greatest triumph.

Col. Williams, who had spoken to Doughty-Wylie shortly before he launched the final attack, found his body lying just inside the 'castle' on top of the hill. He recorded:

I came up shortly after he had fallen; the men round about were full of admiration and sorrow. They told me he was first the whole way up the slope and it was only in the last few yards that some four or five men had got up to and passed him actually over the castle walls; personally, I noticed him on two or three occasions always in front and cheering his men on.

As soon as I came up and realized that he was dead I took his watch, money and a few things I could find and had him buried where he fell. I had this done at once, having seen such disgusting sights of unburied dead in the village that I could not bear to have him lying there. This was all done

An artist's impression of Doughty-Wylie's VC action

hurriedly as I had to reorganize the line and think of further advance or digging in; we just buried him as he lay and I said The Lord's Prayer over his grave and bid him goodbye. That night when things had quietened down I asked Unwin [Cdr. E. Unwin VC] to have a temporary cross put up to mark his grave.

The following morning the Munsters' regimental chaplain climbed the hill, soon to be renamed Fort Doughty-Wylie, and read the burial service over the lone grave.

Doughty-Wylie's achievement in rescuing a seemingly lost cause made a profound impression both on the survivors of his gallant band and on the senior commanders who watched events unfold from the battleships standing offshore. Of the former, Capt. Nightingale wrote:

When he took command of them, they were exhausted with the strain of the landing and depressed with what they had already experienced; but the last he saw of them was at the moment when these same men realised the day was won, and rest close at hand, both of which they knew they owed to his gallant leadership.

Doughty-Wylie's lone grave at Gallipoli

Sir Ian Hamilton, conscious, no doubt, of the great debt he owed to his staff officer, wrote in eulogy of Doughty-Wylie's exploit:

> The death of a hero strips victory of her wings. Alas, for Doughty-Wylie! Alas, for that faithful disciple of Charles Gordon; protector of the poor and of the helpless; noblest of those knights ever ready to lay down their lives to uphold the fair fame of England. Braver soldier never drew sword. He had no hatred of the enemy. His spirit did not need that ugly stimulant. Tenderness and pity filled his heart and yet he had the overflowing enthusiasm and contempt of death which alone can give troops the volition to attack when they have been crouching so long under a pitiless fire. Doughty-Wylie was no flash-in-the-pan VC winner. He was a steadfast hero . . . Now as he would have wished to die, so he has died.

It was, of course, the stuff of legend and, in the hands of the Press, ever eager to find new heroes, that was precisely what it became. First reports of the action, based on accounts supplied by wounded soldiers in Cairo, were cabled to the London newspapers on 7 May. Nine days later, beneath such headlines as

'Bravest of the brave' and 'Nameless hero of Sed-le-Bahr' [*sic*], they identified the gallant officer as Doughty-Wylie. Rather in the way that seventy years later Lt. Col. 'H' Jones would become lionized long before any official recognition was made, so Doughty-Wylie became the Gallipoli Campaign's first hero, overshadowing all others involved in the gallant break-out from the beach at Sedd el Bahr.

There would be no posthumous honours for Grimshaw or Addison. Beckwith, of the Hampshires, received a DSO, as did Stoney, although this was connected with operations later in the campaign. Only the actions of Garth Walford were deemed to have rivalled those of Doughty-Wylie, and their names were linked together in a joint citation for the award of their posthumous VCs which was published in the *London Gazette* on 23 June 1915. They were the first Victoria Crosses of the campaign to be announced. The citation read:

> On the morning of the 26th April, 1915, subsequent to a landing having been effected on the beach at a point on the Gallipoli Peninsula, during which both Brigadier-General and Brigade-Major had been killed, Lieutenant Colonel Doughty-Wylie and Captain Walford organised and led an attack through and on both sides of the village of Sedd el Bahr on the Old Castle at the top of the hill inland. The enemy's position was very strongly held and entrenched, and defended with concealed machine guns and pom-poms. It was mainly due to the initiative, skill and great gallantry of these two officers that the attack was a complete success. Both were killed in the moment of victory.

Five months after the awards were made, on 17 November, a small boat came alongside the rusting hulk of the *River Clyde*. In it was a single woman. Using the old 'wreck ship' as a pier, she went ashore, walked through the village of Sedd el Bahr and on up to the crest of Hill 141, where she placed a large wreath on the white cross standing at the head of the lone grave overlooking the bay.

Lilian Doughty-Wylie had come to pay her last respects to her husband. She was the only woman to set foot on the peninsula during the eight-month long campaign.

Charles Hotham Montagu Doughty-Wylie, the highest ranking officer to win the Victoria Cross during the Gallipoli Campaign, was born at Theberton Hall, Suffolk, on 23 July 1868, the eldest son of Henry Montagu Doughty, JP, and Edith Rebecca (née Cameron). His father, a retired naval officer, was a barrister and lord of the manor of Theberton. Among his more celebrated relatives were his grandfather on his mother's side who was Chief Justice of Vancouver Island, and his uncle, the Arabian explorer Charles Doughty.

Educated at Winchester and Sandhurst, the young Charles Doughty was commissioned a second lieutenant in the Royal Welch Fusiliers on 21 September 1889. Promoted lieutenant the following year, he first saw action in the Hazara Expedition of 1891, in which he also received his first wound. His next fifteen years of military service reads like a roll call of the British Empire's colonial conflicts; Chitral on the North-west Frontier of India (1895), Crete (1896), the Sudan (1898–9), South Africa (1900), Tientsin, China (1900) and Somaliland (1903–4). Along the way, he collected a cluster of campaign medals, a second wound and promotion to the rank of captain in the 2nd Battalion, Royal Welch Fusiliers.

His military career to this point was nothing if not varied. He served as transport officer during the relief of Chitral, was a brigade-major with the Egyptian Army during Kitchener's reconquest of the Sudan, for which he received the Order of the Medjidie, 4th Class, led a mounted infantry unit in the Boer War, where he was wounded during an engagement near Vredefort, and raised and commanded a corps of mounted infantry as part of the China Field Force in the wake of the Boxer Rebellion. In 1903 he found himself in the Horn of Africa, commanding a Somali Camel Corps detachment in operations against the so-called Mad Mullah. The fighting in Somaliland was to be his last experience of warfare as a combatant before the Gallipoli Campaign.

In May 1904 he travelled to India on leave where in Bombay, the following month, he married Lilian Oimara Adams Wylie, widow of Lt. Henry Adams, Indian Medical Service. After a holiday spent on the North-west Frontier, Doughty returned to his regiment in Agra. In December he changed his name by deed poll to Doughty-Wylie, and in the following March, the couple returned to England, by way of Baghdad, taking in the archaeological sites in Babylon and Constantinople. Perhaps it was this journey, combined with the experiences of his famous uncle, which gave him a taste for exploring the Near East. Once home, he sought a change from traditional soldiering and his request for political employment was granted. In September 1906 he was appointed British military vice-consul in Konia, a Turkish province in Asia Minor. Shortly after taking up his new post, he was notified of his promotion to major. Later Cilicia was added to his area of jurisdiction, and it was there, during the Armenian massacres of 1909, that he came to the public's notice. It was there also that he was introduced to the woman who would feature prominently in the last years of his life. Doughty-Wylie first met Gertrude Bell in 1907 while she was engaged in an archaeological dig. They continued to correspond and it is probable that they met again in London five years later, but their relationship did not blossom until August 1913 when he visited her family home at Rounton Grange, near Northallerton.

Promoted consul-general as a reward for his services in Adana, Doughty-Wylie was posted to Addis Ababa, where he served until 1912. On the outbreak of the

Balkan War he and his wife went to Constantinople where he worked as Director of the Red Cross units and she served as Superintendent of Nursing Staff. As a result of his experience during the conflict, he was appointed British representative on the commission appointed to delimit the Greek and Albanian frontier. He became the commission's chairman and his services were recognized by his being appointed a Companion of the Order of the Bath (Civil Division).

In 1913 Doughty-Wylie returned to his consulate in Addis Ababa where he became engaged in treaty negotiations with the Ethiopian Government. Before leaving England, he wrote to Gertrude Bell: 'Go I must . . . There's anarchy out there, complete and beastly.' His diplomatic service was brought to a premature end by the outbreak of war and Turkey's entry into the conflict. February 1915 found him in Cairo, en route to England where he hoped to gain active service employment. Gen. Sir John Maxwell, C.-in-C. Egypt, sought permission to make use of the soldier-diplomat, but that same month the former consul-general was ordered to join Sir Ian Hamilton's Staff with the rank of lieutenant colonel.

Doughty-Wylie proceeded to London where he met Gertrude again before taking up his new appointment. He joined Hamilton's GHQ on 18 March, the day of the Navy's attempt to force a way through the Narrows. Four weeks later, on 21 April, the GHQ Staff were temporarily split up, with Doughty-Wylie and Williams taking their places on board the *River Clyde*. Doughty-Wylie was under no illusions about the hazardous nature of the enterprise. 'This is a very interesting show from every point of view', he wrote to his wife's mother, 'but it runs a great many chances however one looks at it'.

News of his death reached Lilian Doughty-Wylie in St Valery-sur-Somme, where she was in charge of a hospital. She confided in her diary: 'The shock was terrible. I don't know quite what I did for the first sixty seconds. Something seemed to tear at the region of my heart. All my life was so much of his life, all his life mine . . .'

Five months later she received his Victoria Cross, which was sent to her with a letter from King George V, regretting that his death had deprived him of the pride of personally conferring the distinction upon him.

Gertrude did not carry out her threats of suicide. Instead, she threw herself into a new career with the Arab Bureau of the British Intelligence Department. Later, she was to play a key role in the installation of Faisal ibn Hussain as king of Iraq. After the war she became director of antiquities, responsible for the archaeological treasures of Babylon and Assyria. She died in 1926, her affair with Doughty-Wylie still a secret outside her family. Access to her correspondence with him was granted only after Lilian's death in 1960.

Dick Doughty-Wylie's VC, together with his many honours and decorations, are now displayed by his former regiment at the Royal Welch Fusiliers' museum in Caernarfon Castle. Alongside them is a miniature portrait of him painted by

The memorial window depicting Doughty-Wylie as St George, Theberton church

his sister Gerty. His last gallant action is recalled today in his home village of Theberton, where his name is recorded on the war memorial outside St Peter's Church. For many years a machine-gun stood guard at the foot of the white cross, but the ravages of time led to its removal and it now figures in a display at the Suffolk Regiment museum in Bury St Edmunds. Inside the church a beautiful stained-glass window depicts the village's heroic son as St George. Of a less decorous nature is the small road, not far from the church, which bears his name.

But it is, most fittingly, on the peninsula itself that his deeds are best recalled by the presence of his solitary grave on the crest of the hill briefly known as Fort Doughty-Wylie in his honour. Of the many individual graves which were scattered across the Gallipoli battlefields, his alone remains on its original site. Flanked by two trees, the grave is a focal point for the legions of visitors who struggle up the slopes of Hill 141 to gaze out across the bay of Sedd el Bahr and to marvel at the gallantry of a man whose inspiring leadership helped turned defeat into victory all those years ago.

Garth Neville Walford, who played such an important role in the battle for Sedd el Bahr, was born on 27 May 1882, at Frimley, Surrey, the only son of Col. Neville Lloyd Walford, RA.

He attended the prep school run by A.H. Evans at Newbury before entering Harrow, his father's old school, in the autumn of 1895. Walford joined the large boarding house known as The Grove. An entrance scholar, he was invariably near the top of his class except for a period in late 1896 and throughout 1897 when he appears to have been dogged by ill health. He was repeatedly absent from the terminal examinations and remained in the Second Remove of the fifth form throughout this period. Walford's work was regularly commended to the headmaster, and led to his winning a prize while in the First Remove of the fifth.

Although he did not obtain one of the major school prizes, in 1900 he did win the Sayer Scholarship, originally established to fund one place at Caius College, Cambridge, and went to Balliol, Oxford. Unlike so many future VCs, he showed little aptitude for sport beyond playing Harrow football for his house.

Walford joined the Royal Artillery in 1902, where his abilities were quickly recognized when he topped the list of university candidates. His first appointment was in the militia, in December of that same year. He was appointed second lieutenant in December 1905, and two years later was married to Betty Trefusis, the daughter of an army officer. The couple had two daughters.

When war broke out Walford was at the Staff College and he went out to France in the middle of August, where he served with the 27th Brigade, Royal Field Artillery. During the retreat from Mons, he was twice fortunate to escape shell bursts close by him. One caused superficial wounds to both arms, and another blew off his cap without harming him. He saw action at the battle of the Aisne in September, and was evacuated sick later that month. Promoted to captain on 30 October 1914, he returned to his brigade at Ypres, where he held a number of temporary staff appointments. In January 1915 he was summoned home to take up a new appointment, as brigade-major RA, with the newly constituted 29th Division destined for the Dardanelles. After a brief spell at Leamington Spa, where the Divisional Artillery was formed, Walford sailed for Egypt in March 1915. He arrived in Lemnos, with the artillery headquarters staff, on 12 April and in the period immediately prior to the landings Walford joined a party of senior officers to observe a naval bombardment of their objectives. It was during this operation that Walford had his first experience of Turkish gunnery. He noted: 'I saw one shell fall about a thousand yards away and I don't think anything else was much nearer. One felt pretty safe, as we were loaded up with generals and admirals, and they wouldn't risk the Turks making a bag like that.'

Like so many of his colleagues among the expeditionary force, Walford was filled with romantic zeal for the venture which lay ahead of them. Inspired by the epic nature of the enterprise and the grandeur of its classical setting, he was moved to write a verse entitled 'The Last Crusade'. It began:

> Once more revives the never-dying war
> Of East and West: through this one entry gate
> Between two worlds have armies alternate
> Swept forth to conquest an alien shore . . .

By 21 April, his mind clearly focused on that 'alien shore', Walford was ready for the 'great adventure'. Once again, the past collided with the present, as he wrote in his last letter home: 'Well we are off in a day or two if the weather stays

Capt. Walford's grave, Gallipoli

fine; just like the Greek fleet going to Troy, people collected from all over the known world; we have even got our wooden horse, which I will explain later on. As far as the intelligence reports tell us, however, there seems to be no Helen.' Five days later, he was dead.

Walford was buried close to where he fell, just outside the walls of the Old Fort in Sedd el Bahr. A large cross beside a ruined house marked his grave during the campaign, but later his remains were reinterred in a Commonwealth war cemetery on the peninsula. Today Walford is also remembered on a brass plaque in Chagford Church, Devon, and at the Regent Hotel, Royal Leamington Spa, where he was based in early 1915.

In a letter written the day after the success at V Beach, largely inspired by Doughty-Wylie and Walford, Gen. Hunter-Weston (GOC 29th Division) insisted that 'no honour could be too high for them'. Referring to his avowed intention to recommend them for a 'suitable posthumous reward', he added: 'They achieved the impossible. They showed themselves Englishmen in the old mould. I esteem it an honour and a privilege to have known such gallant men.'

W. COSGROVE
Near Sedd el Bahr, 26 April 1915

Cpl. W. Cosgrove

Historians have tended to dwell on the contributions made by Doughty-Wylie and Walford to the success at V Beach, ignoring the influential part played by a 26-year-old junior NCO in the forefront of the assault. Yet it was the gallantry displayed by Cpl. William Cosgrove that undoubtedly helped turn the tide in favour of the assaulting force, faced with the desperate mission of clearing the Turks out of their positions commanding the beach.

At 6 ft 6 in Cosgrove was a giant of a man. His unit, the 1st Royal Munster Fusiliers, had been in the van of the assault from the *River Clyde*. On the first day no unit had performed more bravely or suffered more grievously. Of the three companies who charged out from the sallyports cut in the side of the *River Clyde*, 70 per cent were killed or wounded. Those who succeeded in making it ashore could advance no further than the 8-ft-high sandy bank, some 10 yd from the shoreline, which afforded a measure of cover from the raking machine-gun fire. About 25 yd on, up a slight rise, belts of barbed wire entanglements barred the way. Between bank and wire the bodies of five men of the Munsters bore mute testimony to the accuracy of the Turkish fire and the apparent futility of further advance.

The dazed survivors, huddled below the bank, held their position throughout the rest of the day and night. Most were exhausted; their endurance tested beyond the limit by a day of slaughter and intolerable strain. Capt. G.D. Stoney, the military landing officer who went ashore with Lt. Col. Doughty-Wylie on the morning of 26 April, found the few remaining officers reluctant to move forward.

Although by late morning the village of Sedd el Bahr had been largely cleared, the centre of V Beach was still covered by Turkish machine-guns and riflemen to the front and along both flanks. There also remained the seemingly impossible task of forcing a path through the barbed wire barrier strung across the slope above them. According to Cosgrove, who was among those sheltering beneath the sandy ledge on the foreshore, the wire entanglements 'ran in every direction, and were fixed to stout posts that were more than my own height'.

Stoney, however, was determined to carry out his orders to advance in conjunction with Doughty-Wylie's planned assault on the right. He walked along the beach, collecting officerless parties. All fit men were to advance along the left of the village, past houses which still hid snipers, to link up with Doughty-Wylie's men who were preparing to attack Hill 141 from the edge of the village. It was no easy task organizing the scattered groups. Any movement along the foreshore invited instant Turkish retaliation, and it was not until nearly 1.30 p.m. that Stoney was ready. Leading the assault were a party of Munster Fusiliers with orders to cut a way through the wire. They included Cpl. Cosgrove, who was well aware of his poor chances of survival. He later stated:

I thought, when I heard the work I was detailed for, that I would never again have the opportunity of a day's fighting. However, the work was there; it had to be done, for on its success rested the safety of many men, as well as the opportunity it would afford them of helping to throw back the Turks.

Our job was to dash ahead, face the trenches bristling with rifles and machine guns, and destroy the wire entanglements – that is, to cut them here and there with our pliers. Fifty men were detailed for the work; poor Sergeant Major Bennett led us, but just as we made the dash – oh, such a storm of lead was concentrated on us, for the Turks knew of our intention.

Our Sergeant Major was killed – a bullet through the brain. I then took charge; shouted to the boys to come on. From the village near at hand there came a terrible fire to swell the murderous hail of bullets from the trenches. In the village they fired from doors and windows, and from that advantage they could comfortably take aim.

The dash was quite 100 yards, and I don't know whether I ran or prayed the faster – I wanted to try and succeed in my work, and I also wanted to have the benefit of dying with a prayer in my mind. I can tell you it is not fortunately given to everyone to note the incidents that seem to be the last in your life, and you never feeling better or stronger.

Well, some of us got close up to the wire, and we started to cut it with pliers. You might as well try and snip Cloyne Round Tower with a lady's scissors, and you would not hurt yourself either. The wire was of great strength, strained as tight as a fiddle-string, and so full of spikes or thorns that you could not get the cutters between.

'Heavens,' said I, 'we're done'; a moment later I threw the pliers from me. 'Pull them up,' I roared, 'put your arms round them and pull them out of the ground.' I dashed at the first one; heaved and strained, and then it came into my arms and same as you'd lift a child. I believe there was wild cheering when they saw what I was at, but I only heard the screech of the bullets and saw dust rising all round from where they hit.

I could not tell how many I pulled up. I did my best, and the boys that were left with me were every bit as good as myself, and I do wish that they all got some recognition.

When the wire was down the rest of the lads came on like 'devils,' and not withstanding the pulverising fire, they reached the trenches. They met a brave honourable foe in the Turks, and I am sorry that such decent fighting men were brought into the row by such dirty tricksters as the Germans. They gave us great resistance, but we got to their trenches, and won about 200 yards length by 20 yards deep, and 700 yards from the shore . . .

A machine gun sent some bullets into me, and strange, I was wounded before I reached the trench, though I did not realise it. When I got to the trench I did my own part, and later collapsed. One of the bullets struck me in the side, and passed clean through me. It struck the left hook of my tunic, then entered my body, took a couple of splinters off my backbone, but of course did not injure the spinal column, and passed out on my right side, knocking off the other belt hook. I was taken up feeling pretty bad, when I came to my senses, and considered seriously wounded. I was removed to Malta Hospital, where

An artist's impression of Cosgrove's VC action

there were two operations performed, and the splinters of my backbone removed. I was about 16 stone weight at the Dardanelles, but I am now down in weight, but not too used up . . .

Cosgrove's extraordinary exploit in the face of what appeared to be almost certain death was witnessed by many men, both on shore and aboard the *River Clyde*. Referring to the courage of 'an Irish giant', the ship's surgeon, Burrowes Kelly, noted in his diary: 'The manner in which the man worked out in the open will never be forgotten by those who were fortunate to witness it.'

Four days after the action, 2nd Lt. H.A. Brown, of the 1st Royal Munster Fusiliers, reported to the officer commanding W Company, 'a most conspicuous act of bravery displayed by Corp. Cosgrove'. Brown stated:

I was ordered by a staff captain to collect all the men of my Battn. that were on the beach as a general advance at all costs had to be made to take hill No. 141. After a great effort I managed to collect about 40 NCOs and men.

On a given signal I advanced over very exposed ground being under the fire of 2 machine guns and snipers.

After we had advanced 40 yards from the beach we were held up by about 60 yards of thickly constructed barbed wire entanglement.

Having only one pair of wire cutters our progress was very slow getting through though Pte Bryant was doing his best to cut a passage through the wire. Corp. Cosgrove seeing our difficulty jumped into the wire and hauled down the heavy wooden stakes to which the wire was attached to a distance of about 30 yds long in quite a short space of time.

I personally consider he deserves the height of praise for such a courageous act and was much impressed to see him though wounded in the back leading his section shortly before the enemy were driven from their trenches and the fort captured.

Brown's report, which differs somewhat from Cosgrove's version, formed the basis of a recommendation for the Victoria Cross, which was strongly endorsed by Gen. Hunter-Weston (GOC, 29th Division). 'By this gallantry', he wrote, 'he contributed not a little to the success of the all important operation of clearing the heights commanding the beach, an apparently impossible task'.

Cosgrove's VC, however, was not gazetted until 23 August, two months after the announcement of the other two V Beach VCs to Doughty-Wylie and Walford. The delay may have been caused by Cosgrove's recommendation being linked to those for the Lancashire Fusiliers at W Beach which were the subject of so much official debate. His citation read:

For most conspicuous bravery in the leading of his section with great dash during our attack from the beach to the east of Cape Helles, on the Turkish positions, on the 26th April, 1915.

Corporal Cosgrove on this occasion pulled down the posts of the enemy's high wire entanglements single-handed, notwithstanding a terrific fire from both front and flanks, thereby greatly contributing to the successful clearing of the heights.

Sgt. Cosgrove, right, shortly after his VC was announced

At the time of the announcement, Cosgrove, who had been invalided home, was still recuperating in an army camp, near his home village of Aghada in southern Ireland.

William Cosgrove, later to be fêted as the 'East Cork giant', was born on 1 October 1888 at Ballinookera, near the little fishing hamlet of Aghada, County Cork, one of five sons to farmer Michael Cosgrove and Mary (née Morrissey).

A sister, Mary Catherine, died aged thirteen, from tuberculosis. Life was harsh for the Cosgrove family, as it was for many others living in the rural communities of southern Ireland in the last decade of the nineteenth century. Thousands were driven to seek a better life in the United States and Australia. Among the emigrants was Cosgrove's father who, leaving behind his wife and children, journeyed to Australia.

Mary Cosgrove and her six small children moved to a cottage in nearby Peafield. William attended the local school at Ballinrostig where his academic career was undistinguished. As soon as he was old enough he left to become an apprentice butcher, working in Whitegate, a neighbouring village on the edge of Cork Harbour. At around this time, William's father returned from Australia and the reunited family moved to Ballinookera. It was from here that three of William's brothers, Dan, Ned and David, joined the exodus of young Irishmen to the United States; one to become a racehorse breeder, another to join the police force and the other to become a high-ranking official in the postal service. Only William and his youngest brother, Joseph, who would later become a farmer, remained. William, however, was seeking out fresh horizons of his own. As an apprentice butcher, he regularly delivered meat to Fort Carlisle army camp. A popular, if shy, youngster, he frequently returned from these errands with a cart full of singing children. As the years passed, his thoughts turned increasingly towards the Army as a career, and in 1910 he took the plunge, enlisting in the 1st Royal Munster Fusiliers.

William Cosgrove served four years with the unit in India and Burma. The outbreak of war found the battalion quartered in Rangoon, where they spent the monsoon occupying a string of outposts along the river estuary. In November 1914 they were ordered back to England, arriving in the following January. Two months later, the Munsters left their billets in Coventry bound for the Dardanelles where, during the two-day battle for V Beach, they sustained approximately 600 casualties.

Cosgrove was one of those evacuated to Malta, before being sent home to Ireland. The announcement of his VC made him the centre of attention wherever he went. Promoted sergeant, he remained for a while in his native land, the military authorities being anxious to exploit the celebrity status of a hero in their midst. Such diversions from real soldiering, however, were not to Cosgrove's liking. At one garden party, organized by local dignatories, the regimental band struck up a waltz, but the hero of the hour was nowhere to be seen. A villager recalled: 'Cosgrove remained outside the gate, near the lodge where I lived and played with us children. He was a very shy man, who hated to be fussed over.'

After the war, Cosgrove soldiered on with the Munsters, and when the creation of the Irish Free State in 1922 brought about the disbandment of his regiment, he decided to transfer to a British Army unit, the Royal Northumberland Fusiliers. Six years later, he transferred to the 6th (Burma) Battalion, University Training Corps, based in Rangoon. By then in his forties, Cosgrove was still a powerfully built man, who was well-known for his disinclination to discuss his exploits at Cape Helles.

An expert shot, he helped the Rangoon UTC achieve third place in the Imperial Universities' Shoot two years in succession. In 1934, Staff Sergeant Instructor Cosgrove retired from the Army which had been his way of life for so long. Shortly afterwards, his health, apparently so strong despite his wartime injuries, began to fail. It was discovered that splinters of shrapnel, which surgeons had failed to detect during the operations on his back wound in Malta, were slowly but relentlessly killing him. His Gallipoli wounds caused a drastic muscle shrinkage and regular treatment at Millbank military hospital, London, slowed but could not halt his decline.

On 14 July 1936, after a ten-month battle against ill health, William Cosgrove died at Millbank Hospital, his brother Joseph by his side. During his final months of suffering, his services were recognized by two further awards, the Meritorious Service Medal and the King George V Jubilee Medal. Three days after his death, his remains were brought into Cork Harbour aboard the

SS *Innisfallen*. At the dockside, 300 members of the Munster Comrades Association formed a guard of honour. Later that afternoon, veterans from the disbanded regiment shouldered their comrade's coffin to the family burial ground in Upper Aghada. As villagers and old soldiers stood in silence, a bugler played the Last Post. Among the many wreaths was one from the Leinster Regiment OCA. The inscription on it read: 'In Loving Remembrance of a great Irish soldier.'

Almost forty years later, Cosgrove's gallantry was headline news again when his VC, together with his other medals (1914–15 Star, British War Medal, Victory Medal with Oak Leaf Mention in Dispatches, Army Long Service and Good Conduct Medal and Meritorious Service Medal), was sold at auction for the then world record price of £2,300. Since then they have been resold and are understood to be in private ownership.

William Cosgrove's courageous actions were not forgotten in his own country. Two years after his death a public appeal raised sufficient funds to place an impressive memorial over his grave. Today the tall Celtic cross bears eloquent testimony to the pride felt by the people of Cork for the soldier they called the 'Irish giant'.

W.R. PARKER

400 Plateau, Anzac sector, 30 April–2 May 1915

L/Cpl. W. Parker

Rain fell in torrents from a black sky as the lines of Royal Marines trudged uncertainly through the maze of gullies and hills that formed the precarious beach-head at Anzac Cove. The landing of the Portsmouth and Chatham Battalions of the RM Brigade, the first stage in the relief of the exhausted remnants of the 1st and 3rd Australian Brigades, had started at 4.00 p.m. on Wednesday 28 April.

So parlous was the state of many Australian units that the Marines were led straight to the frontline. There was no time to carry out a reconnaissance of the positions or the ground ahead of them and no time to learn from the hard-earned experience of the men they were replacing. In the rain-sodden darkness the inevitable tension was compounded by confusion as guides lost their way. Expecting to take over established trenches, the Marines found instead shallow, isolated burrows which more closely resembled pot-holes. These inadequate scrapes in the parched ground above Anzac beach represented the straggling, disconnected perimeter stretching across McLaurin's Hill and the northern sector of Lone Pine Plateau. Among the key positions taken over by the Marines were Courtney's Post and Steele's Post. But such was the chaos that they had little idea of the positions on their flanks, nor of the proximity of the Turkish posts in front of them. What they heard, however, was unnerving enough; the crack of rifle bullets from hidden snipers, the rattle of machine-guns playing on the parapets and the distant sound of Turkish bugle calls.

For their part, the Australians were surprised by the appearance of the Marines, who they had expected to be seasoned fighting men. Instead, they found them, in the words of their Official Historian, 'strangely young and slender'. In fact, the two RMLI battalions consisted largely of raw recruits; volunteers who had answered Lord Kitchener's call to arms the previous autumn. Of their number, reservists accounted for 20 per cent while regulars made up only an estimated 5 per cent. Of the remainder, many of them lads of seventeen and eighteen, few had received more than basic training.

Typical of the Marines, in terms of inexperience if not age, was L/Cpl. Walter Parker. A 33-year-old iron moulder from Stapleford in Nottinghamshire, he had enlisted on 9 September 1914. His training with the Portsmouth Division had been unspectacular. One report, in December, described him as a 'moderate' recruit. Of deeper concern, however, was one serious physical defect – bad eyesight. In normal circumstances, it seems unlikely that he would have progressed beyond the entrance to the recruiting office. However, on 28 April 1915, he found himself on Anzac Beach, as a member of the Portsmouth Battalion's medical team commanded by Surgeon Basil Playne.

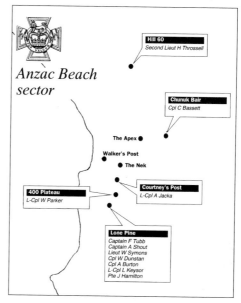

Sketch map showing the location of all the VCs won in the Anzac Beach sector

While Parker and his comrades settled in, advance units from the two Marine battalions discovered just how weak their position was. According to Brig. Gen. C.N. Trotman (GOC, Marine Brigade) the ill-prepared defences were little more than 30 to 50 yd away from the Turkish positions. One Marine officer later complained: 'The trenches were quite isolated with 30 or 40 yards of open ground between them, under an accurate and close range fire'. One of the most exposed of these posts was manned by two platoons from the Portsmouth Battalion's C Company, under the command of Lt. R.W.H.M. Empson and Lt. A.B.F. Alcock. The sixty men making up the garrison had taken over the trench during their first twenty-four hours on the peninsula. Lying in front of the Chatham Battalion's main positions on the extreme left of the Marine Brigade's sector, the post was separated from the nearest friendly position by about 400 yd of bare ground. To reach them in daylight entailed a perilous dash across the open in full view of the nearest Turkish posts. Only at night was there any realistic hope of resupply and relief.

During their first day the Marines were subjected to a few Turkish probing attacks which were all beaten off. In the evening the arrival of the Deal and Nelson Battalions brought the Marine Brigade up to full strength. But any hopes of a lull were soon to be cruelly shattered. In the late afternoon of 30 April

Mustafa Kemal, the aggressive Turkish commander at Anzac, having extended his trenches and brought up five fresh battalions, set in motion his counter-offensive designed at hurling the invaders into the sea. As a prelude to the general attack, riflemen began sniping the perimeter posts at around 4.00 p.m. The pressure quickly intensified on the outlying Marine positions from Courtney's southwards. At 5.00 p.m. some trenches occupied by men of the Chatham Battalion opposite Wire Gully were overrun. Counter-attacks recovered some of the lost posts. Others, found to be untenable, were evacuated. Around midnight reports came in of a Turkish breakthrough at the southern end of McLaurin's Hill, while to the north, the plight of Lt. Empson's post grew desperate.

With casualties mounting steadily and his supply of water and ammunition dwindling, Empson sent a runner back with an urgent message calling for assistance, including medical aid. On receiving the note, his company commander, Capt. A.E. Syson, immediately detailed a party of NCOs and men to deliver the stores. Then he ran down to the medical post. Surgeon Playne was already busy tending the wounded in the frontline, and Syson later recalled: 'I called for a volunteer and immediately L/Cpl. Parker offered to go'. Parker, who had already distinguished himself by his consistent bravery in command of the battalion's stretcher bearers, joined a relief party of ten men under the command of Sgt. M.W. Minter. Setting off under cover of darkness, they came under heavy and accurate fire as soon as they emerged from the trench nearest to Lt. Empson's post. Almost immediately one man was hit and Parker, as the only medic in the party, stayed by him until a stretcher party could take him out. By then he was separated from the rest of Sgt. Minter's party. More disturbingly, it was broad daylight. To attempt to reach the isolated fire trench without the cover of darkness seemed tantamount to committing suicide. And lest there was any doubt in his mind, Parker could see a trail of dead Australians lying in the open between him and Lt. Empson's post.

Parker later recorded how an Australian officer had threatened to shoot him if he did not turn back. But his mind was made up. Disregarding the threat, he leapt over the parapet and sprinted down the slope towards Empson's cut-off trench. The 400 yd of scrub-covered hill was raked by rifle and machine-gun fire. Wounded twice, Parker half-ran, half-stumbled through a rain-filled hollow before plunging into the trench to the cheers of his disbelieving comrades. Only then did he discover that no one else from the relief party had succeeded in getting through. The rest of the ten-strong detachment were either dead or wounded, and Sgt. Minter had abandoned his efforts only after three attempts had ended in failure. Ignoring his own painful injuries, Parker set about treating the wounded in the trench. At dawn, the Turkish pressure had developed into a full-scale attack and in the fierce fighting which followed Lt. Empson was killed.

But the Marines, under the command of Lt. Alcock, held on throughout a scorching day in which their number was reduced to around forty unwounded men.

On 2 May, after a gallant defence lasting four nights and three days, the survivors, who were by then down to their last fifteen rounds, were compelled to withdraw and run the gauntlet of Turkish fire. Once again, Parker proved to be a tower of strength, helping all the wounded men to safety. In so doing he was wounded again, this time more seriously. Hit in the groin and right thigh, and with injuries to his right knee, his shin and chest, he was forced to crawl the final few yards up the slope to the Marines' position. He was on the point of collapse when stretcher bearers from his own battalion reached him. The struggle for Empson's post was over, but the efforts to recognize the gallantry of the Marine medic would take many months more.

Lt. Col. F.W. Luard, CO of the Portsmouth Battalion, cited Parker's heroism in his report of the fighting. A recommendation for the Victoria Cross was immediately made by Maj. C.F. Jerram, staff captain of the RM Brigade. But the dispatches were lost. In September, Lt. Alcock was awarded a Distinguished Service Cross for his gallant leadership. But for Parker, who had survived near-disaster when the hospital ship in which he was being evacuated collided with another vessel in thick fog, there was only a certificate from the GOC to mark his 'gallant and courageous conduct'. His actions, however, had not been forgotten. Writing to Parker later, Maj. Jerram stated: 'When I was on leave, after the evacuation, I met Doctor Playne, who spoke to me very strongly about you; so we collected all the evidence we could and the General put you in again. . . .'

Fortunately, many of the leading participants in the action had survived the campaign, and each one testified to Parker's gallantry. In a letter dated 8 April 1916, Lt. Alcock, DSC wrote: 'The extreme courage with which he carried out his work was excellent and he remained calm and collected under very trying circumstances'. Later that year, Alcock confirmed that Parker was the only member of the relief party to reach his outpost. He added: 'There is no doubt whatsoever that Lance-Cpl Parker knew, as soon as he started, that he was taking the greatest risks possible and that his one idea was to succour the wounded in the isolated trench.'

The campaign to honour Parker found a powerful ally in Brig. Gen. Trotman, who had commanded the RM Brigade at Anzac. On the basis of the new evidence gathered, he considered 'that a Victoria Cross should be awarded'. After a detailed inquiry, the adjutant general of the Royal Marines, David Mercer, agreed. But before it could go forward, the recommendation had one more hurdle to clear. The Marines, concerned with maintaining the high standards of the VC, submitted the papers to the Army Council at the War Office in order that Parker's action could be compared with similar deeds performed during the war. This resulted in a further delay, and it was not until 22 June 1917, more than two years after the action, that the *London Gazette* announced the award of the Victoria Cross to L/Cpl. Walter Richard Parker, RMLI, Royal Naval Division. It was the last VC to be announced for the Gallipoli Campaign. The citation read:

On the night of 30th April–1st May, 1915, a message asking for ammunition, water, and medical stores was received from an isolated fire trench at Gaba Tepe [*sic*].

A party of non-commissioned officers and men were detailed to carry water and ammunition, and, in response to a call for a volunteer from among the stretcher-bearers, Parker at once came forward; he had during the previous three days displayed conspicuous bravery and energy under fire whilst in charge of the battalion stretcher-bearers.

Several men had already been killed in a previous attempt to bring assistance to the men holding the fire trench. To reach this trench it was necessary to traverse an area at least four hundred yards wide, which was completely exposed and swept by rifle fire. It was already daylight when the party emerged from shelter and at once one of the men was wounded; Parker organised a stretcher party, and then going on alone succeeded in reaching the fire trench, all the water and ammunition carriers being either killed or wounded.

After his arrival he rendered assistance to the wounded in the trench, displaying extreme courage and remaining cool and collected in very trying circumstances. The trench had finally to be evacuated, and Parker helped to remove and attend the wounded, although he himself was seriously wounded during this operation.

By the time of the award, Parker was no longer serving in the Marines. Having made a slow recovery from his painful wounds, he returned to duty on 26 April 1916, serving at Command HQ, Ireland. His posting, however, was cut short by sickness. Within weeks, he was being treated for 'brain fever which left his sight badly affected'. He returned to England on 14 May and was invalided out of the services a month later with a war gratuity of £10. Parker found work in a munitions factory, and it was as a civilian that he received his Victoria Cross at an investiture held on the forecourt of Buckingham Palace on 21 July 1917. To mark the award, his former comrades in the Portsmouth Division of the Royal Marines presented him with a marble and gilt clock at a special parade. His wife received a gold regimental brooch. But the signs of his failing health were already apparent. Parker was not well enough to speak, and Brig. Gen. Trotman expressed thanks on his behalf.

A post-war picture of Parker meeting George V

Walter Richard Parker was born on 20 September 1881, at 5 Agnes Street, Grantham, the eldest of eight children to Richard and Kate Parker.

Educated at Grantham elementary school, he was later employed as a coremaker at Stanton Ironworks Foundry. In 1902 he married Olive (née Orchard), the daughter of Stapleford's station-master. They had three sons, all of whom died young, and three daughters.

After the war, Parker struggled bravely to overcome his injuries. He was elected to the local pensions tribunal and became president of the Stapleford branch of the Royal British Legion. His later years, however, were characterized by his declining health. His daughter, Vera Constance, who was born in 1919 and christened in honour of his VC, remembered:

> He was a very sick man for a lot of years . . . When he knew he was dying, he set out to try and get my mother a pension. But the authorities said he had survived too long for his death to have been caused by his war wounds. When his doctor heard, he hit the roof. He said that he had treated him and that he was a complete wreck. He said it was a miracle that he had lived so long.

Walter Parker died at his home in Derby Street, Stapleford, on 28 November 1936, aged fifty-five. His coffin, draped with a Union Jack, was carried to its last resting place in Stapleford Cemetery by eight Royal Marine NCOs from Eastney Barracks, Portsmouth. The first VC hero of Anzac Beach had never courted publicity during his lifetime, but crowds lined the streets of Stapleford to pay their last respects to an unassuming man who had borne his suffering with the same degree of fortitude and courage he had once displayed on the Gallipoli Peninsula.

His Victoria Cross, together with his other decorations, were presented by his family to the Royal Marines Museum, where they now feature in a display honouring the ten Marine recipients of the nation's highest award for valour.

E.C. BOYLE

Sea of Marmora, 27 April–18 May 1915

Lt. Cdr. E. Boyle

The sea was calm and the night dark as HM Submarine E14 twisted between the myriad craft anchored off Cape Helles on her passage up the Dardanelles. It was around 3.00 a.m. on 27 April. Barely an hour and a half had passed since Lt. Cdr. Courtney Boyle had slipped out of Tenedos at the start of his mission to break through the Narrows into the Sea of Marmora, for so long regarded by the Turks as their own private lake.

As the E14 passed the ruined fortress of Sedd el Bahr, the sounds of conflict drifted eerily across the water; the rattle of rifle fire mingling with the cries of men, fighting on the bitterly contested beach-head. Boyle, standing alone and exposed on the open conning-tower, could hear it all. The canvas bridge screen had been removed and all the steel stanchions taken down save one, to give him something to hold on to while navigating a course along the surface.

Occasionally, the night sky was lit by red flashes as the heavy guns from the French battleships thundered across the anchorage. Dead ahead, some eight miles distant, lay the Narrows, bathed in brilliant white light, like a vast stage, while still closer, at the mouth of the Suan Dere river, a single powerful searchlight swept across the water. There was a strange air of unreality. To Boyle's first lieutenant, Edward Stanley, 'it all looked very weird and threatening'. Positioned just below the open conning-tower hatch, Stanley passed Boyle's orders on to the coxswain at the foot of the ladder. He was also in charge of the submarine's gyro compass, a new and important navigational aid considered to require such careful handling that no one else, not even the captain, was allowed to touch it.

Such rules were typical of the meticulous planning which had gone into Boyle's preparation for the hazardous venture into one of the world's most heavily defended stretches of water. Since December 1914, when the small submarine B11, commanded by Lt. Norman Holbrook, ventured half-way up the Narrows to sink an old Turkish battleship below Chanak, three submarines had dared to reach the Sea of Marmora. Two had been sunk and only one, the AE2, an

Australian submarine commanded by an Irishman, had successfully negotiated the Dardanelles. Lt. Cdr. Hew Stoker's foray on 25 April signalled the start of one of the most daring and successful submarine campaigns ever to be waged. But her entry into the Sea of Marmora was of little practical assistance to Boyle, who knew nothing of her experiences. The success or failure of the E14's passage, therefore, would rest wholly on his own plan, based on personal experience and reconnaissances of the approaches to the Dardanelles. Lt. Stanley later noted:

> There was very little guessing . . . as far as possible everything which could ensure success was thought of in advance. The battery was brought up to 100% condition and an hour before starting off was 'fizzing', then ventilated, left topped until within half an hour of diving. Every tank, blow and motor had been examined – all was in tip top condition.

Even with such a high degree of planning, however, there was much that was not known about the obstacles confronting them. As well as at least five rows of mines and numerous vessels patrolling the Narrows, there were reports of shore-sited torpedo tubes, a sunken bridge off Nagara Point and anti-submarine nets. These posed formidable enough problems, but when combined with the natural elements they appeared almost insurmountable. Although the E-class boats were designed to stay submerged for 50 miles, the power of the current, running at 3–5 knots through the narrow bottle-neck linking the Sea of Marmora to the Mediterranean, made it unlikely they would be able to complete the tortuous passage of the 35-mile-long Straits underwater. Nor could they be sure of avoiding all of the moored mines by diving deep. To safely navigate, it was vital to take frequent observations of landmarks which necessarily entailed operating at periscope depth. Even had they been able to remain submerged, the navigation of such a confined waterway dominated by strong-running currents represented one of the most dangerous challenges then known to submariners. In addition, they faced the hazards posed by the

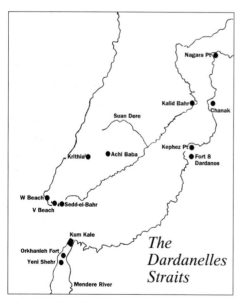

The route through the Narrows

change of water density as the saltwater of the Mediterranean met the freshwater of the Marmora, which could make submarines almost uncontrollable.

It was scarcely surprising, therefore, that when originally asked whether an E-boat could make it through to the Marmora, Boyle had sided with the majority of senior naval officers in delivering a firm 'No'. Only the commander of the E15 had thought it possible, and his attempt resulted in the second submarine loss of the campaign. Since then the AE2 had shown the way, and now it was E14's turn. As the submarine entered the Straits, Lt. Stanley noted 'the crew were extremely calm'. There was no sign of excitement. 'I think really that we were all resigned for the worst and hoped for the best', he added.

At about 4.00 a.m. the E14 was caught in the glare of the searchlight at Suan Dere and almost immediately shells splashed into the sea ahead. Boyle took this as his cue to submerge. In his official report he recorded:

> Dived to 90 feet under the minefield. Rose to 22 feet 1 mile south of Killid Bahr and at 5.15 a.m. passed Chanak, all the forts firing at me. There were a lot of small ships and steamboats patrolling, and I saw one torpedo gunboat, 'Berki-Satvet' class, which I fired at, range about 1,600 yards. I just had time to see a large column of water as high as her mast rise from her quarter where she was presumably hit, when I had to dip again as the men in a small steam boat were leaning over trying to catch hold of the top of my periscope.

It was an extraordinary encounter. Boyle had, in fact, sunk the Turkish gunboat with his second torpedo, but he was fortunate to have escaped without damage from his brush with the steamboat crew. Rounding Nagara Point at 6.30 a.m., he passed beneath a succession of small craft apparently searching for him. At 9.00 a.m., while coming up to periscope depth to get a navigational fix, he spotted a Turkish battleship less than a mile astern, but decided to ignore her and press on towards the Sea of Marmora, which he entered at 10.15 a.m. Boyle was able to observe Turkish efforts to locate him, but not wishing to give his position away, he spent much of his first day submerged. The next day proved a frustrating one with a succession of Turkish patrol craft forcing the E14 to dive whenever the submarine came to the surface to charge her over-worked batteries. Boyle decided to seek out a safer hunting ground, and later that evening moved along the surface to the north-east of Marmora Island.

The next day, 29 April, he spotted a convoy of two troopships escorted by three destroyers. Conditions for attack, however, were far from ideal. He reported:

> Unfortunately, it was a glassy calm and the TBDs [destroyers] sighted my periscope and came for me and opened fire while I was a good way off. I fired

at one transport, range about 1,500 yards, but had to dip before I could see the effect of the shot. (One periscope had had the upper window pane broken by a shot the day before and was useless, and so I could not afford to risk my remaining one being bent).

Half an hour later, when he felt it safe enough to bring E14 to periscope depth, he noted one of the transports 'making for the shore at Sar Kioi with dense columns of yellow smoke pouring from her'.

Later that afternoon the E14 made an unscheduled meeting with AE2, and plans were made for another rendezvous the next day. But Stoker's submarine was sunk the following morning, before she could keep her appointment. The next day the Turks celebrated another success, the destruction of the French submarine *Joule* while attempting to break through the Straits. The crew of E14 would have to continue their efforts alone.

Boyle, meanwhile, was determined to adopt a more aggressive approach towards his most persistent adversaries. As he said in his report: 'I decided to sink a patrol ship as they were always firing at me.' He found his victim at 10.45 a.m. on 1 May, and made short work of it. One torpedo was enough to send the Turkish minelayer *Nour-el-Bahr* to the bottom. Leading Stoker John Haskins wrote in his diary:

The Captain saw two men aboard the mine-layer, cleaning a gun abaft; they saw the torpedo coming straight at them, and they started to run to tell the officer on the bridge. But they were too late. The torpedo hit her and she blew up. By the explosion she made, she must have been full of mines. There was nothing left of her in three minutes. The blast gave us a good shaking up, but nobody minded, as it meant another enemy ship less.

Boyle's reputation was growing rapidly, both among his own crew and the Turks, who attempted to counter the submarine menace by establishing a primitive coast-watching network. Bonfires were lit along the shore as warnings to shipping whenever sightings were made. However, it was bad luck and not smoke signals which denied Boyle of further success on 5 May. On that date, he carried out a textbook attack on a Turkish transport, but his torpedo, which was seen to strike the target, failed to explode. The Turks were becoming increasingly wary. The next day a destroyer and transport turned and fled back towards Constantinople at the sight of E14. Boyle added to their timidity on 8 May when, having stopped and searched two vessels crowded with refugees, he followed a third steamer into the Turkish harbour at Rodosto. He reported: 'She anchored close in shore and was also full of refugees. Approached within 1,200 yards of the shore. I could not see any troops, but they opened a heavy rifle fire on us, hitting the boat several times, so I went away.'

Two days later the E14 surfaced near Kalolimno Island. The sea was clear and Boyle decided to allow the crew some relaxation. But while they were taking a swim, a destroyer hove into view. Leading Stoker Haskins noted: 'There was a hell of a splash as the lads climbed aboard and stood by their diving stations.'

Boyle took E14 down and the destroyer passed directly above. Half an hour later, Boyle sighted two transports being escorted by a single destroyer. In what would prove to be his greatest success of a profitable first patrol in the Marmora, he immediately attacked:

The torpedo fired at the leading transport did not run straight and missed astern. The second torpedo hit the second transport, and there was a terrific explosion. Debris and men were seen falling into the water . . . Unfortunately it was 7.35 p.m. when I fired, and in ten minutes it was quite dark, so I did not see her actually sink. However, she was very much down by the stern when I last saw her, and must have sunk in a very short time.

The crew of the E14 were jubilant. Haskins wrote: 'The lads gave a cheer as the troops aboard the transport jumped overboard in their hundreds.'

What Boyle, in his report, described as a three-masted and two-funnelled ship 'twice as large as any other ship I saw there', was, in fact, the 5,000-ton former White Star liner *Guj Djemal*. She had been packed with 6,000 troops and a field battery, and Boyle was correct in his assumption about her rapid demise.

An artist's impression of E14 sinking the troop transport Guj Djemal

The torpedo attack, on the thirteenth day of the E14's patrol, was to be her last. Boyle had expended nine of his ten torpedoes; the remaining one was found to be faulty. Of the nine, four had resulted in the destruction of a gunboat, minelayer and transport and the almost certain loss of a second transport. Three had either not run true or failed to explode and only two had missed their targets. It was an impressive success rate. Boyle's achievements, however, went far beyond material destruction. Turkish shipping movements were severely disrupted, seriously hampering the transport of men and material to the peninsula. But the impact on civilian morale was even greater. Such was the extent of the hysteria gripping Constantinople, it was considered that the continued presence of the E14 in the Sea of Marmora, even without offensive armament, would contribute significantly to the weakening of Turkish resolve. It appeared to be an accurate assumption. On 13 May the unarmed E14 chased a small steamer with such determination that she ran herself aground. A brief rifle skirmish followed before Boyle left her and headed for Erekli Bay.

The next morning, Boyle decided to employ a new 'weapon' – deception. A dummy gun was rigged up, and was immediately used to help stop a Turkish tug towing a lighter. After an inspection revealed the cargo to be baulks of timber, she was allowed to continue, although reports of her interception could only have served to fuel Turkish anxieties. Later Boyle suffered the frustration of having to allow a convoy consisting of three full transports and one destroyer to pass because of his lack of torpedoes. A busy day ended with the E14 narrowly avoiding disaster after failing to spot a Turkish patrol boat until it was almost too late. Leading Stoker Haskins recorded: 'At 9.10 we had to dive in a hurry. It was very dark, and before we knew what was happening an enemy destroyer appeared right on top of us. It was a near thing.' According to Boyle, the destroyer which almost caught them napping on the surface was 'not more than 400 yards off when sighted'. It was not the first time that the Turks had been in with a chance of catching their quarry, and Boyle was convinced that only their lack of determination spared his vessel from destruction. He noted:

> I think that the Turkish torpedo boats must have been frightened of ramming us, as several times when I tried to remain on the surface at night, they were so close when sighted that it must have been possible to get us if they had so desired. In the day time the atmosphere was so clear that we were practically always in sight from the shore, and these signal fires and smoke columns were always in evidence, so I think our position was always known to the patrols unless we dived most of the day.

By 16 May provisions were running low and water was rationed to one pint per man a day. There were hopes that the submarine would be resupplied by the

E11, but the following day E14 was ordered by wireless to return. On the morning of 18 May, the twenty-first day of his momentous patrol, Boyle brought his boat out of the Dardanelles. Despite having been detected at the very outset of his return trip, and again by the Turkish shore defences at Chanak, he skilfully avoided all obstacles to complete the first double passage. The E14 surfaced close to a French battleship, its decks crowded with cheering sailors. With a destroyer as escort, the submarine, sporting the 'Jolly Roger', entered Kephalo where, according to Haskins, 'we had to go around the whole fleet and they certainly gave us a cheer'.

It had been an outstandingly successful patrol, far exceeding his superiors' hopes. As early as 14 May, Cdre. Roger Keyes had wired the Admiralty praising Boyle and outlining his record of success. Although no official recommendation for honours was made, Keyes had insisted that Boyle 'deserved the greatest credit for his persistent enterprise in remaining in the Sea of Marmora, hunted day and night . . .'. In a subsequent telegraph, Vice-Admiral de Robeck stated: 'It is impossible to do full justice to this great achievement.' The result was one of the swiftest announcements of a VC after the action for which it was gained. News of the honour reached the Mediterranean Fleet on 19 May, two days before it was officially recorded in the *London Gazette* and before Boyle had compiled his own report. Even Keyes was astonished at the speed of events. 'I was hoping they would give him a VC but rather doubted it', he wrote to his wife. 'That they should have done so without our official recommendation was splendid.' In his diary entry for 19 May, Leading Stoker Haskins recorded:

At 6.30 a.m. all hands were turned out and had to fall in on the boat. And then, reading out the citations, they inform[ed] us that our Captain had been awarded the VC and that our second and third officers had been awarded the DSC and that the remainder of the crew had been awarded the DSM each. We gave three cheers for our officers and then at 11.20 a.m. we got on the way for Mudros . . .

For his part, Boyle heaped praise on his crew. He credited much of the E14's success to the 'untiring energy, knowledge of the boat, and general efficiency' of his first lieutenant, Lt. Stanley, and acknowledged the intelligent hard work of his navigator, Acting Lt. Reginald Lawrence, RNR. He also selected for special mention five senior crew members, including Leading Stoker Haskins. His own Victoria Cross citation read:

For most conspicuous bravery, in command of Submarine E14, when he dived his vessel under the enemy's minefields and entered the Sea of Marmora on the 27th April, 1915. In spite of great navigational difficulties from strong

Boyle (top row, centre) and the crew of the E14

currents, of the continual neighbourhood of hostile patrols, and of the hourly danger of attack from the enemy, he continued to operate in the narrow waters of the Straits and succeeded in sinking two Turkish gunboats and one large military transport.

Edward Courtney Boyle, one of the most distinguished submariners of his generation, was born on 23 March 1883 in Carlisle, Cumberland, the son of Lt. Col. Edward Boyle, then serving in the Army Pay Department, and Edith (née Cowley).

Educated at Cheltenham College, he entered HMS *Britannia* in 1897 and became a midshipman the following year. He was an early convert to one of the Navy's newest branches, the Submarine Service. His abilities were such that he was given his first command, a Holland boat, as a 21-year-old sub-lieutenant.

Attractive and intelligent, if somewhat reserved, Boyle's behaviour suggested a casual indifference which was sometimes mistaken for arrogance. To some of his colleagues he gave the impression of being bored by life in the peacetime Navy. Appearances, however, were deceptive. The long-limbed Boyle was one of those rare individuals who could accomplish with relative ease and unruffled calm what others strained to achieve. Charles Brodie, a fellow submariner in the pre-war days, remembered:

> In the period 1905–8 submarines and motor bicycles were new and fascinating if grubby toys, and specialists in both were often dubbed pirates. Boyle knew his submarine as thoroughly and rode his motor bicycle as fast as any, but was more courteous and tidy than most pirates . . . He did not pose, but seemed slightly aloof, ganging his own gait.

His quiet authority and cool efficiency in handling submarines was duly noted. Promotion followed at regular intervals, and a succession of submarine commands followed. At the outbreak of war he was captaining D3 in the 8th Submarine Flotilla. His early North Sea patrols, which included what Keyes described as a 'first class daring reconnaissance' into the shoals inside the Amrum Bank off the north German coast, were recognized by the award of a mention in dispatches. As a further reward, Boyle was promoted lieutenant commander and given command of the E14, one of the Navy's latest submarines. The following March, E14 was among three E-class boats sent from England to operate in the Dardanelles. It would prove to be a happy hunting ground for the modest yet quietly confident Boyle.

Between April and August Boyle and E14 completed three successful cruises into the Sea of Marmora, each journey through the Dardanelles made more dangerous than the previous one by the ever-strengthened Turkish defences. During the return passage at the end of his third patrol, the E14 came perilously close to disaster. Having burst through a new anti-submarine net, she narrowly escaped being hit by two torpedoes fired from the shore, before scraping her way through the Turkish minefields to safety. Perhaps it was an omen. The E14 and her captain were withdrawn from the fray and given a well-earned rest.

In all, Boyle had spent seventy days in the Marmora, and as well as enduring the prolonged strain of command in hostile waters, he had, like many of his crew, suffered bouts of dysentery and illness. The Royal Navy recognized his services by promoting him to commander, while Britain's allies showered him with decorations. The French made him a Chevalier of the Legion of Honour and the Italians gave him their Order of St Maurice and St Lazarus. But apart from the VC given for his first patrol, Boyle surprisingly received no further awards from his own country.

He continued to serve in submarines. By 1917 he was once more operating in the North Sea, in command of the new boat J5, in a flotilla which included the

Navy's Baltic ace, Cdr. Max Horton, DSO and Bar. There were, however, reminders of his Dardanelles days. That same year, Boyle fought and lost a £30,000 claim in an Admiralty prize court for the sinking of the *Guj Djemal*.

The end of the war found him in command of the Australian Submarine Flotilla. Two years later he was promoted captain.

During the next ten years, Boyle alternated sea-going commands with shore duties. He commanded, in turn, the cruisers HMS *Birmingham* and *Carysfort* and the aging battleship *Iron Duke*, while for two years he served as King's Harbour Master at Devonport. Promoted rear-admiral in October 1932, he retired on a Good Service Pension. During the Second World War he served for a time as flag officer in charge, London.

In an active retirement, Rear-Admiral Boyle, a childless widower who lived at Sunningdale Hotel, became an enthusiastic member of the local golf club. He died on 16 December 1967, as a result of injuries sustained the previous day when he was knocked down by a lorry on a pedestrian crossing.

Twenty-one years later, members of the Boyle family provided a fitting epitaph to the life of one of the Navy's most gifted pioneer submariners, when they presented their heroic forebear's Victoria Cross to HMS *Dolphin*, headquarters of the 1st Submarine Squadron at Gosport.

M.E. NASMITH

Sea of Marmora, 19 May–7 June 1915

Lt. Cdr. M. Nasmith

In the early evening of 18 May 1915, Lt. Cdr. Martin Nasmith, captain of the submarine E11, boarded the battleship *Lord Nelson* in Kephalo harbour. The 32-year-old submariner, a favourite of Roger Keyes, had been invited to dine with Vice-Admiral de Robeck prior to taking his boat up the Dardanelles. It was a pleasant enough duty, but uppermost in his mind was a meeting with his friend Courtney Boyle, fresh from his triumphant patrol.

Nasmith had already laid his own plans for his passage through the Narrows, arrangements which were greatly assisted by an aerial reconnaissance he had made. But he was eager to learn from his fellow submariner's experiences. Boyle, weary yet evidently elated, had barely had a chance to recover from his patrol, and while able to pass on news of the latest Turkish counter-measures in the Sea of Marmora he was unable to supply many precise details about the siting of searchlights and leading marks through the Straits. Later, after the meal during which Boyle had recounted his exploits to the distinguished gathering, Nasmith received his final briefing from Keyes. The Commodore's parting words would go down in submarine history. 'Well then', he told Nasmith, 'go and run amok in the Marmora!'

Nasmith, of all submariners, scarcely needed such exhortations. The commander who was reputed to possess the best 'periscope eye' in the Navy was determined to take up where Boyle had left off. He was also desperate to make up for a series of disappointments which had so far blighted his war career. The previous October he had been thwarted, first by mechanical problems and then by alerted shore defences, in his attempt to take the E11 into the Baltic. Even his journey to the Dardanelles had been beset with difficulties. Had it not been for a delay at Malta caused by having to replace his main motor, Nasmith, considered by most senior officers to be the pick of the submarine commanders despatched to the Mediterranean Fleet, would almost certainly have been the first to attempt the passage of the Straits.

Charles Brodie wrote of him: 'A few others might be classed with him on peace attack form, but by strength of character and sheer single-minded zeal he had won already a position among us all his own.' A term-mate of Boyle's at HMS *Britannia*, Nasmith had served as a midshipman on the *Renown* alongside his fellow submariner. Both combined caution with daring, but of the two Nasmith was the more natural leader. To those who knew him well, his eventual success appeared assured. What nobody could have predicted as he proceeded into the Straits at 2.45 a.m. on 19 May was the extent of that success.

Nasmith's extraordinary first cruise in the Sea of Marmora has justifiably entered the annals of naval history as an epic of submarine warfare. During his twenty-one-day patrol he accounted for eleven ships sunk, including a large gunboat and two transports. But, by far his most spectacular coup, was his penetration of Constantinople harbour. It was a startling attack, which has been likened to an enemy submarine venturing into the Pool of London, and had clearly been in Nasmith's mind from the outset of his patrol. Whereas Boyle had chosen to operate mainly at the western end of the Marmora, Nasmith prowled further eastwards, to the approaches of Turkey's ancient capital. He chalked up his first success on 23 May when, with a single torpedo, he sank the Turkish gunboat *Pelenk-i-Dria*, anchored off Constantinople. The crew of the sinking vessel were not short of courage. Even as their boat was going down, they succeeded in putting a shot through the E11's forward periscope. However, Nasmith's coolly delivered attack, within sight of the city's tall minarets, was merely a warning of things to come.

The next day proved to be the most successful of Nasmith's first Dardanelles patrol. It began when the E11 stopped a small steamer whose passengers included an American journalist, Raymond Gram Swing. Nasmith's first lieutenant, Lt. Guy D'Oyly Hughes, who was sent on board with a demolition charge, gave the quick-thinking reporter a brief, impromptu interview in which he claimed the E11 to be one of eleven submarines operating in the Marmora before ordering him into the steamer's lifeboats and firing the charge. Shortly after an explosion tore through the vessel another ship was spotted. Nasmith pursued the heavily laden store-ship into Rodosto harbour and put a torpedo into her as she lay beside the pier. Once again his periscope became the target for some accurate Turkish shooting. In his report, he noted:

Owing to the shallowness of the water it was necessary to expose a considerable amount of periscope to rifle fire, although the boat was bumping along the bottom. One bullet struck the lower tube and made a big indentation but fortunately did not penetrate.

Leaving Rodosto Bay, the E11 came across a paddle steamer carrying a supply of barbed wire. Hailed to stop, the vessel bravely made an attempt to ram the submarine. Nasmith successfully evaded his unlikely attacker and chased her on to a beach beneath some cliffs along the bay's northern shore. His report continues:

> We were just preparing a demolition charge for her when a party of horsemen appeared on the cliff above and opened a hot rifle fire on the conning-tower. We were forced to beat a hasty retreat.

From a safe distance, E11 sent a torpedo towards the grounded paddle-steamer, but it missed, passing along the vessel's side and exploding on the shore. It had been an eventful day; two ships sunk, one forced to beach herself while the E11 had survived a ramming attempt and close-range fire from harbour guards and Turkish cavalrymen! The next twenty-four hours, however, were to see even these exploits upstaged.

Having left Rodosto Bay on the evening of 24 May, Nasmith recharged his batteries and proceeded along the surface eastwards. He had decided this was the moment to test the Turkish defences inside Constantinople harbour. At 6.00 a.m. he dived unobserved near Oxia Island and made his way past an American guardship into the harbour which was filled with shipping. Taking care to follow a course he had seen being taken by a steamer on his previous reconnaissance two days earlier, he searched for likely targets. He picked out a large vessel lying alongside the arsenal. Just ahead of her, Nasmith observed a smaller vessel. Then, he settled into his attack:

> 12.35 p.m. Fired Port Bow Tube. Torpedo failed to run. Fired Starboard Bow torpedo and observed track heading for larger vessel. Unable to observe the effect owing to being swept ashore by cross tide and the presence of what I took to be a Brennan torpedo. [It is now understood that no Brennan exists in Constantinople and it is probable that the torpedo sighted was the first one discharged which by now had blown out its tail plug and was running with a capsized Gyro.] Two explosions were heard, so it is probable that the stray torpedo found a mark as well as the one directed at the ship lying alongside the arsenal. Dived to 75 feet and turned to get out. Grounded heavily at 70 feet and bounced quickly up to 40 feet. Further rise was checked by going full speed astern and flooding internal tanks. The Ship's head then swung from SSE through East and North to West. It was therefore concluded that the vessel was resting on the shoal under the Leander Tower, and being turned round by the current. Her head was then brought to South and the motors started ahead, the boat bumping gently down into 85 feet of water. After bumping for

An artist's impression of E11's raid into Constantinople harbour

some time at this depth the boat was brought off the bottom. On bringing her to the surface about 20 minutes later she was found to be well clear of the entrance.

Later it was learned that a troop-carrying barge had been sunk by the second torpedo, the explosion severely damaging the nearby transport *Stamboul* which had to be run ashore. The first 'rogue' torpedo, having narrowly missed destroying the E11, struck a wharf, blowing away a large section. The dramatic effect of the raid was immense and immediately felt. Troopships were hastily evacuated and vast numbers of people fled into the country as rumours of an invasion circulated. The following day, as the shockwaves continued to reverberate through the city, Nasmith, his great ambition realised, allowed his crew a day off.

His relentless quest for new targets was resumed on 27 May, when he came within an ace of getting in a torpedo attack on the *Barbarossa*, one of two elderly Turkish battleships known to be operating in the Marmora. But as he lined up for a surface shot, Nasmith was forced to dive as one of two escorting destroyers came, in his words, 'either by accident or design almost on top of us'. Later that day E11 enjoyed another narrow escape when she approached a yacht which opened fire at close range with a hidden gun. Luckily, the gunners' aim was not as true as their compatriots aboard the *Pelenk-i-Dria* or the riflemen at Rodosto.

Nasmith, however, remained unshaken. On 28 May he added to his tally a large supply ship, one of a convoy of six vessels steaming along the northern shore. Three days later, he ventured into the Panderma Roads, on the southern coast, and torpedoed a large new steamer belonging to the Rickmers Line. The stricken vessel was towed ashore, listing heavily to port. After a fruitless spell roaming the south-eastern corner of the Marmora, Nasmith notched his next 'kill', an ammunition ship, on 2 June. The explosion caused by his single torpedo was of such ferocity that it appeared to 'lift the whole of her upper deck overboard'.

By now Nasmith was running short of provisions and torpedoes, despite novel if illegal measures which enabled him to recover two which had failed to hit their intended targets by setting them to float at the end of their run. It also appeared as though his luck was wearing thin. On 3 June E11 had her closest call when she was forced by an advancing destroyer to make what Nasmith later confessed was 'a somewhat spectacular dive at full speed from the surface to 20 feet in as many seconds'. Even so, Nasmith still showed little sign of strain. He was preparing to allow D'Oyly-Hughes to carry out his pet project of blowing up a stretch of the Baghdad Railway when a crack was discovered in one of the intermediate shafts between a diesel engine and its main motor. Reluctantly, Nasmith decided it was time to head home.

The journey out, on 7 June, was not without its drama. Having chosen to ignore a large, empty transport anchored by the Moussa Bank in the hope of finding a Turkish battleship or other more tempting targets closer to the Narrows, Nasmith discovered all the anchorages deserted. By then he had travelled beyond Nagara almost as far as Chanak. Most men would have decided to continue their passage home, but not Nasmith. He turned E11 round, headed back up the Straits and sank the transport.

Struggling through the narrow confines of the Straits around Kilid Bahr, the crew had to battle to keep control. An hour later, a scraping noise was heard, similar to that experienced when grounding. Nasmith brought the boat up to 20 feet and to his horror spotted 'a large mine preceding the periscope at a distance of about 20 feet'. The mine's moorings had apparently become entangled in the submarine's port hydroplane and was being dragged along. Without informing anyone of the danger, Nasmith ordered the submarine down deep and proceeded on through the Straits, rising to 20 ft off Kum Kale. There, to the astonishment of his crew, he ordered a succession of strange manoeuvres which eventually resulted in the mine falling clear.

Nasmith's patrol was hailed an outstanding success both in terms of physical damage and the psychological harm done to Turkish morale. As early as 31 May, Keyes had written to his wife praising his new hero. He added: 'I only hope he comes out safely to get the VC he so thoroughly deserves.' The Victoria Cross was duly gazetted on 25 June. As in the case of the E14, the E11's other two officers, Lt. D'Oyly-Hughes and Lt. Robert Brown, received Distinguished Service Crosses while the rest of the crew were given Distinguished Service Medals. The citation accompanying Nasmith's award, which strangely made no mention of his raid on the Turkish capital, read:

> For most conspicuous bravery, in command of one of His Majesty's submarines, while operating in the Sea of Marmora. In the face of great danger, he succeeded in destroying one large Turkish gunboat, two transports, one ammunition ship, and three store-ships, in addition to driving one store-ship ashore. When he had safely passed the most difficult part of his homeward journey he returned again to torpedo a Turkish transport.

Nasmith was promoted commander and went on to complete two further patrols in the Marmora. In their own ways, both were every bit as successful as his first excursion through the Dardanelles and yet, apart from accelerated promotion, Nasmith, like Boyle before him, received no further awards.

During his second patrol, carried out between 5 August and 3 September, he made up for his failure to sink the *Barbarossa* by despatching the aged battleship some five miles north-east of Gallipoli. For a spell Nasmith and Boyle, the twin scourges of the Turks in the Marmora, operated together. It was during this cruise that Lt. D'Oyly-Hughes carried out his famous 'commando-style' raid on the Ismid Railway, a mission left over from the first patrol.

Nasmith's third patrol lasted forty-seven days, a record for submarines operating in the Marmora. By the time E11 made its last entrance into the Narrows the Turks had greatly strengthened their defences, with extra minefields and new nets. But Nasmith was not to be denied his final glory. In all he sank or destroyed eleven steamers, five large sailing vessels and no fewer than thirty smaller craft. On one occasion he rescued forty-two survivors from a destroyer he had torpedoed, later transferring them to a captured sailing vessel.

A few days later, on 14 December, Nasmith repeated his most daring feat with a second raid into the harbour at Constantinople. Spotting a large steamer secured inside the breakwater, Nasmith coolly waited for a small tug towing a string of dhows to pass before sinking her with a single torpedo. There was a brief scare as E11 grounded in shallow water at the end of the breakwater, but Nasmith's luck held good and he managed to bring his boat clear. Incredibly, although the submarine's periscope had been clearly visible for several minutes, not a single gun had opened fire on the hapless boat. Nine days later, the E11 made her way back through the Straits for the last time. The campaign in which she had been one of its most prominent and successful players was over. According to some commentators, the Allied submariners had almost succeeded in bringing Turkey to her knees. Churchill believed 'their exploits constitute . . . the finest examples of submarine action in the whole of the Great War', and it was with bitter disappointment that he noted 'their prowess and devotion were uncrowned by victory'.

There would be only one more attempt to break through the heavily guarded Narrows. On 28 January 1918, while attempting to locate the damaged battle-cruiser *Goeben*, Boyle's old submarine, the E14, now commanded by Lt. Cdr. Geoffrey Saxton White, was spotted and sunk. There were only seven survivors, and based upon evidence supplied on their eventual release from captivity, White was given a posthumous Victoria Cross.

Martin Eric Nasmith, the most successful of Britain's submariners to dare the Dardanelles, was born at 13 Castelnau Gardens, East Barnes, London on 1 April 1883, the eldest son of Martin Nasmith and Caroline (née Beard).

His father was a stockbroker and his two brothers both served in the Army during the Great War, one gaining a Distinguished Service Order and a Military Cross and the other a DSO before his death in action.

Nasmith was educated at Eastman's, Winchester, before joining the *Britannia* in May 1898, at the start of a long and distinguished naval career. As a midshipman aboard the *Renown*, Nasmith volunteered on the same day as his friend Courtney Boyle for submarine service. Their careers continued to run in parallel for the next few years. Nasmith, known as 'Nazims' to his crew, quickly made his mark. A youthful commander of an A-class boat, his technical expertise was such that before the war he was appointed training officer at Fort Blockhouse, the Navy's submarine depot. According to Brodie, Nasmith had been chiefly responsible for the introduction of instrumental aids which made submarine warfare less a matter of inspiration and more a science.

Given command of the E11, Nasmith spent the early part of the war in the North Sea. Having failed in his attempt to join two other E-boats in the Baltic, Nasmith suffered further misfortune when, during an attack on German battle-cruisers returning home from a raid on Hartlepool, he saw his torpedo pass beneath his intended victim. As a result, a despairing Nasmith swore never to drink alcohol or smoke again until he had sunk a battleship; a vow he kept up to his destruction of the *Barbarossa* the following summer.

Posted home, his successes in the Dardanelles made him a popular hero. Nasmith received his VC from George V at Buckingham Palace on 15 January 1916. Six months later he was made the youngest captain in the Royal Navy. By the autumn of 1917 he was commanding a submarine flotilla based at Bantry Bay, Ireland. William Guy Carr, who served as a navigating officer aboard one of his boats, and later wrote one of the most popular histories of the Submarine

Service, remembered him being 'extravagantly admired by his crews, affable and sociable in the ward room'. Guy Carr reckoned: 'He had that rare combination, a delicate sense of the incongruous and an almost ferocious insistence on efficiency.' There were others, however, who noticed the young captain's weakness – a failure to delegate responsibility.

Nevertheless, Nasmith's star continued to burn bright. His war services were recognized by a CB in 1920. Apart from his VC, he had already been made a Chevalier of the Legion of Honour. That same year he married Beatrix Justina Dunbar-Rivers, and took the name Dunbar-Nasmith. They had two sons and a daughter.

By 1928, the wartime submariner had risen to rear-admiral. He was forty-four years old, one of the youngest men to achieve Flag Rank. Further promotions and honours followed. He was made rear-admiral of the Submarine Service in 1929, promoted vice-admiral in 1932 and appointed commander-in-chief, East Indies. Knighted in 1934, Sir Martin Dunbar-Nasmith held one of the Navy's key commands, Plymouth and Western Approaches, at the outbreak of the Second World War. He succeeded Courtney Boyle as flag officer in charge, London in 1942, a post he held until 1946.

After the war he lived in Morayshire, Scotland, and served as vice-chairman of the War Graves Commission and later vice-lieutenant for Morayshire. In retirement, he listed his hobbies as sailing, skiing and forestry.

Admiral Sir Martin Dunbar-Nasmith, who had been created a Knight Commander of the Order of St Michael and St George in 1955, died in Elgin on 29 June 1965, almost fifty years to the day after his gallant leadership had been marked by the award of his nation's supreme honour.

A. JACKA

Courtney's Post, Anzac sector, 19 May 1915

L/Cpl. A. Jacka after being commissioned

At 3.30 a.m. on 19 May 1915, the Turks launched an all-out assault on the Anzac perimeter arcing across the ridges above Ari Burnu. More than 40,000 troops were pitched forward in the greatest single effort to destroy the beach-head.

It was an operation as ill-conceived as any of the Allied attempts to break through the Turkish lines. The mass attack was met by a storm of fire. Only at one place did the Turks breach the defences, but even that minor triumph was short-lived and ended in their dramatic expulsion thanks almost entirely to a single Australian soldier, Acting L/Cpl. Albert Jacka.

On the morning of the Turkish attack, the 14th Battalion were manning Courtney's Post, the central position of three posts established on a vital ridge at the head of a gully which bisected the entire Anzac beach-head. Courtney's took its name from the CO of the 14th Battalion whose task it was to garrison that sector of the 4th Australian Brigade line. It occupied one of the narrowest points on the razor-back ridge known as McLaurin's Hill. Here, friend and foe were separated by only a matter of a few yards. Behind the post, the ground fell away sharply to the beach below.

The 14th Battalion were on the alert, ready for the assault that intelligence reports had forewarned them was imminent. At the time of the attack, Jacka's D Company was in support. Together with about ten members of his platoon, he was standing on a fire-step cut into the front wall of the trench on the left of the position. As the fighting erupted all along the Australian line, a party of Turks took advantage of some dead ground in front of Courtney's to creep to within a few feet of the parapet. From there they bombed the trench, killing two defenders, wounding two more and throwing the remainder into confusion. As they fled from the bombs, the Turks swiftly occupied some 12 yd of trench at the head of Monash Valley. One man, however, refused to run. Jacka, standing behind a traverse in the next-door bay, drilled a volley of warning shots into the back wall of the fire-bay occupied by a then unknown number of Turks. In doing so, he single-handedly barred any further progress north. Meanwhile, other Australians had rallied in a communication trench to prevent a move south, trapping the Turks in the middle.

As news filtered back, Lt. H.N. Boyle, of the 14th, went up the line to investigate. Peering from the corner of the southern communication trench, he was promptly shot in the ear and stunned. Supports were ordered forward, but before they arrived Lt. W.H. Hamilton, of D Company, decided to try and dislodge the Turks on his own. Charging along the communication trench, armed only with a revolver, he was shot dead.

For more than fifteen minutes Jacka remained the only obstacle to a Turkish move northwards. Then he spotted another man approaching along the communication trench where Hamilton's body lay. It was Lt. K.G.W. Crabbe, sent forward to check out Boyle's report. Jacka shouted: 'Back out, Turks in there.' Crabbe called back, asking Jacka whether, if given support, he would charge the Turks. 'Yes', came the reply, 'I want two or three'. Crabbe returned moments later with four volunteers, L/Cpl. Stephen d'Arango, L/Cpl. William Howard and Pte. Frank Poliness, all of A Company, and Pte. Joseph Bickley, of Jacka's company. Having seen them gather in the communication trench opposite, Jacka leapt across the gap in the Turkish-occupied bay to join them. Then, at the agreed moment, he led the small party in a bayonet charge round the bend in the trench and straight at the Turks. They had hardly begun, however, before they were halted by Turkish fire which wounded both Howard and Bickley. Jacka only just managed to reach the shelter of his original position, behind the traverse. There Jacka, recognizing the failure of the attack, bided his time before leaping back into the communication trench.

Together with Lt. Crabbe, Jacka hatched a second and more daring plan. This time, while Crabbe and the surviving members of the party distracted the Turks, Jacka aimed to dash along the communication trench running parallel to the fire-bay occupied by the Turks and take them from behind. It was a startlingly simple plan and one which relied heavily on courage and faith in his own abilities. After a lull in which Crabbe obtained two bombs from Brigade HQ, the plan was set in motion. Pte. James McNally, of D Company, began the diversion by hurling the two bombs towards the fire-bay. One missed, bouncing into a neighbouring trench, and the other burst on the parapet, throwing up a cloud of smoke and dust. Riflemen added to the Turks' confusion by firing into the wall of the fire-bay in an effort to convince them that another attack was coming from the north. Jacka, meanwhile, ran the length of the communication trench, cut in behind the fire-bay and climbed out into no man's land. Then, with the Turks' distracted by Crabbe's diversion, he leapt in among them. The ensuing struggle has been told many times, and details of it vary. According to Newton Wanliss, the 14th's historian, Jacka bayonetted the first two Turks, one of them an officer, and shot five more. He also credited the lone Australian with shooting two more as the survivors fled over the parapet. Poliness was said to have shot a further two. When Crabbe entered the recaptured trench, carpeted with dead Turks and Australians, he found Jacka with an unlighted cigarette in his mouth and his face 'flushed by the tremendous excitement he had undergone during the previous hour'. Jacka merely remarked: 'Well, I managed to get the beggars, Sir.'

Two wounded Turks and 26 Turkish rifles were recovered from the body-strewn bay. It had been an extraordinary individual action calling for a high degree of courage and tactical skill. Jacka noted in his diary:

An artist's impression of Jacka's VC action

> Great battle at 3.00 a.m. Turks captured large portion of our trench. D Coy called into the front line. Lieut Hamilton shot dead. I lead a section of men and recaptured the trench. I bayonetted two Turks, shot five, took three prisoners and cleared the whole trench. I held the trench alone for 15 minutes against a heavy attack. Lieut Crabbe informed me that I would be recommended.

Jacka, whose rank of lance-corporal was confirmed on 15 July, was recovering from bouts of diarrhoea and influenza on Imbros when the *London Gazette* of 24 July announced the award of his Victoria Cross. The citation read:

> For most conspicuous bravery on the night of the 19th–20th May, 1915 [*sic*], at Courtney's Post, Gallipoli Peninsula. Lance-Corporal Jacka, while holding a portion of our trench with four other men, was heavily attacked. When all except himself were killed or wounded, the trench was rushed and occupied by seven Turks. Lance-Corporal Jacka at once most gallantly attacked them single-handed, and killed the whole party, five by rifle fire and two with the bayonet.

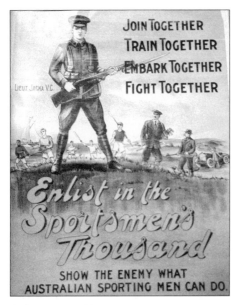

JOIN TOGETHER
TRAIN TOGETHER
EMBARK TOGETHER
FIGHT TOGETHER

LIEUT JACKA V.C.

Enlist in the Sportsmen's Thousand

SHOW THE ENEMY WHAT
AUSTRALIAN SPORTING MEN CAN DO.

Jacka on a recruiting poster

The official account, sprinkled with errors, is a classic example of the unreliability of VC citations. In this case, the mistakes were probably the result of a delay in processing Lt. Crabbe's original verbal recommendation.

When news of the award reached Australia, Jacka became a national hero. As Australia's first Victoria Cross winner of the war, he received £500 and a gold watch offered by John Wren, a prominent Melbourne businessman. Jacka's face was soon to be found adorning magazine covers and recruiting posters. In a matter of months, the volunteer soldier from Wedderburn had come to epitomize the heroic Australian fighting men battling against terrible odds in support of the Mother Country.

Albert Jacka, the man who would later be described as Australia's greatest frontline soldier, was born in Layard, Victoria, on 10 January 1893, the fourth of seven children to timber worker Nathaniel Jacka and his English-born wife Elizabeth (née Kettle).

The family moved to Wedderburn when he was five years old. Educated at the local school, Jacka obtained his standard and merit certificates before taking a job as a labourer, working with his father. At the age of eighteen he joined the Victorian State Forests Department, working at Wedderburn, Cohuna, Koondrook, Lake Charm and Heathcote. Jacka shared his countrymen's enthusiasm for sport and excelled as a cyclist. He enlisted in the AIF at Heathcote on 8 September 1914, but had to re-enlist after his papers were lost. By the end of November, Jacka, having been posted to the 14th Battalion, was made acting lance-corporal. After training at Broadmeadows camp, the unit embarked for Egypt on 22 December. More training followed in the Middle East before the 14th took part in the Gallipoli landings on 25 April 1915.

During the early days on the peninsula, Jacka had a narrow escape when a shell burst above his dugout, mortally wounding the man beside him, but leaving him unharmed. His VC, followed by rapid promotion – he was made corporal on 28 August, sergeant on 12 September and CSM on 14 November –

established him as one of the battalion's leading personalities. To new recruits he had the aura of a modern-day sporting celebrity. E.J. Rule, in his classic war memoir *Jacka's Mob*, described his first meeting with the unit's VC hero:

> To me, Jacka looked the part; he had a medium-sized body, a natty figure, and a determined face with a crooked nose. His feat of polishing off six Turks single-handed certainly took some beating. At that time one characteristic above all endeared him to all underdogs; instead of criming men and bringing them before the officers, his method was: 'I won't crime you, I'll give you a punch on the bloody nose.'

It was this highly individual and unorthodox style of leadership which led to Jacka becoming a revered figure in the 14th. But there were other sides to his character, which brought him into conflict with authority. An ambitious streak combined with an outspokenness, viewed by some of his superior officers as insubordination, stunted his advancement. According to his friends, Jacka fell foul of petty jealousies which prevented him receiving the honours his exploits merited.

Commissioned second lieutenant on 29 April 1916, Jacka accompanied the 14th to France where he continued to serve with the unit until being wounded and badly gassed in May 1918. In that time he had risen to the rank of captain and added a Military Cross and Bar to his VC. However, Charles Bean, Australia's Official War Historian, was not alone in believing Jacka deserved still greater recognition. After his death, Bean wrote:

> Jacka should have come out of the war the most decorated man in the AIF. One does not usually comment on the giving of decorations, but this was an instance in which something obviously went wrong. Everyone who knows the facts, knows that Jacka earned the Victoria Cross three times. In many cases there may be doubt as to what decorations should be awarded, but there could be no real doubt in these.

Bean rated Jacka's courage at Pozières on the Somme in August 1916, and at Bullecourt the following April, as sufficient to have earned him two Bars to his VC. In the event, they brought him a Military Cross and Bar.

In the early morning of 7 August 1916, during the Battle of Pozières, Jacka's platoon was cut off by a German attack which tore through the Australian lines. A grenade rolled into his dugout and killed two men before Jacka led a remarkable counter-attack. The German infantry had thought the battle was over. About forty prisoners from a neighbouring Australian unit were being rounded up when Jacka, followed by seven men, burst among them, shooting and stabbing with bayonets. His unit history recorded:

Jacka, hurled off his feet on different occasions by the terrfic impact of rifle bullets fired at close range, was seven times wounded, once being knocked down by a bullet that passed through his body under the right shoulder, and twice partially stunned by head wounds. He fairly surpassed himself this day, and killed upwards of a score of Germans with his own hand, including some with the bayonet . . . This brilliant counter-attack against an overwhelming and triumphant enemy was completely successful – all the Australian prisoners were released, the whole of the German escort guarding them was killed or dispersed, and in addition 42 unwounded Germans . . . were captured.

Bean called it 'the most dramatic and effective act of individual audacity in the history of the AIF'.

Evacuated to England, Jacka was promoted lieutenant on 18 August and reported dead on 8 September. In fact, he was very much alive and, despite the seriousness of his wounds, he was fit enough to attend a VC investiture at Windsor Castle on 29 September. Jacka was promoted captain on 15 March 1917, and the following month, while serving as battalion intelligence officer, he carried out a number of hazardous patrols in no man's land which culminated in a daring reconnaissance of the German lines on the eve of the Battle of Bullecourt. During this foray, Jacka captured a two-man German patrol single-handed, earning a Bar to his MC.

During the battle for Messines Ridge in June 1917, Jacka led his company with great skill. During their advance, they overran machine-gun posts and captured a German field gun, but his actions went unrecognized. Three months later, after recovering from another wound in July, he distinguished himself again during the fighting near Polygon Wood, when the 14th captured and held its objectives against heavy German counter-attacks. Wanliss wrote:

His reckless valour, his excellent judgement, his skilful tactics, his prompt anticipation of the enemy's movements, and the force and vigour of his battle strokes gained the admiration of all ranks, and inspired everyone with the greatest confidence. Throughout the whole engagement he was an ubiquitous and fearless figure, the very incarnation of a great fighting soldier and a born leader of men. No more fearless or gallant soldier took part in the Great War.

Jacka was recommended for the Distinguished Service Order, but again it was not granted.

The injuries he sustained in May 1918 were of such severity that it was feared he might not survive. But following two operations and a long recuperation, he recovered to receive a hero's home-coming in Australia in September 1919.

Demobilized in January 1920, Jacka established an electrical goods importing and exporting business together with two comrades from the 14th. The venture was heavily financed by John Wren, the businessman who had given Jacka £500 as the first Australian VC winner of the war. The following year Jacka married Frances Veronica Carey, a typist from his office. They settled in St Kilda and later adopted a daughter. In September 1929 Jacka was elected on to St Kilda Council and the following year he became mayor. Much of his civic work was devoted to helping the unemployed, but what few realised at the time was that Jacka's own business had fallen victim of the slump.

His last years witnessed a painful decline; both physically and financially. By August, 1931, when his term as mayor ended, he was worn-out by his civic duties and the vain attempts to keep his sinking business afloat. He soldiered on, taking a job as a salesman for the Anglo-Dominion Soap Company, until in December 1931 he collapsed at a council meeting. He entered Caulfield Military Hospital, where he died of chronic nephritis on 17 January 1932. Jacka was only thirty-nine years old, although visitors to his bedside reckoned he looked nearer sixty. Unknown to many, Jacka had separated from his wife shortly before his final illness. By the time of his death, Bert Jacka had come to epitomize the Australian creed of bluntness, personal bravery and great comradeship to such a degree that almost 6,000 people were reckoned to have filed past his coffin as it lay in state in Anzac House.

After his funeral, a public appeal raised funds for a memorial plaque and sculpture to be placed above his grave in the Presbyterian section of St Kilda cemetery. A further £1,195 was raised to buy his widow a house. Each year a memorial service is held at his grave; originally it was organized by his old comrades in the 14th, although today it is carried on by the local council.

The Jacka legend was perhaps best summed up by E.J. Rule, who wrote:

He was not one of those whose character, manner, or outlook was changed by the high decorations which he had received. His confident, frank, outspoken personality never changed. His leadership in his last battle was as audacious and capable as in his first. He deserved the Victoria Cross as thoroughly at Pozières, Bullecourt and Ypres as at Gallipoli. Not we only, but the brigade, and the whole AIF came to look upon him as a rock of strength that never failed. We of the 14th Battalion never ceased to be thrilled when we heard ourselves referred to in the estaminet or by passing units on the march as 'some of Jacka's mob'.

G.R.D. MOOR

Near Krithia, Helles sector, 6 June 1915

2nd Lt. G.R.D. Moor

By the middle of May, following a fortnight of prolonged fighting, the 29th Division was in sore need of rest and recuperation. Units which had shouldered the main burden of operations since the landings had shrunk to less than half their original number.

The losses sustained by the 2nd Hampshires were typical. On 28 March more than 1,000 officers and men embarked at Avonmouth for the Dardanelles. By May 10th, when the battalion was withdrawn for a brief rest, having endured the bloodbath at V Beach and the two subsequent hastily mounted and ill-prepared attempts to roll back the Turkish forces in front of Krithia, it numbered less than 250 men.

Throughout May the 29th Division's hard-pressed battalions pursued a policy of careful but systematic advance designed to push the Allied lines to within 200 yd of the Turkish front line in readiness for a renewed offensive. As they prepared for the battle to come, the Hampshires received some welcome reinforcements, including a new commanding officer. On 30 May Lt. Col. Weir de Lancy Williams, who had distinguished himself at V Beach alongside Doughty-Wylie and Walford, joined the depleted unit. Williams, who had been given temporary command of the 88th Brigade after the establishment of the Helles beach-head, was the Hampshires' fifth CO since 25 April. The battalion was further strengthened by drafts which brought the unit up to 382 other ranks. Among the arrivals on 17 May were thirty-nine officers and men rejoining the unit from hospital. They included 18-year-old 2nd Lt. G.R. Dallas Moor, one of the youngest officers then serving in the British Army. Nine months earlier, Moor had been studying at Cheltenham College. Now he was a wounded veteran of the battle for the Helles beach-head. He had returned just in time to take part in the general attack to be made at midday on 4 June.

The Third Battle of Krithia, as it was officially termed, was launched with great hope among the British commanders whose confidence appeared restored following the frustration of their original plan. At first their renewed optimism seemed well-founded. Supported by a short bombardment, the assault units of

the 29th Division succeeded in securing their objectives while, in the centre, the
recently arrived 42nd East Lancashire Division achieved a spectacular
breakthrough, advancing to within half a mile of Krithia. However, the failure of
the French assault on the right and its tragic consequences for the Royal Naval
Division brought about the ruination of the offensive.

One of the redeeming features of yet another lost opportunity was the gallant
performance of the over-stretched units of the 29th Division. Of these, the 2nd
Hampshires achieved more than most. Fortified by a stirring speech by their new
CO, in which he expressed the hope that one of them would earn the Regiment's
first Victoria Cross since the storming of the Taku Forts in 1862, the battalion
advanced across Fir Tree Spur, capturing two lines of trenches, H8–H9 and H10,
in the process.

By mid-afternoon the Hampshires' breakthrough had been deepened. The H12
line was secured along the 88th Brigade front and there were reports of
lodgements in a fifth trench line. The repulse of the French, followed in turn by
the retirement of the Naval Division, however, left the most advanced units of
the 42nd Division exposed. Counter-attacks pushed the East Lancashires back,
making some of the 88th Brigade's gains untenable. At 6.00 p.m. the Hampshires
were ordered to withdraw to the H11 line and by nightfall the brigade's line,
running from H11 westwards to a salient created by a section of the H12 line,
was consolidated.

The Hampshires had paid heavily for their success. Almost half of the 300 men
engaged were casualties, with losses particularly severe among officers. In one of
the captured trenches, Lt. Col. Williams came across 2nd Lt. Dallas Moor, who
he described as 'a tall, wild-looking, dark-haired boy of 18'. He later recalled:
'Moor, myself and one other officer were the only officers left untouched. I said
to him: "Well done, boy! Hold what you've got."' An hour afterwards Williams
was wounded, and by the morning of 6 June, Dallas Moor, the youngest and
most junior subaltern of the battalion, had been left in sole command of the 88th
Brigade's right-hand forward sector. The previous day had passed off relatively
quietly. A series of half-hearted Turkish attacks were beaten back by machine-
gun fire. But in the early hours of 6 June the Turks, strengthened by newly
arrived reinforcements, returned to the assault with extraordinary results. Lt.
Col. A.G. Paterson DSO, MC, of the 1st KOSBs, who together with the 1st Essex
were occupying the H12 salient on the left of the 2nd Royal Fusiliers and 2nd
Hampshires, later recorded:

There was a slight mist. At dawn heavy fire broke out and a message came
through that H12 was lost. Almost at the same moment looking away to the
right one saw what appeared to be the whole of our trench garrisons streaming
back in hundreds to the old front line under heavy MG fire.

It was a most extraordinary sight and I shall never forget the sound made by troops coming back – a sort of long drawn-out moan.

An officer of the HQ with us (I am not sure whether it was the Essex or the Borders) ran out towards Nine Tree Copse to rally these troops. They must have rallied quickly as we got in touch with the Essex later in the morning. The Turks took no advantage of this momentary panic.

That they did not do so was almost certainly, in part, due to the Hampshires' young acting CO. Having outflanked the KOSBs' positions on the left of the salient, the Turks burst through the 1st Essex line and, as the survivors fell back on the H11 trench, the men in the second line broke, threatening to unhinge the entire 88th Brigade defence system. The Hampshires' history states:

A disorganised mass of men was being pressed back against the Royal Fusiliers' left, where crowded and narrow trenches impeded any reorganisation of the defence. The situation was becoming critical, officerless men were retreating in confusion when Second Lieutenant G.R.D. Moor . . . dashed across the open from the Hampshires' lines with a few men and stemmed the retirement by vigorous and forcible measures, actually shooting one or two panic-stricken fugitives. He did not stop here: having rallied and reorganised the men in a hollow, he led them back to the lost trench and cleared the Turks out, setting a magnificent example of bravery and resourcefulness . . .

Details of this action, and, in particular, the ruthless methods employed by the young officer to turn back the fleeing troops, are sketchy. Dallas Moor appears to have left no record of the most dramatic event of his young life. Lt. Gen. Sir Beauvoir de Lisle, who had arrived on the peninsula two days earlier to take command of the 29th Division, later stated that Moor 'had to shoot the leading four men, and the remainder came to their senses'. He called it a 'very remarkable performance' and described the young subaltern as 'one of the bravest men I have met in this war'.

With so little evidence to hand, any judgement, even with the benefit of hindsight, appears worthless. But balanced against the desperate measures taken by Moor is the certainty that a disorderly rout of the kind which threatened to overtake the British line would unquestionably have resulted in far higher casualties among the retreating troops.

His subsequent counter-attack, no mean feat in itself considering the shock of the initial panic, dislodged the Turks from their slender hold on the H11 line. The H12 salient, however, remained in Turkish hands. Another attack at about 6.00 p.m. was repulsed with heavy losses.

'That evening', wrote the Hampshires' historian, 'Second Lieutenant Moor had

An artist's impression of Moor's VC action

to be taken to Brigade Headquarters, being completely exhausted'. Moor's role in the battle prompted a congratulatory message from the commanding officer of the 88th Brigade. However, his actions may otherwise have gone unrewarded but for the action of officers from the neighbouring unit, the 2nd Royal Fusiliers. It was they who, having witnessed his desperate efforts to prevent a catastrophe, recommended him for the Victoria Cross.

Moor had been under almost continuous fire for eleven hours, and it was a further fourteen hours before he recovered from the state of collapse brought on by the strain of carrying out his CO's orders to hold his position. Shortly afterwards, the young officer was evacuated to hospital in Malta, suffering from 'exhaustion'. On 24 July the *London Gazette* announced the award of the Victoria Cross to 2nd Lt. Moor. The citation read:

> For most conspicuous bravery and resource on the 5th June, 1915 [sic], during operations south of Krithia, Dardanelles. When a detachment of a battalion on his left, which had lost all its officers, was rapidly retiring before a heavy Turkish attack, Second Lieutenant Moor, immediately grasping the danger to the remainder of the line, dashed back some 200 yards, stemmed the retirement, led back the men and recaptured the lost trench.
>
> This young officer, who only joined the Army in October, 1914, by his personal bravery and presence of mind saved a dangerous situation.

The reason for the erroneous date is unclear. Perhaps an early draft of the recommendation was wrongly dated and the mistake repeated. More understandable was the official reticence over the methods used to stop the troops 'rapidly retiring'.

By August 1915 the Mediterranean Expeditionary Force's youngest VC was back serving with his unit in trenches close to the scene of his gallant action. On 6 August the 2nd Hampshires took part in a diversionary attack in which the H12a, H12 and H13 network of trenches west of the Krithia Nullah were once again the objective. Moor was, fortunately as it transpired, one of the officers 'left out of battle'. The operation was an unmitigated disaster for the Hampshires. More than 240 officers and men were killed for no gains. A further 210 were wounded and Moor was one of only four officers left in the battalion. Despite the appalling losses, which once again left him in temporary command of the battalion, his morale does not appear to have flagged. Maj. John Gillam, who visited the Hampshires in their trenches ten days after the ill-fated attack, noted in his diary how he had been taken to one of the forward positions by 'a cheery young man named Moore [sic], who has recently won the VC'.

Moor stayed with his battalion for another month before suffering a severe bout of dysentery which resulted in him being evacuated on 15 September.

St Berwyns, Braunton, where Moor convalesced

He was invalided to England and spent some time in a London hospital before receiving his VC from George V at Buckingham Palace on 18 October. Shortly afterwards, he visited his mother in Braunton, north Devon, where the local citizens had prepared a special welcome. The *North Devon Journal* reported: 'As Lieut Moor and his mother walked from the platform to the waiting motor car . . . the large crowd gave three hearty cheers, with an additional cheer for Mrs Moor. Lieut Moor, in acknowledgement, rose from his seat in the car and saluted.'

His poor health, however, was painfully apparent. The newspaper noted: 'Lieut Moor, who was looking pale and was evidently very weak, briefly replied that he was very glad to be home.' Later, the young officer was presented with an illuminated address by the chairman of Braunton Parish Council. The address, read out to loud applause, concluded: 'We wish you God-speed and further success in whatever duties you may be called upon to perform in the future.' Lt. Moor, perhaps overawed by the scale of his welcome or suffering from the effects of his illness, simply replied with a single sentence of thanks.

George Raymond Dallas Moor was born on 22 October 1896, at his mother's sister's home in Pollington Street, St Kilda, Australia, the second son of William

Henry Moor, a senior official in the Ceylon Civil Service, and Ella Helen Moor (née Pender).

It appears he was set to follow in the family tradition of colonial service. His father was an auditor general of the Transvaal and an uncle, Sir Ralph Moor, achieved distinction in Southern Nigeria.

Privately educated at Little Appleby, Ryde, on the Isle of Wight, Dallas Moor attended Cheltenham College from September 1910. His original application form, dated 12 November 1909, gave as his intended profession the Egyptian Civil Service.

With his father occupying a key post in Pretoria, Moor became a member of Cheltenham College's Boyne House, where he was noted more for his sporting prowess than his scholarship. His education ended abruptly with the outbreak of war during the school holidays of 1914. In September he attended a recruiting meeting at Braunton, where his mother was living, and the following month he enlisted in the 11th Devonshires. Within days, however, he was commissioned and transferred to the 3rd Battalion of the Hampshire Regiment, his father's old regiment. He was not yet eighteen. 2nd Lt. Moor joined the 2nd Hampshires as it was preparing to embark for the Dardanelles. He survived the landing on 25 April, but was wounded three days later during the advance from the beaches. As well as his VC, Moor was granted a commission in the Regular Army, dated 1 August 1915, for his services at Gallipoli.

After a lengthy period of rest and recuperation following his evacuation from the peninsula, Moor joined the 1st Hampshires on 3 October 1916, serving with them during the final actions on the Somme. He remained with them on the Western Front until 23 December 1917, when a severe arm wound necessitated his evacuation. Returning to England, he was appointed ADC to Maj.-Gen. Williams CB, CMG, DSO, his former CO from Gallipoli days, who was then commanding the 30th Division.

Williams, who had not forgotten his young subaltern's powers of leadership on the battlefield two years earlier, had tried in vain to have Moor posted to his staff when he took command of the division in April 1917. He later stated:

My first thought was for young Moor. I wrote to his Battalion commander asking for him, saying that 'the boy has been at it so long he must want a rest'. His CO wrote back that he could not spare him.

Early in 1918 I heard from him that he was wounded and in England, and though he could not get passed fit he could come to me as ADC. He joined me on March 20th, 1918, during our retreat before the German main attack [sic].

Moor, who had still not yet recovered the full use of his arm, was given the rank of acting general staff officer, grade three (GSO 3) and he quickly adapted to his new role. Williams wrote: 'This officer has a positive contempt for danger, and distinguishes himself on every occasion.' Not for him a safe billet well behind the lines. Williams stated: 'In the open fighting of the last few weeks of the war he was invaluable, day after day reconnoitring well out in front of our most advanced troops.' During the pursuit of the Germans towards the River Scheldt in October 1918, Moor had two narrow escapes from death. Philip Neame, himself a VC holder, who was then serving as GSO I of 30th Division, was with Moor when they rode out with the advance guard. He later wrote:

> We had dismounted and handed our horses to our orderlies while I looked with my field-glass, when I heard the ominous roar of a heavy shell coming through the air. By experience I knew that it was a 5.9 inch howitzer shell, and that it was coming very close. There was no cover at all, so we just stood there. The shell landed with a thud within three yards of our feet: by good fortune it was a dud. Another day Moor and I were walking down a lane with the CRA, Brigadier-General F.F. Lambarde CMG, DSO, when a German field-gun battery bracketed us with two salvoes. Moor and I, as I thought sensibly this time, made to get into the ditch, where there was good cover. Lambarde frightened us by walking straight down the middle of the road without batting an eyelid, and for very shame we went too, while the shells kept on coming, but behind us.

Moor's repeated acts of gallantry were recognized by the awards of a Military Cross and Bar which were both gazetted in the space of ten weeks. The citation for his MC, published on 2 December 1918, stated: 'For conspicuous gallantry and skill. He carried out a daylight reconnaissance all along the divisional front in face of heavy machine-gun fire at close range, in many places well in front of our foremost posts.'

Tragically, however, Moor did not live long enough to receive either award. During the last few days of the war, he fell victim to the influenza epidemic sweeping across Europe. On 3 November 1918, at Mouveaux, in

The illuminated address presented to Moor

France, he succumbed. Only twelve days earlier, he had celebrated his twenty-second birthday.

Lt. Dallas Moor VC, MC and Bar is one of forty-six names recorded on the roll of honour inside Braunton's thirteenth-century church. The village's war dead are also commemorated in the church's Lady chapel. At the nearby museum, a short walk away from St Berwyns, the house where his mother lived, the exhibits include a copy of the illuminated address presented to the young VC winner by the people of Braunton. Among the museum archives is a brief note stating: 'Lt Moor's regiment presented the village of Braunton with a field gun which stood in the park for some years.' According to villagers, the gun remained on display until it rusted away!

In 1961 Dallas Moor's elder brother, Cdr. W. Sylvester Moor RN, a former champion lightweight boxer who had served throughout the First World War, wrote to the Hampshire Regiment: 'I now hold my brother Dallas' Victoria Cross, and as I have no Blood Relations left, would like to present it to the Regiment.'

Today the Cross is displayed at the regimental museum in Winchester in memory of the youngest Army officer VC of the war, who was described by his former chief, Maj.-Gen. Williams, as 'a fine character and as fearless a soldier as ever lived'.

Moor's grave

H. JAMES

Near Gully Ravine, Helles sector, 28 June and 2 July 1915

2nd Lt. H. James

At 11.00 a.m. on 28 June, following a short bombardment, British troops rose from their trenches on both sides of Gully Ravine and surged towards the Turkish lines. The attack, which was intended to emulate the French success at Kereves Dere a week before, was limited to clearly defined objectives and at first all appeared to go well.

On the left, the men of the 29th Division, supported by the Indian Brigade, made swift gains, their progress across five lines of trenches on Gully Spur being marked by the sun glittering on triangles of metal sewn on the men's tunics to aid artillery observers. But on the right, where the untested Scots of the 156th Brigade, from the 52nd Lowland Division, were assigned the task of capturing two lines of trenches on Fir Tree Spur, known as H12a and H12, the story was a depressingly familiar one. The war diary of the 4th Worcestershires, a support unit, reported: '11.00 a.m. The first troops to move to the attack have started and appear to do very well. For some reason or other the 8th Scottish Rifles have retired. . . .' The reason was simple enough. The Turks in trenches, scarcely touched by a preliminary bombardment devoid of HE shells, had slaughtered the attacking battalions as soon as they crested a slight rise separating the two lines. In the space of five minutes twenty-five out of twenty-six officers and 448 men of the 8th Scottish Rifles were killed or wounded. The unit's losses were greater than those sustained by any of the assault battalions on the first day of the Somme. The saps leading out into no man's land were choked with dead and wounded. Yet still the attack went on. Not realizing the full extent of the 156th Brigade's repulse, General de Lisle (GOC, 29th Division) signalled: 'H12 is to be taken at all costs, if necessary you will send forward your reserve battalion.'

In a display of courage bordering on desperation, the 7th Scottish Rifles leapt out of their trenches and charged through a storm of fire to capture a section of the H12a line. A barrier, later known as Southern Barricade, was erected and a series of bombing attacks beaten off. Another small party seized a stretch of the H12 trench on the left, where a block was flung up, to be known as the Northern Barricade. But the two lines facing the shattered 8th Scottish Rifles remained firmly in Turkish hands. A renewed attempt to take them resulted only in more casualties, among them Brig. Gen. William Scott-Moncrieff, who was killed at the head of Sap No. 29 leading his last reserves into action.

Incredibly, it was decided to continue the assault into the afternoon. The Essex and the 5th Royal Scots, from the 88th Brigade, were pushed forward and at 4.00 p.m. the Royal Scots, using Saps No. 29 and 30 for cover, launched another futile attack over ground already strewn with the dead of the Scottish Rifles. Shell-fire and machine-guns destroyed the attack before it had really begun. One subaltern emerging from Sap No. 30 with only three men of his platoon still unscathed saw beyond a barricade 'many men with fierce bearded faces and he realised that to lead his three men against such a throng of foes would be an act of insane folly. Accordingly he withdrew . . .'

Attached to the 5th Royal Scots was Lt. Herbert James, a 26-year-old subaltern from the 4th Worcestershires, who had been commissioned from the ranks in the autumn of 1914. James had only returned to the peninsula twelve days earlier after recovering from wounds sustained during the April fighting. He had been sent to the Royal Scots as a liaison officer, with the job of helping his battalion exploit any success. When the Royal Scots' attack foundered, James was sent forward by the battalion's CO in order to assist the assault. But by the time he arrived, the frontline trenches were crowded with wounded and dazed survivors. All the unit's officers having become casualties, James took over command and set about restoring order. Then he made his way back to battalion HQ before returning with reinforcements. When he arrived back, he discovered that a Turkish counter-attack had shattered the defence. So once again he re-established the line and held it until nightfall.

During the next three days fighting continued on both sides of Gully Ravine. But the Turks in H12a and H12, who had successfully repulsed the Lowland Scots on 28 June, continued to hold out. Two days after the first failed assault, the 88th Brigade took over from the exhausted 156th and arrangements were made to pinch out the salient. The attack, postponed from 1 July to the following day, was to be carried out by parties from the 4th Worcestershires and the 2nd Hampshires. None of the detachments involved were larger than a company.

In view of the shortage of shells, it was decided a bombing attack along the existing saps would stand a better chance of success than another full-scale assault across the open. Two saps in the centre of the line were assigned to the Worcesters. The Hampshires were allotted two saps on the left. In command of one of the Worcesters' detachments was Lt. James, who had gained first-hand knowledge of the ground during his attachment to the Royal Scots.

The attack was launched at 9.00 a.m. Two below-strength companies of the Hampshires advanced beyond the Northern and Southern Barricades established in H12a and H12. Their official history recorded:

W Company gained about 20 yards in H12a. Further they could not go: rifle fire from the next trench behind and enfilade fire from a communication trench commanded a bend round which it was impossible to advance, so a barricade was made. X also made about the same distance in H12 and established another barricade, where also much bombing developed . . .

The Worcesters, with smaller parties each consisting of about thirty men, initially fared better. Having left the cover of the saps, they sprinted across the open, overran the Turkish sap heads and sent the surprised defenders reeling back. Lt. James led his bombers along the left-hand sap while Lt. J. Mould led his first attack along the right sap. James pushed well forward, but his progress was hampered by the large number of dead bodies clogging the trench. The grisly post resembled a charnel-house. Since the battle of 4 June, fighting had raged along it off and on for a month and soldiers of all ranks lay in heaps, some half-buried by earth with more recent victims sprawled on top. The 4th Worcesters' official account recorded:

The bombers advanced up the sap head to the trench junction at its further end. There the enemy were waiting, and a furious bombing fight ensued. The enemy were well provided with bombs (the British forces had at that date only 'jam-tin' bombs, the Turks were supplied with spherical bombs of archaic appearance, but of much greater effect) and in rapid succession the men of Lieut James' party were struck down. Presently, only four were left standing – the subaltern, one lance-corporal and two privates. These four maintained an obstinate fight, hoping for reinforcements . . .

James had sent one of his men back with a message calling for assistance, but unknown to him he had been killed. Meanwhile, the bomb fight reached its climax. A number of Turkish bombs were thrown back before they could explode, but then one burst among them, killing the two privates and peppering James and L/Cpl. R. Reece with fragments. Ordering Reece to return for reinforcements, James decided to try and hang on alone. According to the Worcesters' account:

The Turks were organising a counter-attack. A cluster of bayonets could be seen over the top of the trench. Presently came a shower of bombs and the bayonets moved forward. Before that attack the subaltern fell back along the winding trench, holding back the pursuit by bombing from each successive bend. The enemy followed. Halfway back along the saphead, Lieut James came to a point where a heap of dead bodies blocked the trench. There, he found one of his bombers, Private Parry, lying wounded. To protect him, Lieut James turned to bay. Hastily forming a low barricade of sandbags (at that point there was a small 'dump' of bombs and sandbags on top of dead bodies) the subaltern organised a temporary defence.

With two rifles and a sack of bombs, Lieut James held the trench single-handed, alternately lying behind his barricade to fire then rising to bomb the Turks after his rifle had driven them back behind cover. Amid a shower of bombs he held his ground until the arrival of reinforcements headed by Sgt-Major C. Felix.

With the reinforcements came L/Cpl. Reece, who joined his officer at the temporary block while a secure barricade was constructed behind them. Finally, after Pte. Parry had been removed, James and Reece pulled back behind the new defensive barrier. Shortly afterwards, the Turkish attack petered out. Just how long James waged his single-handed battle is not clear. His unit's historian stated: 'The exact length of time . . . can never be known, but during that time he expended nearly the whole of his sack of bombs.' Throughout his splendid rearguard action Lt. Mould had waged a similarly gallant but hopeless struggle on the right for which he later received a Military Cross.

By early afternoon the action was over. The battalion war diary stated:

An artist's impression of James's VC action

'2.30 p.m. After repeated attempts we have been unable to gain H12 and H12a. Total casualties three killed and twelve wounded.' The two positions inside the salient remained in Turkish hands to the end of the campaign. Apart from cuts and bruises sustained in the bomb fight, Lt. James came out miraculously unscathed. He was recommended for the Victoria Cross, and, while the papers made their way along official channels, he was promoted adjutant.

Two months later, on 6 August, during the battle for the Vineyard, his battalion was almost destroyed. The following day he went forward to investigate reports that some wounded were still lying out in no man's land with a view to sending out a rescue party. Lt. Col. C.A. Bolton later recalled: 'Lieut James left me and I did not see him again until next morning, when he reported that there had been wounded in no man's land and that to save a patrol he had gone out and brought them in himself – two men badly hit and unable to move.'

Three weeks later, while the remnants of the battalion were resting on Imbros, news came through of James' VC award. The citation, published in the *London Gazette* on 1 September, stated:

> For most conspicuous bravery during the operations in the Southern Zone of the Gallipoli Peninsula. On 28th June, when a portion of the regiment had been checked, owing to all the officers being put out of action, Second Lieutenant James, who belonged to a neighbouring unit, entirely on his own initiative, gathered together a body of men and led them forward under heavy shell and rifle fire. He then returned, organised a second party and again advanced. His gallant example put fresh life into the attack. On 3rd July [*sic*], in the same locality, Second Lieutenant James headed a party of bomb throwers up a Turkish communication trench and after nearly all his bomb throwers had been killed or wounded, he remained alone at the head of the trench and kept back the enemy single-handed until a barrier had been built behind him and the trench secured. He was throughout exposed to murderous fire.

L/Cpl. Reece was awarded a Distinguished Conduct Medal for his part in the second action.

On the night of 27/28 September James was wounded in the foot while visiting one of his battalion's advanced sap heads. The injury necessitated his evacuation, and after treatment the new VC hero was sent home on a month's convalescence leave. He slipped into Birmingham almost unnoticed and, throughout his stay, he politely but steadfastly refused to discuss his experiences. He could not, however, evade completely the public adulation. During December, in a ceremony orchestrated by the city's Lord Mayor Neville Chamberlain, the future British Prime Minister, he received his fellow citizens' acclaim in a crowded Victoria Square.

Herbert James, the first member of the Worcestershire Regiment to win the VC in the war, was born on 13 November 1888 in Ladywood, Birmingham, the son of Mr and Mrs Walter James. His father ran a jewellery engraving business in Warstone Lane.

Herbert James was educated at Smethwick Central School, and appeared destined for the teaching profession. After leaving school he taught at the Bearwood Road and Brasshouse Lane schools, and preparations were made for him to attend college for further training. But James had other plans. On 13 April 1919, aged twenty, he joined the Army on a short service enlistment as a trooper in the 21st Lancers, famous for its vainglorious charge at Omdurman in 1898. He joined his regiment in May 1909 and went with it to Egypt in 1910 for a two-year tour of duty followed by a spell in India.

1909 -

James was promoted lance-corporal on 14 July 1911. Even in the Army, he continued with his studies, and his talent for languages won him numerous prizes. He intended to make a career in the Civil Service after his Army days were over, but, like so many plans, it was overtaken by the war.

By the autumn of 1914 the War Office, faced with the task of recruiting a New Army, found it necessary to increase the number of commissions offered to Regular Army NCOs. James was a prime candidate, and on 9 November 1914, after having spent five years and 208 days in the ranks, L/Cpl. James became 2nd Lt. James of the 4th Worcestershires. He returned to England to join the unit, largely consisting of men from his home city of Birmingham, and embarked with the battalion on 22 March 1915 for the Dardanelles.

The main body of the 4th Worcesters landed at W Beach on 25 April and the unit played a key role in effecting the link-up with the troops on V Beach the following day. It was during this fierce fighting that James was severely wounded in the head. He was evacuated to Malta, his name appearing in the Mediterranean Expeditionary Force's first casualty list alongside two other Gallipoli VCs, Garth Walford and Cuthbert Bromley.

After being evacuated from the peninsula for the last time in September, Lt. James was transferred to the 1st Worcestershires where he was given command of B Company. He went to France in March 1916 and served with the battalion on the Somme in July 1916. During the fighting around the village of Contalmaison Lt. James was wounded again. Evacuated to a hospital on the Isle of Wight, he was then moved to the mainland where he recuperated. Two months later, on 5 September, he married Gladys Beatrice Lillicrap at Stoke Damerel parish church, Devonport.

Little more is recorded of his subsequent war service. He returned to duty on 18 August 1917 as a general staff officer, grade three, with the rank of temporary captain. On 1 April 1918 he was promoted to the rank of brigade-major. James was awarded the French Croix de Guerre on 1 May 1917 and the Military Cross on 16 October 1918, although there is no mention in any official records of the acts for which the decorations were granted. He also received two mentions in dispatches, gazetted on 20 May and 20 December 1918, and the honourary award of the Panamanian Medal de la Solidaridad, which was not approved until 17 February 1920.

Capt. James VC, MC remained in the Army after the war, his Civil Service ambitions apparently forgotten. On 21 December 1920 he transferred to the East

Lancashire Regiment with the rank of captain and brevet major. He served in the West Indies before entering the Staff College. He then took up a post as a staff captain at the War Office. He had a stint as a brigade major in the Aldershot Command from October 1927 to November 1928 and it was during that spell of duty that he transferred to the York and Lancaster Regiment with the rank of major.

He separated from his first wife, and married Jessy Amy England in a quiet ceremony in London on 26 November 1929. The following March the *London Gazette* announced that Maj. James was retiring from the Army due to ill health. Maj. James' son, A.H. James, who later followed his father into the Worcestershires and rose to the rank of major, wrote of his father:

> He was a dedicated and very efficient soldier, but a shy withdrawn man who found it difficult to get on with other people. He was invalided out of the Army . . . due to ill health brought on by a head wound which he got in France. I believe he would have risen very high in the Army but for this.

Little more is recorded of Maj. James' life. By the late 1950s he was living apart from his second wife in a rented bedsit in Brunswick Gardens, Kensington. He lived there for the last fifteen months of his life a virtual recluse, buying and selling paintings. In August 1958 he suffered a heart attack and, according to newspaper reports, was found five days later by his landlord lying on the floor of his close-shuttered room on the point of starvation. Maj. James was taken to hospital, where he died on 15 August. The following day newspapers carried the tragic story. In one, the landlord's sister told how her brother had found him surrounded by paintings, many of them stacked together. 'My brother picked up a book in the room', she said. 'It was a complete list of VCs and it fell open at a page marked in pencil. The line was against Major James' name, and that was the first we knew of his record.'

G.R. O'SULLIVAN AND J. SOMERS

Near Gully Ravine, Helles sector, 18–19 June and 1–2 July 1915

55 Capt. G. O'Sullivan

Cpl. J. Somers

18 June 1915, the hundredth anniversary of Wellington's victory on the field of Waterloo, was marked by a modest celebration at Sir Ian Hamilton's headquarters on Imbros. Over a dish of crayfish, Hamilton and his eternally ebullient chief lieutenant, Gen. Hunter-Weston, wallowed in past glories. Suitably inspired, Hamilton sent a wire delivering greetings to all Wellingtonians under his command. Yet try as he might, he was not able to set aside his mounting difficulties on the peninsula. After his meal, the GOC noted: 'Have just heard that after a heavy bombardment the Turks made an attack and that fighting is going on now.'

With little sense of history, the Turks had indeed contrived to spoil the party by launching a fierce assault on a recently captured extension of the British line at the eastern edge of Gully Ravine. Approximately 70 yd of 'Turkey Trench', a length of the old Turkish frontline that had defied all attempts at capture on 4 June, had been wrested from their grip in a minor operation seven days earlier. But the Turks were not prepared to surrender the position without a struggle. Shortly after 6.30 p.m. on 18 June, heavy shelling was reported by forward units of the 2nd South Wales Borderers manning the trench. It was the beginning of what was, by Gallipoli standards, a fearsome bombardment. Later estimates put the number of HE shells directed at the trench at approximately 500 within the space of little more than half an hour. Parapets were shattered and telephone communications destroyed. At 7.30 p.m.

an orderly brought out the message: 'Men all right, trenches and parapets badly damaged'. Then came reports of the first Turkish attack. It was easily driven off, but the second assault, launched shortly before 9.00 p.m., penetrated the north-west sector, killing and wounding most of the occupants. With their senior officer fatally wounded, the survivors fled in the face of a Turkish bomb attack. 'Turkey Trench' was in Turkish hands once more and the Borderers' withdrawal had left a dangerous gap in the line.

The Turkish threat was felt immediately by the Borderers' neighbouring unit, the 1st Royal Inniskilling Fusiliers. A shower of bombs fell on a position occupied by B Company, forcing them to give up 30 yd of trench. Orders were swiftly issued for the gap 'to be made good by force and to be maintained by force'. It was at this point in proceedings that Capt. Gerald O'Sullivan intervened. Leading A Company of the Inniskillings, together with one platoon from C Company, he moved forward to the support of the most threatened units. By 9.45 p.m. O'Sullivan and his men, armed with a meagre supply of jam-tin bombs, had regained his battalion's lost fire-trench and had joined with a party of South Wales Borderers in bombing their way along 30 yd of Turkey Trench. The Turks retaliated with a bombing assault of their own in which they regained roughly 20 yd. As the battle ebbed and flowed along the bomb-blasted trench, O'Sullivan called for help to stem the counter-thrust.

An attempt to reach the head of Turkey Trench via a newly dug sap ended in failure. But O'Sullivan, desperately pressed, refused to budge from his toe-hold and plans were made for a fresh attack by the South Wales Borderers to relieve pressure. Postponed until 3.30 a.m., by which time 30 yd of Turkey Trench had been won and lost again, the attack was stopped in no man's land. Shortly afterwards, Brig. Gen. W.R. Marshall (GOC, 87th Brigade) took personal command and, after talking with officers on the spot, ordered a further assault to be carried out by a combined force of Borderers and Inniskillings. Once again, O'Sullivan led the way. The Inniskillings' war diary states:

4.30 a.m. Capt O'Sullivan with bomb party of about 6 men together with SWB bomb party drove enemy down Turkish sap. Enemy then endeavoured to evacuate sap by retiring across the open, but were shot down by rapid fire from A and B Coys. Remainder of enemy in Turkish Sap (13) taken prisoners.

As might be suspected, it was not quite as simple as that. According to Lt. Col. H.G. Casson (CO 2nd South Wales Borderers) the first bomb and bayonet attack was defeated, and it was only a renewed effort in the grey light of dawn which finally shattered Turkish resistance. Even then, the battle raged for another five hours. By 5.15 a.m. 30 yd had been recaptured, and by 10.00 a.m. the head of Turkey Trench was at last reached.

An artist's impression of O'Sullivan's VC action

The cost of holding the 70-yd-long trench was 175 dead, wounded and missing among the two British battalions. Turkish casualties were even higher. A total of 91 bodies were counted within ten yards of Turkey Trench. Many more could be vaguely seen, if not accurately computed, lying out in the open. Col. Casson estimated the Turkish dead at over 200. As the full story of the confused fight was pieced together, the prominent role played by Gerald O'Sullivan emerged as the most gallant and influential. In the words of the 87th Brigade's war diarist, the Irish captain had 'behaved magnificently throughout'. The result was a recommendation for the award of a Victoria Cross.

Gerald Robert O'Sullivan was born at Frankfield, near Douglas, County Cork, on 8 November 1888, the son of Lt. Col. George Lidwell O'Sullivan and his wife Charlotte (née Hiddingh). His father had served in the Argyll and Sutherland Highlanders and his mother was of South African descent.

'Jerry' O'Sullivan spent most of his boyhood in Dublin. Intended for a naval career, he entered Wimbledon College in 1899. A headstrong boy, he insisted on joining the school's Army department. The matter was only resolved by the intervention of the college rector, who declared 'he was a boy, and not an Army student'.

In the under-stated language of a college account, the young O'Sullivan was a 'somewhat controversial character'. According to school records,

> his daring, but rash characteristics, which were only too evident when he was playing football also accompanied him during his study, for as an Army student [he had finally achieved his ambition in 1904], he distinguished himself by quarrelling with A.H. Mankelow [later to become Captain Mankelow MC] in the laboratory, and fighting him there and then.

Leaving Wimbledon College in June 1906, O'Sullivan pursued his military ambitions. He attended RMC Sandhurst, and was commissioned into the Royal Inniskilling Fusiliers on 9 May 1909. He joined the 2nd Battalion in Dublin, and later that year embarked for Tientsin, China. O'Sullivan spent the next three years in China, turbulent years which included the revolution of 1911, before being transferred with his battalion to Secunderabad, in Central India.

Brought back to England shortly after the outbreak of war in August 1914, the 1st Inniskillings helped form the 29th Division, destined for operations in the Dardanelles. O'Sullivan was serving as a company commander when his battalion landed at X Beach on 25 April 1915. He came through the early fighting unscathed, and with his reputation greatly enhanced. After the action of 18 June in which O'Sullivan had distinguished himself, the Inniskillings played a key role in the Battle of Gully Ravine. In one of the campaign's most spectacular advances, they achieved all their objectives on 28 June, capturing and consolidating two trenches, J10 and J11, on the western edge of the ravine.

The next day the battalion took over a vital trench known as J11a which ran parallel to the coast, linking the Indian Brigade in the advanced J12 trenchline with the main British position on Gully Spur. Lt. Col. E.J. Buckley, in temporary command of the Inniskillings, was ordered to hold J11a 'at all costs'. To strengthen the position he ordered a new trench be dug, connecting J12 from near the Western Birdcage, a wired barricade about 180 yd west of the ravine, to Border Trench, north of J11. Working parties began constructing what later became known as 'Inniskilling Inch' under cover of darkness on 30 June. It proved a dangerous as well as arduous task. Mistaken for Turks, they came under fire from the men manning J12. Fortunately, there were no casualties and the following evening, after a quiet day in the coastal sector, the men of B Company continued the work. At first all went well. When Col. Buckley toured the position at 8.00 p.m. everything appeared peaceful. At 9.30 p.m., however, events took a dramatic turn for the worse. Col. Buckley later reported:

A wounded officer came in to Battalion headquarters and stated that the Turks were attacking in force – that B Company was cut up and that the assaulting party were moving in the direction of Border Trench.

I telephoned immediately to OC Borders and to Bde headquarters; to the latter I stated that for the moment the situation was not at all clear and that I was counter-attacking to clear it up. (The officer who had brought in the information was very young and excited and all I could be sure about was that B Company had been suddenly attacked.) I asked at the same time that the Bde Reserve Coy should be put at my disposal.

I sent forward Capt O'Sullivan's Company, supported by ½ company of Capt Edden's Company, with instructions to disengage B Company, of which a few wounded men had now returned, and to inform me of the situation.

I at the same time moved a Company into an old Turkish Fort which was just East of, and about the centre of, J11a (my first line) and directed the Bde Reserve Company to rendezvous in J11a [sic].

Capt O'Sullivan took his Company down J11a (which was held by ½ Company) with the intention of moving down J12 to the Birdcage where the left of B Company rested and then cover the retirement of what was left of that Company.

Capt Edden moved his force in a direct line towards the Birdcage so as to be ready to support Capt O'Sullivan.

On arriving at the junction of J11a and J12 Capt O'Sullivan found the situation changed as J12 was occupied by the Turks, who were in the act of driving out the Gurkhas [2/10th Gurkha Rifles]. He decided to carry out his original plan to move down J12 to relieve B Company and to attack the Turks in J12 and recapture the trench.

He immediately attacked, leading the storming party. Accompanied by Cpl Somers, he advanced in the open along the parapet of the trench, bombing the interior as he regained it. The Turks bombed back and from where I was I could distinctly see the flashes of the Turkish bombs, generally two to Capt O'Sullivan's one. We had only the jam-pot bomb . . . while the Turks had quite a useful bomb.

Capt O'Sullivan cleared the trench as far as the Birdcage and, leaving a garrison in the trench, proceeded to disengage B Company, leaving Capt Edden to continue the attack on the Turks.

The bitter fighting in the J12 trench bore a striking similarity to the battle waged for Turkey Trench two weeks before. Twice O'Sullivan's men drove the Turks out of the Gurkhas' position only to be ejected. But at the third attempt they succeeded in hanging on. By then O'Sullivan had been compelled to relinquish command due to a serious bullet wound in the leg.

Throughout the night action, O'Sullivan's boldest ally had been a junior NCO, Cpl. James Somers, a 21-year-old Irishman from County Cavan. It was later said of him that his unerring accuracy as a bombthrower owed much to his prowess as a cricketer. Somers later told how he had remained at an angle in the trench and was determined to 'hold his end up'. Armed with a healthy supply of bombs, he was able to stop each successive rush made by the Turks. In a letter to his father, he stated:

I beat the Turks out of our trench single-handed and had four awful hours at night. The Turks swarmed in from all roads, but I gave them a rough time of it, still holding the trench . . . It is certain sure we are beating the Turks all right. In the trench I came out of, it was shocking to see the dead. They lay, about 3,000 Turks, in front of our trench, and the smell was absolutely chronic. You know when the sun has been shining on those bodies for three or four days it makes a horrible smell; a person would not mind if it was possible to bury them. But no, you dare not put your nose outside the trench, and if you did, you would be a dead man . . .

Subsequently, in a newspaper interview Somers estimated that he had personally accounted for at least eighty Turks, killed or wounded. The account, published in *The Times*, described the continuation of the battle for J12, presumably after O'Sullivan's departure. It stated:

Just before dawn he [Somers] stole away, and brought up a bombing party he had charge of, and all next day he and his men fought on sharing the zig-zag trench with the enemy. He had one narrow escape on the morning of July 2nd – a splinter struck him across the spine, but he held his men together and rained the bombs until he fell from loss of blood and fatigue in the afternoon. By that time, however, the trench had been captured. The Turks retreated crying 'Allah! Allah!' and 'we gave them La! La!', said Somers with great glee.

In fact, the result was a good deal less conclusive. O'Sullivan's courageous counter-attack had indeed regained the lost position, but the success was short-lived. Following O'Sullivan's serious leg wound, command of the Inniskillings had devolved upon Capt. Edden. In his report on the action, Col. Buckley explained the confusion which marred their triumph:

> Capt Edden pressed his attack and cleared the trench as far as the Nullah and for about 100 yards up the Nullah towards J13. He sent a runner to inform me of the position and to ask for instructions but most unfortunately the runner lost his way and did not arrive till after daylight.
>
> At dawn, Capt Edden was personally at the spot where J12 joins the Nullah and he then signalled with a large Turkish Artillery flag which he had found there, hoping that I would understand where he was and send him instructions.
>
> The signalling, however, only drew some Artillery fire – Capt Edden thought from our guns and in absence of instructions he considered he had no right to risk his small party further, his original orders having been carried out, and withdrew without being in any way pressed across the open to Battalion headquarters. I had seen the signalling but as I had no idea that Capt Edden had got to the Nullah, I thought it was an act of bravado on the part of the Turks. Had the position been realised it would have given us the Nullah . . .

Instead, they fell back to the old barricade in J12, leaving the deserted stretch of trench joining the nullah for the Turks to reoccupy shortly afterwards.

The fight cost the Inniskillings six men dead and thirty-seven wounded. Despite the action's unsatisfactory conclusion, senior commanders were impressed by the tenacity displayed by the Irishmen. At 9.00 a.m. on 2 July Col. Buckley received a telegram from Maj.-Gen. de Lisle (GOC 29th Division) which simply stated: 'Well done Inniskillings'. Three hours later the remnants of Captain O'Sullivan's gallant company were finally relieved. 'That day', Col. Buckley later recounted, 'I promoted Corpl Somers to Sergeant on the field and recommended him and Capt O'Sullivan for the VC and Capt Edden for the DSO'.

Although there were other awards for gallantry displayed during the fight, a DSO for Capt. Edden was not among them. The 29-year-old commander of D

Company was later killed in action on 21 August. His only reward for his Gallipoli services was a posthumous mention in dispatches, announced on 5 November.

Shortly after the action, O'Sullivan and the newly promoted Somers were evacuated to Egypt. Somers was admitted to a hospital in Cairo on 18 July, and later sent to England to recuperate from the effects of the injuries to his back caused by bomb splinters. O'Sullivan remained in Egypt where he made a rapid recovery. A fellow patient later recorded:

> Gerald arrived in my hospital ward at 19 General Hospital one evening, I think about 12th July but I am not certain of the date. He had a bullet wound high up in his leg which had only just missed the femoral artery. He was soon able to get up and we used to go out a great deal together. With a certain amount of difficulty, owing to red tape regulations, we went to Mass together on the two or three Sundays we were together. He had a rosary he always carried on him and had on his chair by his bed, rather a large one, and I think he wore a medal around his neck.

O'Sullivan reported back to his battalion on 11 August, having been away less than six weeks. His return coincided with the 29th Division's move to Suvla Bay, in readiness for the big push aimed at regaining the initiative in the northern sector. As part of the general offensive planned to take place on 21 August, the sorely depleted Inniskillings were given the task of seizing Hill 70, otherwise known as Scimitar Hill. Two days before the attack, Maj. R.H. Scott, of the 6th Inniskillings, who were serving at Suvla Bay, paid a courtesy call on the 1st Battalion. He later recalled:

> Capt Pike in command (with two bullets in him that he would not wait to have taken out), and Capt O'Sullivan, who had just heard that he had got the VC [sic], were, with all the others, in the greatest form and ready for another go at Johnny Turk. It took me a long time finding where they were that day, but we spent much longer a few nights afterwards looking for Capts Pike and O'Sullivan out in front, and never found them.

The disastrous battle of 21 August was the setting for the last glorious chapter in the short life of Gerald O'Sullivan; a desperate encounter crowned by a display of leadership destined to be immortalized by his regiment.

On that day O'Sullivan led his company through a hurricane of fire onto the crest of Hill 70, only to be forced back by enfilading artillery fire. Some 400 yd beneath the hilltop he gathered together the survivors in a gully and urged them to make 'one more charge for the honour of the Old Regiment'. The effect of his impassioned appeal was electrifying. According to the Inniskillings' history, 'every man who could responded, and a little band of fifty rushed against the crest. Of that band only one, a wounded sergeant, came back'. O'Sullivan's fate remained a mystery for several weeks after the battle. Eventually, the unit's new CO wrote to his mother:

> It seems tolerably certain that he was killed, and killed outright by being hit in the head as the assaulting line reached the furthest line of the enemy's trenches on the 21st of August. He was seen to fall in the trench wounded, as was thought for some days, but a private who got back and says he was next to your son, is positive that he was killed outright.

Seven days after O'Sullivan's last charge, a train pulled into the small country town of Cloughjordan, in County Tipperary. The station was a sea of cheering people, and above the din a band welcomed home their conquering hero. News of Sgt Somers' VC recommendation had leaked out, prompting a wave of premature celebrations in which the young NCO was showered with praise and gifts, including a cheque for fifty guineas. On 1 September the *London Gazette* announced what the citizens of Cloughjordan had taken for granted, that No. 10512, Sgt. James Somers had won the Victoria Cross. The citation stated:

> For most conspicuous bravery on the night of the 1st–2nd July, 1915, in the southern zone of the Gallipoli Peninsula, when, owing to hostile bombing, some of our troops had retired from a sap, Sergeant Somers remained alone on the spot until a party brought up bombs. He then climbed over into the Turkish trench, and bombed the Turks with great effect. Later on, he advanced into the open under very heavy fire, and held back the enemy by throwing bombs into their flank until a barricade had been established. During this period he frequently ran to and from our trenches to obtain fresh supplies of bombs. By his great gallantry and coolness Sergeant Somers was largely instrumental in effecting the recapture of a portion of our trench which had been lost.

The same gazette carried the following citation for Capt. Gerald O'Sullivan's VC:

> For most conspicuous bravery during operations south-west of Krithia, on the Gallipoli Peninsula.
> On the night of the 1st–2nd July, 1915, when it was essential that a portion of a trench which had been lost should be regained, Captain O'Sullivan, although not belonging to the troops at this point volunteered to lead a party of bomb throwers to effect the recapture.

He advanced in the open under a very heavy fire, and in order to throw his bombs with greater effect, got up on the parapet, where he was completely exposed to the fire of the enemy occupying the trench. He was finally wounded, but not before his inspiring example had led on his party to make further efforts, which resulted in the recapture of the trench.

On the night of 18th–19th June, 1915, Captain O'Sullivan saved a critical situation in the same locality by his great personal gallantry and good leading.

O'Sullivan's name is listed on the Helles memorial to the missing, and also appears on the war memorial in Dorchester. His mother was living at Rowan House, Dorchester, and his posthumous VC was sent to her on 26 September 1916.

James Somers was hailed as Tipperary's first VC winner of the war. In fact, although his family moved to Cloughjordan before the war, he was born in Church Street, Belturbet, County Cavan on 12 June 1894, the son of Robert and Charlotte (née Boyre) Somers. Somers' father was sexton of the town's Protestant church and his mother had previously been employed as a parlour maid.

Variously described as 'a light, wiry fellow' and 'a well-built, good-looking young fellow', Somers' first job was as a footman in Bantry House. Domestic service, however, appears not to have been to his liking, and on 14 January 1913 he joined the Special Reserve of the Royal Munster Fusiliers. During the early days of the war he served with the 2nd Battalion, Royal Inniskilling Fusiliers in Belgium and France. He was severely wounded during the great retreat from Mons. The precise nature of his injuries are unclear. One report refers to a shrapnel wound to his knee and another quotes him as having 'stopped three bullets'. Whatever the truth, they were serious enough for him to be evacuated, and he spent Christmas, 1914 at home with his parents. Later, he returned to Ireland as a member of a party detailed to guard German prisoners of war.

Transferred to the 1st Battalion, Somers went through all the early fighting on the peninsula, surviving unscathed until the action of 1–2 July. Like so many VC winners, the announcement of his award brought him brief fame. Among the many gifts presented to him were an illuminated address and £240 raised by the people living in and around Tipperary. The climax of his triumphant homecoming came on 14 October 1915, when he travelled to Buckingham Palace to receive his Cross from the king.

Little is recorded of Somers' subsequent career. There are no references to him in any accounts concerning the Inniskillings after 1915. On 1 April 1917 he transferred to the Royal Army Service Corps and was given a new Army number, M/39117. It can only be speculated that this was a consequence of his injuries sustained at Gallipoli. What is certain is that he served for a spell on the Western Front. By the spring of 1918, however, Sgt. Somers was back in Ireland. From the flimsy evidence available, it would appear that he had suffered a breakdown in health, almost certainly as a result of gas poisoning while in France. Conjecture remains, however, as to the precise cause of his death, on 7 May 1918, at his parents' home in Cloughjordan. Local newspapers reported his 'death was due to lung trouble contracted in France some months ago'. His former regiment listed him as dying from 'the effects of gas poisoning in France'. His family, however, maintained that he was the victim of an accident. Some months prior to his death, they said he had returned to Ireland as an instructor. And they claimed it was while demonstrating the use of gas that his lungs were irreparably damaged due to a leaking cylinder.

Sgt. James Somers was buried with full military honours in Modreeny Church of Ireland cemetery. His coffin was draped in a Union Jack and carried to its last resting place on a gun carriage. Shops were closed and blinds drawn as the funeral procession, led by the Pipe Band of the Cameron Highlanders, made its mournful way through the streets. Three years earlier those same streets had been crowded with well-wishers, welcoming home their local hero. The *Nenagh News* recorded that an immense number of people 'of all classes and creeds' attended the funeral. A firing party fired a final salute as the coffin was lowered into the ground, beneath a headstone bearing a simple inscription taken from the Second Book of Samuel:

He stood and defended. The Lord wrought a great wonder.

L.M. KEYSOR, W.J. SYMONS,
A.S. BURTON, F.H. TUBB,
W. DUNSTAN, J. HAMILTON AND
A.J. SHOUT

Lone Pine, Anzac sector, 7–9 August 1915

In the days following the landing at Anzac, the Turks began constructing an elaborate system of trenches on the southern crown of 400 Plateau. Protected by scattered wire entanglements, the frontline trenches were deep and almost entirely covered by heavy baulks of timber.

The ridge, which had seen much heavy fighting during the first month of the campaign, was known by the Turks as Kanli Sirt, or Bloody Ridge. The Australians, however, had their own name for the position which emerged some 60–150 yd in front of them. Shortly after the landing, artillery observers searching for landmarks had noticed a solitary pine tree standing in splendid isolation on the scrub-covered ridge. Adapting the title of a popular song, they called it the 'Lonesome Pine', and the name, in its abbreviated form, had stuck. So formidable was the Lone Pine position, that the sector's Turkish commanders considered it impregnable to direct assault. Yet in August 1915 the Australian commanders were preparing to do just that. The capture of the Lone Pine position became one of the main objectives for a series of attacks to be delivered against the Turks at Anzac with the intention of diverting Turkish attentions and reserves away from the new landings at Suvla Bay, a few miles to the north.

In the late afternoon of 6 August the Australians launched one of the campaign's most boldly conceived attacks. Rushing across the open, the 2nd, 3rd and 4th Battalions, all from the 1st (New South Wales) Brigade, took the Turks by complete surprise. Within half an hour they had achieved, at a fearful cost, their objectives. The seemingly secure Lone Pine position had indeed fallen to direct assault. But the real test was yet to come. By 7.00 p.m., as the initial wave of frenzied fighting subsided, a number of scattered posts were established in the heart of the captured position. The brigade's reserve unit, the 1st Battalion, was ordered forward in readiness for the counter-attacks which the operation was designed to provoke.

Top row, left to right: L/Cpl. L. Keysor, Lt. J. Symons painted by his wife, Cpl. A. Burton. Middle row, left to right: Lt. F. Tubb, Cpl. W. Dunstan, Pte. J. Hamilton. Bottom left: Capt. A. Shout.

Capt. H. Jacobs took the leading company over the open and into Lone Pine. They were met by Lt. Col. R. Scobie, commanding the 2nd Battalion, who directed most of the new arrivals to the right of the position. Among the reinforcements was L/Cpl. Leonard Keysor, a much-travelled, 29-year-old Jewish Londoner who had arrived on the peninsula by way of Canada and Sydney, Australia. Keysor's company was divided among the barricaded posts at the head of a depression towards the rear of the Lone Pine network, known as The Cup. These hastily erected posts, many of them named after the senior officer responsible for their defence, represented the furthest Australian incursions and became the focus of the fiercest fighting of the battle. The bombing duels which characterized the sanguinary struggle started during the night and were directed chiefly at the posts overlooking The Cup.

Although in better-sited positions, the Australians here, as elsewhere in Lone Pine, were at a serious disadvantage when it came to the quality and quantity of bombs. While the Turks were well-supplied with spherical steel grenades the size of cricket balls, the Australians had to make do with their home-made missiles, the so-called jam-pot bombs which frequently proved as dangerous to the thrower as their intended victims.

During his time on the peninsula, Leonard Keysor had become well versed in the art of bombing, and was widely acknowledged as an expert in this form of fighting. Throughout the night of 6/7 August he and his fellow bombers held their own against the uncoordinated Turkish probing attacks. However, pressure on the advanced posts on the right flank intensified during the morning. The Turks succeeded in establishing themselves in a hollow between two of the Australian posts and from there they began to shower bombs on the defenders. The deficiencies in the supply of bombs and the technique of bombing were being felt by the Australians. Even so, they succeeded in beating off one Turkish attack, and in the lull that followed Col. Scobie toured the threatened sector. Preparations were made to link the isolated posts into one trench-line, but before this could be done the Turks launched a second major attack.

The assault was supported by artillery fire which caused a number of casualties. One shell burst in the trench, killing the post commander, Lt. F.J. Cox of the 1st Battalion, and the men beside him. An hour later, at noon, the full weight of the attack fell upon two barricaded positions known as Cook's and Youden's posts. The two junior officers in command quickly became casualties and bombs began raining on the defenders from all directions. It was then that L/Cpl. Keysor's gallantry reached a peak. Scorning what little shelter existed, he worked miracles in nullifying the effect of the bombs, smothering the exploding missiles with sandbags and his own coat. When the burning fuses appeared long enough, he adopted the riskier though more satisfying course of returning the bombs to their owners. Frequently, he astonished his comrades by catching

Turkish bombs in mid-flight and hurling them back. It was an extraordinary feat and it put fresh heart into the defenders at a most critical moment.

The more exposed posts, however, could not hold out indefinitely, and Col. Scobie ordered a retirement to the main position while he remained to cover the withdrawal. A few moments later, the gallant CO of the 2nd Battalion was killed by a grenade burst. The Turks swept past the demolished barricades to be halted by Capt. Jacobs just short of the main position. His men occupied a barricaded trench, later known as 'Jacob's Trench', and resisted a succession of Turkish attacks which lasted into the evening. Bombing continued throughout the night, and the following day, 8 August, the weary survivors, by then commanded by Capt. Cecil Sasse of the 1st Battalion, withstood more attacks in which the irrepressible Keysor again figured prominently.

Although he had been wounded the previous day, and was hit again on the 8th, Keysor refused to leave. Instead, he continued to hurl bombs, by then in more plentiful supply, until his unit was relieved in the afternoon by the 7th Battalion. So ended what has been described as 'one of the most spectacular individual feats of the war'.

Keysor's deed had been one of sustained gallantry over a period of fifty hours of unrelenting and nerve-sapping Turkish pressure. His resourceful resistance in the face of repeated bombing attacks had materially influenced the outcome of the fierce fighting in the southern sector. That he survived with only two wounds must have been as much a surprise to himself as his comrades. Not long after the battle, Keysor was evacuated to England, suffering from a bout of enteric fever. He was convalescing when the *London Gazette* of 15 October announced that his courage had been recognized by one of the seven Victoria Crosses to be given to the defenders of the captured Lone Pine position. The citation read:

An artist's impression of Keysor's VC action

For most conspicuous bravery and devotion to duty at Lone Pine trenches, in the Gallipoli Peninsula. On August 7th, 1915, he was in a trench which was being heavily bombed by the enemy. He picked up two live bombs and threw them back at the enemy at great risk to his own life, and continued throwing bombs, although himself wounded, thereby saving a portion of the trench which it was most important to hold.

On August 8th, at the same place, Private Keysor successfully bombed the enemy out of a position from which a temporary mastery over his own trench had been obtained, and was again wounded. Although marked for hospital, he declined to leave, and volunteered to throw bombs for another company which had lost its bomb-throwers. He continued to bomb the enemy till the situation was relieved.

Keysor received his Cross from George V at an investiture in Buckingham Palace on 15 January 1916.

Relief came to the exhausted survivors of the 1st and 2nd Battalions on the afternoon of 8 August. Lt. Col. Harold Elliott, a peacetime lawyer noted for his great energy and explosive temper, led the 7th (Victoria) Battalion into Lone Pine at about 1.30 p.m. and by 3.00 p.m. he had taken charge of the southern half of the captured trench system. The transfer went smoothly and Elliott took advantage of the lull to tour the position. He had brought three companies, A, C, and D, with him, leaving a fourth, B Company, under the command of Capt. Fred Tubb in reserve at Brown's Dip in the old Australian frontline. Elliott divided his sector into two with the left flank, running from Goldenstedt's to Woods' post, under the command of Lt. William Symons, and the more isolated Jacob's Trench position on the right, commanded by Lt. G.J.C. Dyett.

Jacob's Trench consisted of three posts and was partially covered with a wire-mesh screen and timber roof. The defenders, many of them recently arrived drafts, had two machine-guns with which to counter any Turkish infantry assault. It was upon them that the next blow fell. A short, violent bombardment was followed by a bombing attack which took a heavy toll of the defenders crowded together in the trench. Intermittent bombing developed into a major attack launched at about 7.00 p.m. and which threatened to swamp the southern sector.

Lt. Symons, the D Company commander in charge on the left, was engaged in a desperate fight at Goldenstedt's Post with its commanding view of The Cup. The Turkish bombers were able to shelter beneath a few wooden beams, and Australian losses were heavy as the Turks repeatedly forced their way over the low barricade into the main trench. Each time, however, they were ejected by a counter-attack force which Symons wisely held in reserve in a small dug-out, the entrance of which was covered by wire mesh to keep out Turkish bombs. The struggle went on for much of the night until around 2.00 a.m., when the Turkish bombers were finally driven from their head-cover.

Meanwhile, the number of casualties sustained in Jacob's Trench had compelled Elliott to bring up his reserve company, with Capt. Tubb taking over from the wounded Lt. Dyett. By the early hours of 9 August, as the Turks moved forward to renew their assault, the southern sector of Lone Pine had been split into three sub-units; Lt. Symons, after his gruelling contest at Goldenstedt's, still held the left flank posts, with Capt. Tubb's B Company in the middle and Lt. J.M. West commanding the isolated right flank position.

The attack, when it came at 4 00 a.m., was furious and extended from Sasse's Sap in the north to Jacob's Trench in the south. In Lt. Symons' sector the fighting was of a frenzied nature. Once more the Turks concentrated their efforts on dislodging the Australians from Goldenstedt's. Symons, leading his men by personal example, succeeded briefly in subduing the Turks by hurling Lotbinière bombs, a missile which consisted of slabs of gun-cotton tied to small wooden boards and which were more familiarly known as 'hair-brush bombs'.

As the Turkish waves lapped along the southern perimeter, Elliott's chief concern was for his exposed right flank, where the Turks had succeeded in wiping out the garrison of a newly constructed trench designed to protect Jacob's Trench. At the second attempt, the Turks drove the survivors out of this vital position and resisted an effort to recapture it. With his entire position thus threatened, Elliott turned to Lt. Symons, whose cheery optimism had deeply impressed him. Handing the company commander his revolver, Elliott ordered him to retake Jacob's Trench with the words: 'I don't expect to see you again. But we must not lose that post.'

Accompanied by Cpl. G. Ball and Cpl. J.H. Wadeson, Symons led a rush which cleared Jacob's Trench. Two Turks fell to his borrowed revolver and Symons barely had time to reconstruct the trench barricade before a counter-attack was launched. Beset from three directions, Symons requested and was granted permission to withdraw his men beneath a portion of overhead cover at the western end of the trench. The Turks occupied the remaining 15 yd of open trench and then began their relentless efforts to eject Symons' party. Twice they set fire to the timber roofing, but on both occasions Symons countered with a charge which sent the Turks scurrying away and allowed time for the flames to be extinguished. In one of his forays, he brought back a machine-gun which had been abandoned.

The Turks, knowing the importance of the position, made one last effort to overwhelm the defenders. However, their attempt to encircle Symons' men was foiled when their movement across a stretch of ground in what had been no man's land was spotted by Australians in the old frontline and elsewhere in Lone Pine. It was just as well, for casualties had reached alarming proportions among Symons' party. By 6.30 p.m. the heaviest Turkish counter-attack of the battle for Lone Pine had died away, leaving the Australians in their hard-won position.

On 11 August, three days after the remnants of his battalion were relieved, Lt. Symons wrote to his mother:

Since last writing I have had a rough time, as you will perhaps have heard. The New South Wales boys charged the enemy's trenches, and by the dint of hard and strenuous fighting captured them. It was simply grand watching them bayonetting and shooting the Turks. They were standing on the top of the enemy's trenches and prodding Abdul with the bayonet, just like a woman putting a hatpin in her hat or a butcher boning a roast. They then dropped into their trenches . . . Two nights after, the Turks attacked and tried to recapture their trench, but were driven out again. Our battalion was sent to assist them and I went in with a company of 141 men, and the other companies had about a similar number. Anyway, Abdul decided to take his trench at all costs, but in vain. They came once and dropped about 1,000 bombs in our trenches, and I am sorry to say they did a great deal of damage, but I think that we did decidedly more with ours, for we were better throwers than they were, and more accurate. They were in greater numbers.

The first attack was at about 3.30 a.m. They came at us in hundreds, and made a special point of my position. I only had about 40 men with me in the firing line, the others being in reserve or else casualties. We had to set our teeth and drive them back, which the lads did with great credit. When I came to muster we had only about 15 left, and I got some of my reserve in and made up the strength again. It was just in time for another attack, which was equally unsuccessful. They were sent away with great loss, but I had to build up again.

By this time the bottom of our trench was filled in some places four or five feet deep with dead and wounded Turks and our brave lads. They were just coming for a third time, when a couple of shells were distributed among them by our artillery, and they must have thought discretion was the better part of valour, as they 'imshied', leaving us still masters of the position. I was left with about 40 men of my company, and I don't think one of the remaining men was unwounded.

I can tell you I was not sorry that they were not game enough for the last attack. Well, you can just imagine the pluck and endurance of our men after about four months' fighting to get into a hole like that and come out successfully. They are heroes, every one.

I was fortunate to escape practically whole, although losing my other officers wounded and killed. Well, mother, I hope you are all well. As for myself, I feel a little tired, but with a couple of nights' rest I will be fit for them again.

In fact, Symons had been wounded. At one point during the fighting a Turkish bullet had shattered the butt of his rifle, peppering his left hand with splinters. Ten days after the 7th Battalion left Lone Pine, Lt. Col. Elliott filed an official recommendation for the Victoria Cross for the gallant commander of D Company.

Symons remained with his unit until he contracted a bout of enteric fever which undermined his health. Evacuated to England, he arrived in an enfeebled state, having been reduced from 12 to 8 stone. He spent two months in hospital and one month in a convalescent home. It was while recovering from sickness that he learned of his VC award. The citation, contained in the *London Gazette* of 15 October, stated:

> For most conspicuous bravery on the night of August 8–9th, 1915, at Lone Pine trenches, in the Gallipoli Peninsula. He was in command of the right section of the newly-captured trenches held by his battalion, and repelled several counter-attacks with great coolness. At about 5.00 a.m. on the 9th August a series of determined attacks were made by the enemy on an isolated sap, and six officers were in succession killed or severely wounded, a portion of the sap was lost. Lieutenant Symons then led a charge and retook the lost sap, shooting two Turks with his revolver. The sap was under hostile fire from three sides, and Lieutenant Symons withdrew some 15 yards to a spot where some overhead cover could be obtained and in the face of heavy fire built up a sand barricade. The enemy succeeded in setting fire to the fascines and woodwork of the head cover, but Lieutenant Symons extinguished the fire and rebuilt the barricade. His coolness and determination finally compelled the enemy to discontinue the attacks.

Symons had recovered sufficiently by 4 December to attend a Buckingham Palace investiture where he received his Cross from the King. Among the recipients was Percy Hansen VC, MC, who had won his Cross at Suvla Bay. As he pinned the VC on Symons' tunic, the King remarked: 'I am proud to decorate an Australian with this Cross. You may be interested to know that the intrinsic worth of this bronze cross is only 5½d. I hope you will live long to wear it.'

Fred Tubb had been in the old Australian frontline for two days when three companies of his battalion filed passed on their way to reinforce the Lone Pine position. Initially held back in readiness to assault the Turkish trenches on Johnston's Jolly, his company had been consigned to the role of spectators.

Yet those forty-eight hours had taken their toll. Few had been able to sleep and Turkish shellfire had already reduced their number. On August 8 the commander of B Company, 7th Battalion, noted in his diary:

> 0540. Shells are falling thick amongst us; one fell on my back after striking a few feet away . . . Tired and sleepy, we are all fagged; the strain is wearying. Just lost my Sgt Major Baker from nerves and shock. Pvte Willis also. Another Sgt Major of B Coy outed. It is stiff luck for just as I get the Coy going I lose the men I need most . . .

His company, bolstered three days earlier by the arrival of fifty reinforcements, remained in reserve in the Pimple throughout a tense afternoon made increasingly uncomfortable by the attention of the Turkish gunners. Tubb recorded that 'Shrapnell [sic] is coming like out of a watering can, splattering all round me as I wait for instructions'.

At last, orders came for him to advance into the Lone Pine trenches. Sending one platoon into the firing line at 8.00 p.m., he followed with the remainder of his company and reported to Brig. N.M. Smyth. He was given command of a captured trench on the left of the position and then followed a depressing night as he and his men watched a steady stream of dead and wounded men being carried past them on their way out of Lone Pine. In his diary he provided his own concise account of his stay in the captured position:

Monday/Tuesday 10/8/15. Here I am sitting down in a dugout near the beach ready to go to Lemnos or Mudros. (I am wounded but not too bad.) It would take a book to describe what happened since yesterday morning. I have no notes of it but can supply most particulars. At Stand To, 0400 yesterday the fun started. I was whipped round with my Coy to the firing line. The enemy was attacking. Well they attacked us three times but we licked them. I was put in charge of the 7th firing line section. We had a ding-dong scrap which off and on lasted till 4 in the afternoon when we were relieved by the 5th Bn and what was left of us came down to this bivouac. We went in 670 strong and we came out 320. All the officers except the CO and Capt Layh were hit, even the Q. Master Hopkinson. I was extremely lucky and feel grateful for being alive and able to write. Four of the old officers, Capt Ross, Lt Swift, Hornby and Kurring came to me after we had been going for some time. Lt West, Fisher and Young, Edwards and Capt Ross were outed. My luck was in, all the time. It is miraculous that I am alive. Three different times I was blown yards away from bombs. Our trenches were filled with the dead, mostly ours. Burton of Euroa deserved the highest award for his gallant action for three times filling a breach in the parapet till they killed him. Dunstan and Oates, Ellis, Caddy, Webb, Silver, Keating also did magnificent work. Ellis was killed whilst throwing back enemy bombs before they exploded. . . . We were glad to get out . . . I cannot write of details but many of our brave boys were blown to pieces. As fast as we put men in to fill the breaches they were out. I kept sending for reinforcements and bombs, all our bomb throwers were killed and so were those that volunteered to fill their places. To cut a long story short, we beat the enemy. Three times he attacked. Once he nearly got us. We yelled and yelled and the black devils turned and we knocked 'em over like rabbits. I was wounded three times but got my injuries attended to and kept going. I am suffering a bit now from reaction. The doc has fixed my head, and arm up. My left eye is painful but otherwise I am fit . . . I reckon I'll be A1 again in a week for my injuries are slight. By jove it was some scrap and a lot more of our good old 7th are gone. The Brigadier came to see me this morning, congratulating me, etc. My haversacks are shattered; the iron rations inside one of them are smashed to pieces. Anyway the CO is very pleased with me and so is the Brigadier so I feel happy as Larry.

Tubb had replaced Symons in command of the Goldenstedt's barricade when the latter was ordered to retake the lost posts in Jacob's Trench. He had ten men with him, two of whom, Corporals Webb and Wright, were given the task of smothering or throwing back any enemy bombs while the remainder manned the parapet. According to Charles Bean, the Australian Official Historian:

A few of the enemy, shouting 'Allah', had in the first rush scrambled into the Australian trench, but had been shot or bayoneted. Tubb and his men now fired at them over the parapet, shooting all who came up Goldenstedt's Trench or who attempted to creep over the open. Tubb, using his revolver, exposed himself recklessly over the parapet, and his example caused his men to do the same. 'Good boy!' he shouted, slapping the back of one of them who by kneeling on the parapet had shot a sheltering Turk. As the same man said later: 'With him up there you couldn't think of getting your head down.'

But one by one the men who were catching bombs were mutilated. Wright clutched at one which burst in his face and killed him. Webb, an orphan from Essendon, continued to catch them, but presently both his hands were blown away, and, after walking out of the Pine he died at Brown's Dip. At one moment several bombs burst simultaneously in Tubb's recess. Four men in it were killed or wounded; a fifth was blown down and his rifle shattered. Tubb, bleeding from bomb-wounds in arm and scalp, continued to fight, supported in the end only by a Ballarat recruit, Corporal Dunstan, and a personal friend of his own, Corporal Burton, of Euroa. At this stage there occurred at the barricade a violent explosion which threw back the defenders and tumbled down the sandbags. It was conjectured that the Turks had fired an explosive charge with the object of destroying the barrier. Tubb, however, drove them off, and Dunstan and Burton were helping to rebuild the barrier when a bomb fell between them, killing Burton and temporarily blinding his comrade. Tubb obtained further men from the next post, Tubb's Corner; but the enemy's attack weakened, the Turks continuing to bomb and fire rifles into the air, but never again attempting to rush the barricade.

Like Symons' defence of the same sector, Tubb's stand came at a critical moment and certainly prevented a Turkish breakthrough at this point. In a letter to the sister

An artist's impression of Tubb, Dunstan and Burton's VC action

of Cpl. F. Wright, who was killed alongside Tubb, Col. Elliott cited the gallantry shown by Tubb, Dunstan, Burton, Webb and Wright. He concluded:

I recommended all these boys for the VC. Tubb, Dunstan and Burton got VCs, Webb the Distinguished Service Medal [*sic*]. No doubt, had your brother lived, he would have got the DCM if not the VC. There are so many brave deeds that it is almost impossible to receive recognition for them.

The *London Gazette* of 15 October carried the citations for the three VCs. Tubb's read:

For most conspicuous bravery and devotion to duty at Lone Pine trenches, in the Gallipoli Peninsula, on 9 August 1915. In the early morning the enemy made a determined counter-attack on the centre of the newly captured trench held by Lieutenant [*sic*] Tubb. They advanced up a sap and blew in a sandbag barricade, leaving only one foot of it standing, but Lieutenant Tubb led his men back, repulsed the enemy, and rebuilt the barricade. Supported by strong bombing parties the enemy succeeded in twice blowing in the barricades, but on each occasion Lieutenant Tubb, although wounded in the head and arm, held his ground with the greatest coolness and rebuilt it, and finally succeeded in maintaining his position under very heavy bomb fire.

The joint citation for Burton and Dunstan stated:

For most conspicuous bravery at Lone Pine trenches, in the Gallipoli Peninsula, on August 9th, 1915. In the early morning the enemy made a determined counter-attack on the centre of the newly captured trench held by Lieutenant Tubb, Corporals Burton and Dunstan, and a few men. They advanced up a sap and blew in a sandbag barricade, leaving only one foot standing, but Lieutenant Tubb, with the two corporals, repulsed the enemy and rebuilt the barricade, although Lieutenant Tubb was wounded in the head and arm and Corporal Burton was killed by a bomb while most gallantly building up the parapet under a hail of bombs.

As the storm broke around Tubb's barricade, the northern sector at Sasse's Sap, a key artery leading into the heart of the Australian-held portion of Lone Pine, became the focus of renewed Turkish pressure. A bombing attack against the sap which formed the junction between the 3rd and 4th Australian Battalions began shortly after 4.00 a.m. as part of the Turks' general assault. It was preceded by intense machine-gun and rifle fire which ripped through the sandbag barriers and shattered the improvised periscopes serving as an early warning system.

While every man who could be spared was attempting to replace the wrecked barricades, the Turks succeeded in bombing their way into Sasse's Sap. A bold counter-attack swiftly sealed the breach. But the relief was only temporary. A second powerful thrust swept over the 4½-ft tall barricade and Turkish infantry began pouring unchecked along Sasse's Sap towards the centre of Lone Pine on a line leading directly to the 1st Australian Brigade's advanced headquarters together with that of the battle-weary 3rd Battalion.

The battalion's adjutant, Capt. Owen Howell-Price, was the first to detect the threat to the sector's main command post. As the first streaks of dawn lit the grey sky, he pushed a periscope over the sandbag parapet in headquarters trench and was shocked to see Turks advancing along the nearby Sasse's Sap. Leaning over the parapet, he emptied his revolver into them while his batman, Pte. P.H. Ward, opened fire with his rifle. Turning to the men closest to him, Howell-Price ordered a party to climb out and strike at the Turks in the flank while also preventing any advance across the open. Six men, Lt. E.W.G. Wren, Sgt. W. Adams, Pte. J. Hamilton, Pte. T. Jenkin, Pte. V.B. Perkins and Pte. Ward, scrambled out on their dangerous mission as Howell-Price launched his own counter-attack. Accompanied by Brig. Gen. Nevill Smyth, who had won a VC fighting the Dervishes in Kitchener's reconquest of the Sudan, Maj. D. McConaghy, senior surviving officer of the 3rd Battalion, and a member of the Brigade Staff, Howell-Price rushed to the entrance of Sasse's Sap. They arrived just in time. The Turks were 15 yd away, advancing three-deep, in column formation. In a remarkable confrontation, resembling a Hollywood-style Wild West shoot-out, Howell-Price and his distinguished band fired into the leading ranks. Howell-Price accounted for at least three while one Turk narrowly missed him. Taken by surprise, the Turks were thrown into total confusion by the fire from Lt. Wren's party. A well-aimed shot by Pte. Ward killed a Turkish bomber whose missile exploded among his own men. A similar fate befell those Turks who attempted to bomb the 4th Battalion positions from Sasse's Sap.

Most prominent among the handful of Australian sharp-shooters lying out in the open was a 19 year old from Penshurst, New South Wales, whose courage had already been noted during the Lone Pine fighting. John Hamilton had gone over the top with the 3rd Battalion on the first day, and during the bitter fighting which followed he played a key role in the bombing duels which became such a deadly feature of the battle. As well as hurling improvised jam-tin bombs at the Turks, Hamilton, like Keysor of the 1st Battalion, picked up enemy bombs and threw them back before they exploded. One of his fellow bombers, Sgt. C.O. Clark, explained:

It was soon perceived that a couple of seconds elapsed between the landing of the cricket ball bombs and the explosion. So the policy of returning the bombs was adopted with most satisfactory results, although the practice occasionally led to casualties in our own ranks.

The extraordinary spirit of the Australian bombers was revealed by Lt. A.F. Burrett:

Two of my bombers – Norton and Hamilton – the latter won his VC there – were up on the parapet throwing bombs as fast as they could light them. One burst prematurely in Norton's hands, and blew both of them to fragments. We sent him back to the dressing station. Next morning a doctor said to me: 'Good God! It's wonderful. That man Norton is the gamest thing that ever breathed. After I had finished fixing him up for the beach he said "Goodbye Doc, old sport. Sorry I can't shake hands." '

Having survived innumerable bomb fights which maimed and killed so many of his comrades, Hamilton proved himself equally adept with a rifle. From an exposed position on top of the parapet, he sniped the Turks as they attempted to bomb the Australians from Sasse's Sap. Alone of the six who had ventured into the open under Howell-Price's orders, Hamilton held his position. Protected by a few sandbags, he lay out on the parapet observing Turkish movements and shouting back instructions telling his comrades where to direct their bombs. For six hours he continued to target the Turks as well as sniping anything that moved along the sap.

By 10.00 a.m. the danger had passed sufficiently to allow Hamilton to slip back into the 3rd Battalion's headquarters trench. Shortly afterwards his unit was

An artist's impression of Hamilton's VC action

relieved by the 1st Battalion. In three days' close-quarter fighting, the 3rd had been reduced to a shadow of its old self. Of the 883 men at the time of the assault, less than 300 marched out.

When so many had performed feats of daring and acts of courage were commonplace, it was perhaps an invidious task to single out individuals for honours. Even so, the awards to members of the 3rd Battalion were miserly in the extreme. Howell-Price's gallantry and initiative was recognized by the award of a Military Cross and his batman, Pte. Ward, received a Distinguished Conduct Medal. The consistent valour of John Hamilton could not, however, be ignored. Throughout the defence he had shown scant regard for his own safety, and his repeated acts of bravery had materially affected the outcome of the fighting in his sector. On 15 October 1915 the *London Gazette* announced the award of the Victoria Cross to No. 943, Pte. John Hamilton. Inexplicably, given the number of witnesses, the citation ignored his bombing exploits. It stated:

> For most conspicuous bravery on the 9th August, 1915, in the Gallipoli Peninsula. During a heavy bombing attack by the enemy on the newly captured position at Lone Pine, Private Hamilton, with utter disregard of personal safety, exposed himself under heavy fire on the parados, in order to secure a better fire position against the enemy's bomb-throwers. His coolness and daring example had an immediate effect. The defence was encouraged, and the enemy driven off with heavy loss.

The arrival of the 1st Battalion for its third and final tour on the morning of 9 August marked the return to Lone Pine of one of Anzac's most legendary and popular characters. Alfred Shout, a captain of eleven days and a veteran of the Boer War, had proved himself one of the most resourceful junior leaders in the 1st Australian Brigade, where his name was already a byword for courage. In the thick of the fighting since the landing, he had been twice wounded and twice honoured with a Military Cross, the first to a member of the 1st Battalion, and a mention in dispatches. Universally admired, he combined daring with a highly developed tactical awareness. According to one of his men, 'He never risked his life for no purpose, but just to see him walking calmly along the trenches in the thick of an attack, or stalking through the undergrowth as though there were no such things as bullets, was enough to give a man a good heart for fighting'.

It was an inspiring brand of leadership which affected all who came in contact with him. Charles Bean, the Official Australian War Historian who was at Anzac as a war correspondent, wrote: 'Since the day of his arrival he had been the heart and soul of this section of the firing line, and his invincible buoyancy and cheerfulness had been a great help to the men.'

Not long after the 1st Battalion completed their relief of the 3rd Battalion, the

An artist's impression of Shout's VC action

Turks renewed their attack, recapturing a stretch of Sasse's Sap, the scene of Owen Howell-Price's desperate stand earlier in the day. To allow such an incursion to remain uncontested within his battalion's sector was an anathema to Shout. His response was swift and wholly in keeping with his reputation. With his friend Capt. Cecil Sasse, he gathered three men to carry sandbags with which to build trench blocks and then helped himself to a supply of bombs before charging the hapless Turks. They scarcely knew what hit them. In one short section, Shout bombed and killed eight and routed the remainder. Sasse, armed with a rifle, was credited with shooting a dozen. Their advance, conducted in short hops, won back approximately 20 yd of the sap, strewn with dead and wounded Turks. Then they halted and established a new trench barricade. Sasse was elated by their success, and that afternoon, after talking with Shout, they decided to repeat the operation and extend the Australian grip on the sap. For their second foray they took eight men to carry sandbags and an extra supply of bombs. In a report of the action written shortly afterwards, Bean stated:

They started together, Captain Sasse with a rifle and Captain Shout with bombs. Captain Shout had a good look round to see the position, and then pushed the barricade down.

They went forward two abreast, Captain Sasse shooting and Captain Shout bombing. As Captain Shout's bombs fell those following could hear the bustle of accoutrements and cries.

Finally, they reached a point where they decided it was suitable to build a last barricade. Captain Shout, who all the time was laughing and joking and cheering his men on, resolved to make a big throw before the final dash. He tried to light three bombs at once, so that they might be quickly thrown, and the Turks prevented from hindering the building of the barricade. He ignited all three bombs, and threw one. Then either the second or third burst as it was leaving his hand, and shattered one hand and most of the other, destroying one eye, laid his cheek open, and scorched his breast and leg.

Captain Shout nevertheless, remained conscious, talked cheerfully, drank tea and sent a message to his wife.

Immediately afterwards, Shout was evacuated, but three days later, on his thirty-third birthday, he succumbed to his terrible wounds aboard the hospital ship *Euralia* and was buried at sea. Tragically, a clerical mix-up led to his wife being informed that a report of his death was wrong and that he had been wounded and was returning to Australia.

Lt. Col. A.J. Bennett, commanding officer of the 1st Battalion throughout the Lone Pine fighting, wrote to Shout's widow:

I desire to express to you, though quite inadequately, our very deep sympathy with you in the loss of your husband, the late Captain Shout, as true a gentleman and as brave as ever wore the uniform of his King. Numerous acts of conspicuous brilliant conduct had already brought Captain Shout into favourable notice, and he had already, though so short a time in the field, had the Military Cross conferred upon him. In the storming, capture, and defence of the enemy's stronghold, known as Lone Pine, this brilliant officer was again unapproachable in his splendid leadership, and it was while in the act of again bombing the enemy out of their trenches that he sustained the injuries from which he subsequently died. So outstanding was Captain Shout's devotion to duty that I had recommended him for the most glorious distinction of the Victoria Cross, before he was wounded, and this recommendation has been approved by the general officer commanding, and, melancholy satisfaction though it be, I hope to see his name honoured by enrolment in the band of heroes who have won the VC.

Col. Bennett's original recommendation was clearly based on Shout's exploits during the morning of 9 August. Following his death, the recommendation was redrafted. It is clear, however, from Bennett's letter that he considered Shout to have earned his VC even before he embarked upon his final, fatal charge along Sasse's Sap.

The posthumous award was gazetted, together with the other Lone Pine VCs, on 15 October. The citation read:

For most conspicuous bravery at Lone Pine trenches, in the Gallipoli Peninsula. On the morning of 9th August, 1915, with a very small pary, Captain Shout charged down the trenches strongly occupied by the enemy, and personally threw four bombs among them, killing eight and routing the remainder. In the afternoon of the same day, from the position gained in the morning, he captured a further length of trench under similar conditions, and continued personally to bomb the enemy at close range, under very heavy fire, until he was severely wounded, losing his right hand and left eye. This most gallant officer has since succumbed to his injuries.

Capt. Cecil Duncan Sasse, Shout's gallant companion on both his bombing missions, received the Distinguished Service Order for his courageous leadership at Lone Pine, although, strangely, his citation referred only to his actions on 6–7 August and made no mention of the events of 9 August in which he shared. Sasse's Sap was never fully recaptured.

On 20 November 1915 the governor general, Sir Ronald Munro Ferguson, unveiled a memorial plaque in hour of Shout at Darlington Town Hall, Sydney. The tablet is now displayed at Victoria Barracks Museum, Paddington.

❖❖❖

Leonard Maurice Keysor, erroneously spelt Keyzor in his VC citation, was born in Lanhill Road, Paddington, London, on 3 November 1885, the son of Benjamin Keysor, a clock importer.

Educated at Tonnleigh Castle, Ramsgate, Keysor emigrated to Canada in 1904. He settled there for ten years until his restless spirit led him to Australia, where he had a sister. He had been in Sydney, living with his relatives in Bayswater Road, Darlinghurst, for barely three months when war broke out. He enlisted in the 1st Battalion on 18 August 1914, the day after the unit was formed at Victoria Barracks, Sydney, and gave his occupation as a clerk. Keysor embarked with the 1st Battalion on 18 October, bound for Egypt. He took part in the landings on 25 April 1915, and was promoted lance-corporal in June.

After his VC award, he rejoined the 1st Battalion in France and took part in the heavy fighting around Pozières on the Somme in the summer of 1916. On 17 November he transferred to the 42nd Battalion and the following month was promoted sergeant. He served with the unit for the remainder of the war, being commissioned on 13 January 1917. Keysor was wounded again on 28 March and 26 May 1918. In October Lt. Keysor returned to Australia as part of a recruiting drive. A pro-conscription campaigner, he had little time to make an impact before the war ended. Discharged on 12 December as being medically unfit, he resumed his work as a clerk.

Two years later he returned to London to join his father's business and on 21 July 1921 he married Gladys Benjamin at the Hill Street synagogue. In 1927 Keysor was persuaded to re-enact his bomb-throwing exploits for a film called *For Valour*. The venture, however, went awry when one of the bombs filled with flash powder exploded near to Keysor. He had to be treated in hospital for cuts and burns. It was an incident wholly out of keeping with his post-war life. A shy man, he ventured only reluctantly into the public sphere. In a rare interview given during the 1940s, Keysor, by then white-haired and deaf, described himself as a 'common or garden clock importer', and insisted that 'the war was the only adventure I ever had'.

Leonard Keysor died of cancer on 12 October 1951, aged sixty-five. He was cremated after a memorial service at the Liberal Jewish synagogue in St John's Wood, London. His Victoria Cross was bought by the Australian Returned Services League in 1977 and it now forms part of the collection at the Australian War Memorial in Canberra.

William John Symons was born on 12 July 1889, at Eaglehawk, Victoria, the eldest son of William Samson Symons and Mary Emma (née Manning). His parents were of Cornish descent, and his father, who was a Methodist lay preacher, worked as a miner.

Lt. J. Symons

The family lived in Tarriff Street, and William, known to his friends as 'Curley' Symons, attended Eaglehawk State School. He was a member of the Eaglehawk West Methodist Band of Hope, and the church played a big part in his formative years. He was also a teetotaller. Tragedy struck in 1904 when his father died suddenly at the age of forty-two, leaving William, at fourteen, as head of the family. To help support them, he took a job driving a grocer's cart and, together with his old grey horse, he became a familiar figure in Eaglehawk. Two years later, he moved with his mother and four brothers to Brunswick, Melbourne. He joined the militia and soon all his spare time was devoted to soldiering, firstly in the 5th Australian Volunteer Regiment and then in the 60th Infantry, where he held the rank of colour sergeant.

When war broke out, he was living with his family at 8 Burkett Street, East Brunswick. On 17 August 1914 he left his job, working behind the counter at Messrs McDougall and Sons' grocery stores in Sydney Road, and enlisted. Posted to A Company of the 7th Battalion as colour sergeant, he embarked with his unit for Egypt on 18 October.

Symons was promoted to acting regimental quartermaster sergeant sixteen days before his unit landed at Anzac Beach. He came through the initial fighting unscathed and later recorded:

The fire was terribly hot, and, as soon as we had advanced a certain distance, Colonel Elliott sent back a message, 'We are digging in', but he received an order to press on at once, and so on we went. As a matter of fact, we went up straight in the face of a point-blank fire from Turkish machine-guns and artillery. Of 1,100 odd who landed, we mustered, after two days' continuous fighting, only 300, and a good number of these were wounded.

As a result of the heavy losses, Symons was commissioned second lieutenant on 26 April. He came through the ill-starred Second Battle of Krithia, in which his unit again suffered heavily, and was promoted lieutenant on 2 July. During the defence of Lone Pine, Symons commanded D Company, of whom four-fifths were volunteers from Bendigo. He returned to Australia in March 1916 to rapturous receptions throughout Victoria. A contemporary newspaper report described him as 'tall and well-built, but a trifle thin as the result of his illness. He has a quiet, active manner, and talks freely with the people he knows, but is absolutely silent when approached on the subject of how he earned the coveted VC'. At Bendigo he was greeted at the railway station by relatives together with the Citizens' Band, who provided a musical escort to the Town Hall where 300 townspeople and 50 returned ex-servicemen were waiting to honour him.

Symons did not return to the 7th Battalion. He was posted to a newly raised Victorian unit, the 37th Battalion, which formed part of the 10th Brigade. Made captain, he was given command of D Company, consisting largely of farmworkers who felt proud to be led by a man they considered a 'dinkum' soldier. According to that unit's history, 'Symon's free and easy devil-may-care attitude appealed to all ranks'. The 37th Battalion arrived in France in November 1916 and Capt. Symons was wounded during the 10th Brigade's so-called 'Big Raid' carried out on 27 February 1917. Back with his unit by April, he narrowly escaped death a month later when two shells hit his dug-out without harming him. On 7 June, however, he was badly gassed as he led his company forward for the assault on Messines Ridge. He rejoined the battalion in January 1918 and served with it during the heavy fighting which followed the German offensive in March.

On 15 August, having adopted the surname of Penn-Symons, he married Isobel Anna Hockley, eldest daughter of Mr and Mrs H.E. Hockley, of Kenton, Hayling, at St Mary's Church, South Hayling in Hampshire. An artist of note, his bride could claim descent from the Spanish aristocracy. The day after their wedding, they sailed for Australia, arriving in October. Capt. Penn-Symons VC was discharged from the Australian Imperial Force on 7 December 1918, although he continued to serve as a captain in the 59th Infantry Regiment until transferred to the reserve of officers in July of 1922. They then returned to England and settled close to his wife's family home in Kenton.

Penn-Symons began a successful business career, gathering a clutch of directorships in a number of firms ranging from fur dyeing to sport stadium management. During the Second World War, with Britain threatened by German invasion, he was one of thousands of First World War veterans to enlist in the

Local Defence Volunteers. He was given command of the 12th Battalion, Leicestershire Home Guard, and held his appointment until 1944. He also served, during this period, on the Leicestershire Military Interviewing Board.

Lt. Col. William Penn-Symons VC died on 24 June 1948 in London as a result of a brain tumour and was survived by his wife and three daughters. In December 1967 his widow, claiming poor circumstances, sold his decorations at public auction for £800. The 7th Battalion Association persuaded the Australian Returned Services League to launch a public appeal and the Victoria Cross was purchased and presented to the Australian War Memorial at Canberra.

Alexander Stewart Burton was twenty-two when he was killed in the act of winning the first posthumous Victoria Cross to an Australian serviceman.

He was born on 20 January 1893, in Kyneton, the son of native-born Victorians Alfred Edward Burton and Isabella (née Briggs). His father was a grocer and an elder of the Presbyterian Church.

At an early age, Alex Burton and his family moved to Euroa, where he attended the state school, acquiring a reputation as a keen sportsman and useful member of the church choir and town band. After leaving school, he joined the firm of A. Miller & Co., where his father was a partner, taking a job in the ironmongery department. In 1911, aged eighteen, he began his period of compulsory military service. Among his circle of friends was a farmer from the nearby town of Longwood by the name of Fred Tubb. When war broke out Tubb led twenty-seven men from the district to Seymour to enlist. Among them was Alex Burton. They travelled to Broadmeadows, on the outskirts of Melbourne, and two months later Burton embarked with his unit, the 7th Battalion, for Egypt, where he underwent more training in preparation for the Dardanelles operations.

A throat infection kept him out of the landings on 25 April. He eventually landed on the peninsula a week later and, according to Press accounts, he remained in the trenches for all but two weeks of the last four months of his life. Slightly wounded in June, he was promoted lance corporal in July and shortly afterwards made full corporal.

His courageous actions alongside his friend and company commander, Fred Tubb, at Lone Pine won him universal praise. Tubb later said of him:

> He was a bonny boy and always did what he was told. With his quiet smile he was always there. I made him lance corporal [*sic*] at Lonesome Pine, and for four or five days he did responsible work well. In the 'show' there was not a better man on the Peninsula than Burton. Just before he died he looked up at me, smiled quietly, and was then killed. His was a fine death, and I almost wish I had died too.

William Dunstan, who shared the risks and the honours with Burton, generously gave much of the credit to his dead comrade. 'I don't know that I did anything out of the way', he said, 'but Burton won it all right.'

News of Burton's death reached his parents in the first week of September and the *Euroa Gazette* sounded a jingoistic note when it recorded: 'Mingled with the sorrow of his relatives, there should be pride that, at any rate, he showed no "white feather", but answered his country's call nobly and at once.'

The Victoria Cross, announced six weeks later, was sent to his father with a letter from the king. Dated 12 January 1916, it read: 'It is a matter of sincere regret to me that the death of Corporal Alexander Stewart Burton deprived me of the pride of personally conferring upon him the Victoria Cross, the greatest of all military distinctions'. Burton's father wore the medal at a homecoming reception for Fred Tubb in April 1916, when he told the audience he was wearing it 'for his boy's sake', and pledged always to wear it on special occasions.

Alex Burton has no known grave. He is commemorated on the Lone Pine memorial. He is also remembered in Euroa, where, on 16 December 1934, Lord Huntingfield, Governor of Victoria, dedicated three English oak trees to the memory of the district's three VC winners – Burton, Fred Tubb and Leslie Maygar, who won his award during the Boer War. At the same time two hills along the highway leading to Longwood were christened Tubb Hill and Maygar Hill, while the Euroa Bridge was named Burton Bridge.

Fifty years later, when road works threatened the destruction of the oaks, three more trees were planted in front of Euroa Civic Hall and dedicated in memory of the three VC winners. Burton's VC, which had been worn with such paternal pride by his father, was presented by the family to the Australian War Memorial in 1967.

Frederick Harold Tubb was born on 28 November 1881 at St Helena, Longwood in Victoria, the fifth of ten children, to Harry Tubb and Emma Eliza (née Abbott). Both his parents were English-born, and his family could trace its ancestors back to thirteenth-century Cornwall. Tubb's parents, both of whom were teachers, settled in Longwood in 1875, a year after they were married. They lived in a two-storey house, originally built as a hotel, which Tubb's father, being a keen student of Napoleon, named St Helena. As well as teaching at the old and new Longwood State schools, the Tubbs took a 320-acre holding between the old and new town. Fred Tubb attended his father's school, obtaining his merit certificate, and then managed the family's farm before working his own land at Longwood.

At 5 ft 5¾ in, he was the smallest of the four sons (another son had died aged six) but possessed a competitive streak which made him a successful sportsman.

Giving a brief resumé of his life and interests, shortly after his VC award, he stated:

> Have played all games since I was able, and at 16 played senior football. Very keen and fond of sport, and have always taken a prominent part in Victoria ... Very fond of shooting, and have a good record for rifle, game and trap-shooting (at pigeons, starlings etc). Have been on the land all my life, on my father's property ... also have landed interest myself.

An extrovert whose popularity was not confined to male company, Tubb shared his father's interest in military affairs. On 20 June 1900, while his elder brother Frank was serving with the Australian Contingent against the Boers, he joined the Victorian Mounted Rifles. Later, he recalled: 'We supplied all our own horses, outfit, uniforms, etc. No pay of any sort.' After two years' service, he joined the Commonwealth Light Horse and served with them for nine years, rising to sergeant.

> When the Australian Compulsory Service came into force I transferred to the 60th Battn. of Infantry [November 1911], because I was then in that area. As the Citizen Force grew our area was strong enough to form a Battalion [the 58th] under Lieut-Colonel H.E. Elliott. He was the CO of the 58th when I got my commission and transferred to the 7th Battalion, Australian Imperial Force.

Fred Tubb was commissioned second lieutenant on 2 December 1912, and enlisted in the AIF on 24 August 1914. Appointed 7th Battalion Transport Officer, he accompanied the unit to Egypt where he was promoted lieutenant on 1 February 1915. Although he embarked with the battalion to take part in the landings, Tubb remained aboard ship with the transport and returned with it to Egypt. He did not set foot on the peninsula until 6 July, when he arrived as a replacement B Company commander. A month later, on the day of the assault on the Lone Pine position, Tubb was promoted captain.

After the battle, Tubb was treated for his injuries at the 2nd Australian Field Ambulance station on the beach at Anzac. On 11 August, after a day-long wait, he was evacuated aboard the hospital ship *Gascon*. In his diary he noted: 'I don't like going away for many reasons, but the doctor and the CO say I must and that I am not to come back till I am quite well. The CO was grand about it.' Taken first to Malta and then England, he was staying at Lady Clementine Waring's convalescent home in Lennel when his VC was announced. Some time afterwards, Lady Waring remembered:

> I can see him now, his whole personality radiating vitality and energy ... He came with two other Australians, all three had been wounded at Gallipoli. On

that first evening it was whispered to me that he had been recommended for the VC . . . I can see his wrathful face and blazing eyes as he turned to refute the statement: he was ever modest . . . The life of the convalescent is necessarily uneventful, yet it is in a hospital that one so speedily realises and appreciates these characters, like 'Tubby's', were cheerful, helpful and resourceful.

Tubb spent the day of his VC award with officers of the King's Own Scottish Borderers in Berwick. On his way back to Lennel, his car was intercepted at Coldstream Bridge and he was carried off to a reception organized by Lady Waring. She recalled:

'Tubby' remained speechless, overwhelmed. Finally in a broken voice, he murmured a few incoherent words of thanks, and espying my small two-seater car nearby, leaped in with an imploring 'For God's sake get me out of this!' and whirled off through the gates.

Tubb's recovery was slow and painful. An emergency appendicectomy left an incision hernia, which proved a source of great discomfort, and he was invalided home to Australia. He arrived to a hero's welcome in April 1916. Crowds greeted him at Euroa and Longwood. The *Euroa Gazette* estimated that almost every resident for miles around attended his home-coming at Longwood which was 'en fête' for the occasion. As a band played 'Home, Sweet Home', Tubb was carried from the station, which had been decorated in his honour, and deposited onto a specially constructed platform. Later, at a civic banquet, Tubb told of the exploits of his fellow citizens and concluded: 'I am a very lucky man and hope soon to get back. I want nothing better than for more Euroa and Longwood boys to come back with me.'

Despite his pleas, however, Tubb did not immediately return to the 7th Battalion. In May 1916 he was sent as a bombing instructor to Duntroon Military College. This was followed by a tour of army camps. Eventually, he persuaded a medical board to pass him fit for active service and he rejoined his unit in France in December 1916. Two months later, he was promoted major.

On 20 September 1917, during the Third Battle of Ypres, Maj. Tubb led his company in an attack on a group of nine German pillboxes south of Polygon Wood. The day before he had been in considerable pain from his hernia and his brother, and fellow officer Frank, was authorized to replace him for the attack, but he had refused to stand down. Fred Tubb, leading his company with his customary dash, captured and consolidated their objective. Shortly afterwards he was wounded by a sniper and while being carried to the rear for treatment his stretcher party was caught in a British barrage. Tubb was mortally wounded and

Tubb's grave

died later that evening at a dressing station. He was buried in the Lijessenthoek military cemetery, Belgium.

The news of his death cast a shadow over his home town of Longwood. The sanctuary of the church was draped with flags, white flowers and black hangings, and an officer's sword and laurel wreath were placed on the Litany desk. At a memorial service, attended by a congregation almost as large as the home-coming crowds, the rector took as his text St Paul's words: 'I have fought a good fight. I have finished my course, I have kept the faith.'

Lady Waring, with whom Tubb had spent his last English leave as a guest at Lennel, later wrote: 'The manner of his death came as no surprise to those who knew his gallant spirit, and I, for one, feel certain it is the death "Tubby" would have desired.'

William Dunstan, the only one of the three VC winners from the defence of Goldenstedt's Post to survive the war, was born on 8 March 1895, at Ballarat East, in Victoria. He was the fourth child, and third son, born to bootmaker William John Dunstan and Henrietta (née Mitchell). His father was born in Ballarat of Cornish mining stock.

The family lived in Cameron Street, Golden Point, and William attended the Golden Point State School. An intelligent boy, he attended the local church, where his father was a leading figure, and belonged to the Golden Point Gymnasium Club. He left school aged fifteen, and became a clerk at Snows drapers in Ballarat. His great interest, however, was military matters, and the following year he joined the Army cadets, rising to the rank of cadet captain before transferring to the 70th (Ballarat) Battalion as one of the youngest lieutenants in the Citizen Forces.

When war broke out he was serving as Adjutant of the 70th Battalion. His unit spent the early days of the war digging trenches around Queenscliff,

Portalington and Point Nepean, where the only excitement was the seizure of Australia's first prize ship, the German merchantman *Pfalz*. Dunstan's initial attempt to join the AIF was rejected on account of his age. But so desperate was he to get into action, he quit his job, resigned his commission in the Citizen Forces and on 2 June 1915 enlisted as a private. He was courting his future bride, Marjorie Carnell, at the time, and family legend has it that her mother, who evidently considered the Dunstans figured rather low on the social ladder, told him: 'You can marry my daughter if you come back with the VC.' Apocryphal or not, Dunstan left Australia on 17 June as an acting sergeant in the 6th Reinforcements of the 7th Battalion.

Following a brief stay in Egypt, Dunstan joined Lt. Tubb's B Company a few days before the attack on Lone Pine. He swiftly made his mark. During his short period on the peninsula, he was twice mentioned in dispatches and was promoted corporal on 3 August. Badly wounded in the head during the defence of Goldenstedt's Post, Dunstan was blind when he was evacuated from the peninsula less than a fortnight after joining the 7th Battalion. He was invalided back to Australia, where he gradually regained his sight. But he would say nothing of his actions at Lone Pine. The first word of his exploit came from Chaplain William McKenzie, the legendary 'Fighting Mac'. In a letter from the peninsula, intended to ease his parents' concern about the state of his injuries, McKenzie wrote:

Willie Dunstan met me the day of his arrival here. I urged him to write home right away, which he did. I was sorry that he had not been delayed one week longer. However, he was awfully glad to be in it – the charge which eventuated at Lone Pine Ridge on 6th August. While he was not in it, nor any of the 2nd Victorian Brigade, they came in to relieve us on 9th and 10th, and they had a very trying time with bombs from the Turks. They suffered terribly, and had over 300 casualties. I may say that Willie and another did such fine work in bomb-throwing and held out in a trench against a very determined attack of the Turks, that both are recommended for the Victoria Cross. The other young man was eventually killed. Willie was severely wounded with bomb wounds, but not at all dangerously. He will suffer considerable pain for a couple of weeks, or even four, but will probably be as right as possible again in six or seven weeks' time. He proved himself a capable, intelligent, intrepid young warrior in his first fight. It was one of the most desperate and stubborn nature. There is no need whatever to worry about him. He is doing all right. There is every reason to feel proud of such a son.

A little over a month after his return to Australia, the announcement of his VC turned him, much against his will, into a local celebrity. A total abstainer and

A special edition of the Ballarat Courier, *featuring Cpl. Dunstan on the front page*

staunch Methodist, he found the media attention overwhelming. Cajoled into attending a reception at the Coliseum, Ballarat, he confessed to one civic dignatory: 'I would rather again stand before the Turkish guns and bombs than appear before the big crowd in the Coliseum . . . What have I done? What is it all about?' Dunstan appears to have been genuinely surprised and embarrassed by his award and the fuss it created. Civic honours were showered upon him. His old employers presented him with a gift of fifty guineas, but Dunstan could take no more. When it was announced that a memorial fund was to be opened in his honour, he wrote declining it. In a letter, published in the local Press, he explained:

> I cannot see where there is any necessity for such a course, and, secondly, I think the public have quite enough calls on their purse . . . I only did my duty and one does not wish to be recompensed for that. I do not wish to appear ungrateful, but I really could not accept any such public offering . . . I consider I am more than fortunate in being able to return to my home and receive such honors [sic], which I am sure, are due to hundreds of other Australian soldiers, who may not, like myself, have had the opportunity of coming into the limelight, or, perhaps, had the opportunity but have been killed.

One ceremony he could not avoid was the presentation of his Victoria Cross. The investiture, performed on the steps of Parliament House, Melbourne, on 9 June 1916, was one of the largest and grandest staged during the war. After receiving his Cross from the governor general, Sir Ronald Crawford Munro Ferguson, he acknowledged the congratulations of the crowds, who included Dame Nellie Melba, and then made a dash to escape their attention.

Dunstan had been discharged from the AIF on 1 February 1916. Immediately, he rejoined the Citizen Forces as a lieutenant and area officer based at Ballarat. He served as acting brigade major of the 18th Infantry Brigade and, in 1921, he transferred to the 6th Battalion. Placed on the unattached list in 1923, he joined the reserve of officers in 1928 and retired with the rank of lieutenant.

On 9 November 1918, Dunstan married his pre-war sweetheart, Marjorie Carnell, in Ballarat East. The newly-weds spent their honeymoon in St Kilda, watching the Armistice celebrations from their hotel room window. Unlike so many of the war's heroes, Dunstan did not slip back into obscurity. Instead, he forged a new and successful career in commerce. After a period spent working in the repatriation department, he joined Keith Murdoch's Herald & Weekly Times Ltd as an accountant in 1921. Within thirteen years he had become administration general manager for the entire Herald Group, a post he held for nineteen years until his war wounds forced him to resign and accept a directorship. According to his son Keith, who became a journalist and author, Dunstan was gregarious, a man with an immense number of friends and as general manager of the Herald & Weekly Times Ltd quite dynamic in business. Immediately World War II broke out he contacted General Blamey and expected to be given a command. He was disgusted when he was rejected on medical grounds.

In fact, the painful legacy of his VC action remained with him until the end. His son has written:

> He had shrapnel permanently in his brain and for the rest of his life he suffered from terrible headaches. When the headaches came there was no sleep and as children we were told to move very quietly about the house. The entire household was aware of his suffering.

For whatever reasons, Dunstan rarely if ever discussed his war experiences, even with members of his family. His VC, together with his other decorations, remained, for the most part, hidden in a cupboard under the stairs.

A keen racegoer and active supporter of the Australian turf, Dunstan was, with fellow VC holder Rupert Moon, co-owner of a racehorse called Maid of Money. It was while returning from the Caulfield Races, on 2 March 1957, that the last-surviving member of Tubb's gallant band collapsed and died of a heart attack.

More than 800 people attended a memorial service in Christ Church, South Yarra. They included seven VC holders from the First World War. A mile-long cortège followed Dunstan's ashes to their last resting place at Springvale crematorium, where a guard of honour from the 1st Armoured Regiment fired a three-volley salute. Among the many tributes was one from the prime minister, Robert Menzies, a close personal friend, who said: 'We have lost a man who was brave, capable and friendly.' Lt. Gen. Sir Sydney Rowell, a former chief of the Australian General Staff, added: 'He was one of the most modest VC winners the world will ever know . . . One had to know Bill Dunstan well to realise the depths of his character and personal modesty.'

The only member of the 3rd Battalion to win the Victoria Cross during the First World War, **John Hamilton** was born in Orange, New South Wales on 24 January 1896. He was the son of William Hamilton and his wife Catherine (née Fox).

Details of his education are not recorded, but Hamilton went to work as a teenager for his father, who had a butcher's business in Penshurst. He served in the militia before enlisting as a private in the Australian Imperial Force on 15 September 1914. Posted to the 3rd Battalion, he sailed for Egypt the following month.

Hamilton took part in the landing on 25 April and went through the early fighting before being evacuated suffering from a bout of influenza at the end of May. He rejoined the 3rd Battalion on 2 June and remained with the unit throughout the August battles.

After a spell in England, during which he received his VC, Hamilton proceeded to France with his unit. Promoted corporal on 3 May 1916, he fought at Pozières, Mouquet Farm and Flers during the Somme offensive. His services with the 3rd Battalion were further recognized by promotion to sergeant in May 1917, and a recommendation for a commission. On 5 July 1918 he was posted to No. 5 Officer Cadet Battalion based at Cambridge, England. Thus ended his active war service. Incredibly, during his three years of frontline service there is no record of him ever being wounded. Hamilton was commissioned second lieutenant two months after the Armistice and rejoined the 3rd Battalion as a lieutenant in April 1919. Three months later he returned to Australia and was demobilized on 12 September 1919.

Hamilton after being commissioned

The butcher's boy who came home an officer with a Victoria Cross settled at Tempe, Sydney, and took a job as a docker. He continued to work in the port for thirty years, as docker, shipping clerk, storeman and packer. An active member of the Waterside Workers' Federation, he was Labour nominee for the post of Sydney branch secretary in 1952.

The outbreak of the Second World War had seen him back in uniform. He was given his commissioned rank back and served with the 16th Garrison Battalion in Australia from June 1940 to September 1942. Hamilton served overseas with the 3rd Pioneer Battalion in New Guinea, before transferring to the Australian Labour Companies. In 1944 he joined the Army Labour Service, being promoted captain in October. With his unit, he supported the Australian forces who landed on Bougainville in July 1945. Hamilton returned to Sydney in April 1946 and four months later his second spell of military service was officially terminated.

Jack Hamilton VC, the last survivor of the seven Australians to win the Cross at Lone Pine, died of cerebro-vascular disease in the Repatriation General Hospital, Concord, Sydney, on 27 February 1961. After a private funeral, he was buried in Woronora cemetery. His wife Myrtle died in 1975 and ten years later, on the 70th anniversary of his VC action, his only son Alwyn presented his father's medals to the Australian War Memorial.

Alfred John Shout, hailed as one of Australia's greatest heroes of the Gallipoli campaign, was, in fact, a New Zealander by birth. He was born on 8 August 1882 in Wellington, the son of John Shout, a London-born cook, and his Irish wife Agnes (née McGovern). Little is known of his early life. He was still in his teens when he embarked with the New Zealand contingent to fight the Boers.

He served with distinction in the Border Horse, was twice wounded and, on one occasion, reported as killed in action. His gallantry was marked by a mention in dispatches and promotion to sergeant for a deed set out in Army Orders on 23 February 1901 as follows: 'At Thabaksberg, on 29th January, 1901 – Displayed great courage and assisted greatly in keeping men together. Under a heavy fire he brought out of the firing-line a wounded man of the 17th Battery, RFA, and took him to a place of safety.'

It is possible that Shout remained in South Africa after the war. Certainly, in 1903, he joined the Cape Field Artillery, as a sergeant. He emigrated to Australia in 1907 and settled in the Sydney suburb of Darlington where he worked as a carpenter and joiner. Shout pursued his military interests by joining a militia unit, the 29th Infantry Regiment, otherwise known as the Australian Rifles. A fine shot, Shout was a familiar figure at the Randwick rifle range and was a mainstay of the 29th Infantry Club. Commissioned a second lieutenant in the militia on 16 June 1914, he enlisted in the Australian Imperial Force on 27 August. By then Shout had married Rose Alice and the couple had a 9-year-old daughter.

Shortly after the outbreak of war the 29th was swallowed up by the newly constituted 1st Battalion, AIF, and Shout was posted as second lieutenant to F Company, commanded by Lt. Cecil Sasse. The battalion embarked for Egypt on 18 October and shortly after its arrival the unit was re-formed into four companies, with Shout becoming a platoon commander in D Company. In February 1915 he was promoted lieutenant and it was with this rank that he landed at Anzac on 25 April.

Shout played a significant part in the confused and costly fighting to secure the beach-head. On the first day he fought a rearguard action on Baby 700 and later that same day he led a mixed party of stragglers to support the thin Australian line on Walker's Ridge. Two days later, having toiled without a break since the landing, he replaced a wounded officer and held a threatened sector on Walker's Ridge. One of his men later recorded:

There were only two officers left – Lieutenants Shout and Harrison – and our position was desperate. The gallantry of both was remarkable, but Lieutenant Shout was a hero. Wounded himself several times, he kept picking up wounded men and carrying them out of the firing line. I saw him carry fully a dozen men away. Then another bullet struck him in the arm, and it fell useless by his side. Still he would not go to the rear. 'I am here with you boys to the finish', was the only reply he would make. We all thought too, that it was to be a finish for us. The Turks were attacking us in thousands. We were not properly entrenched, and we were hopelessly outnumbered. A little later Lieutentant Shout was wounded again, and fell down. It was cruel to see him. He struggled and struggled until he got to his feet, refusing all entreaties to go to the rear. Then he staggered and fell and tried to rise again. At last some men seized him and carried him away, still protesting.

For his gallant leadership, Shout was awarded the Military Cross. The citation stated:

On 27th April, 1915, during operations near Gaba Tepe, for showing conspicuous courage and ability in organising and leading his men in thick, bushy country under very heavy fire. He frequently had to expose himself to locate the enemy and led a bayonet charge at a critical moment.

Shout was not seriously wounded and was soon reunited with his unit. On 11 May he was wounded again and, for his work since the landing, he was mentioned in Sir Ian Hamilton's dispatches of 29 June. A month later he was promoted captain and a week afterwards led his men into Lone Pine. The three-day battle which followed was one of the fiercest waged on the peninsula. Judged as a diversionary *A memorial to Capt. Shout in Australia*

operation designed to distract Turkish attentions from the Allies' main objective on Chunuk Bair, the attack must be counted a success. However, the Australians paid a fearful price for their victory. More than 2,000 men of the 1st Australian Division were killed, wounded or posted missing – 340 of them from the 1st Battalion. None among those who died was mourned more than Alfred Shout.

Charles Bean, who knew him and knew of the respect in which he was held, has probably come closer than anyone to reflecting the spirit of Australia's most decorated soldier at Gallipoli. Writing of him after his last exceptional action at Lone Pine, he said: 'Shout was one of the gamest officers that ever lived, from the first day ready for any adventure, plunging into the thick of it, light-hearted and laughing . . .'

C.R.G. BASSETT

Rhododendron Spur, Anzac Beach sector,
8–10 August 1915

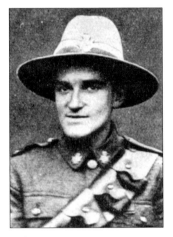

Cpl. C. Bassett

At first light on 8 August 1915 the commanding heights of Chunuk Bair, overlooking the Anzac beach-head, were seized by a New Zealand battalion, supported by a British New Army unit, without a shot being fired and without the loss of a single man. It was one of the most dramatic coups of the campaign. For a brief moment, it appeared that Sir Ian Hamilton's bold plans would be crowned by success. From the former Turkish trench on the crest of this strategically important ridge, the men of the Wellington Regiment and the 7th Gloucesters could look back towards the Anzac beach-head, while ahead of them, tantalizingly close, could be seen a ribbon of shimmering blue marking the course of the Narrows, the prime objective of Hamilton's expeditionary force.

The occupation of the hills above Anzac represented the corner-stone of Hamilton's August offensive. All the other operations, including those at Suvla Bay, were of secondary importance. The plan to seize them involved two brigade-strength columns exploiting gaps torn in the Turkish lines by a covering force. They were to strike at night, deep into the heart of Turkish territory, in order to be ready to storm the heights at dawn on 7 August. It was an audacious plan, but one made even more hazardous by the maze of gullies and hills which had to be negotiated in darkness.

The right assaulting column was detailed to reach the summit of Chunuk Bair, then thought to be devoid of Turkish troops, by way of Rhododendron Spur, which took its name from the profusion of wild flowers carpeting its slopes. Commanded by Brig. F.E. Johnston, the column consisted of the New Zealand Infantry Brigade, supported by the 26th Indian Mountain Battery and No. 1 Field Company, NZ Engineers. During their march, they were to be joined by another New Zealand battalion.

The force set out from Anzac on the night of 6 August. By daybreak, however, the column was still short of its objective. Although only a handful of Turks had been encountered on the night march, one of the New Zealand units had become lost, resulting in a delay which would prove costly. As the column approached Chunuk Bair on the morning of 7 August, Johnston could see that, contrary to expectation, the heights were occupied. In fact, Johnston's force vastly outnumbered the few defenders, but there followed a further unaccountable delay before the attack was launched, by which time the Turks had brought up sufficient reinforcements to beat off the assault.

The Auckland Battalion and the 2/10th Gurkhas, a unit which had attached itself to Johnston's column after losing touch with its own command, were almost annihilated on the open slopes running from the centre of Rhododendron Spur towards Chunuk Bair. Johnston set up his headquarters in a cup-shaped depression about 60 yd wide, within 300 yd of the summit. From this position, later known as the Apex, he set about planning a renewed assault. Unfortunately, although the Apex offered cover from the Turkish-held heights, it presented little room for deploying an attacking force. The ground between Johnston's position and Chunuk Bair afforded no better protection. Apart from an abandoned Turkish trench 100 yd further along the spur, the slopes were totally devoid of cover.

Yet at 4.15 a.m. the following morning, when the second attack went in, having been preceded by a violent naval bombardment, the New Zealanders advanced unopposed. The men of the Wellington Battalion found the crest of Chunuk Bair deserted, save for a single Turkish machine-gun section. The rest of the garrison had withdrawn to escape the bombardment. For two hours the new occupants were left in splendid isolation. However, after coming under machine-gun fire from the flanks, the Wellingtons' commanding officer decided to withdraw the bulk of his men from the crest and dig a new trench along the reverse slopes. It was a move which irrevocably altered the course of the fighting, and although the battalion resisted a series of Turkish attacks throughout the morning, their grip on the crest became increasingly precarious.

At Brigade HQ in the Apex, Johnston, who was not in communication with his men on the crest, was growing increasingly alarmed at developments. He therefore decided to send forward a small section from the Divisional Signals Company. Among their number was a small, slim-built Aucklander, who had been working as a bank clerk until war broke out.

Cpl. Cyril Bassett had already survived one close call during the Chunuk Bair operation, when a stray bullet had embedded itself in his boot without touching his foot. On the previous day, he had volunteered to run a telephone forward with the Aucklanders, but the failure of their attack made it a futile gesture. Now Johnston placed him in command of a party of signallers who were to be followed an hour later by another section led by Spr. B.L. Dignan. Their mission involved climbing the exposed slopes of Rhododendron Spur, and braving the

Artist's impression of Bassett's VC action

Turkish machine-gun and rifle fire being directed from the neighbouring heights, Hill Q and Point 971. The sight which greeted them as they left the Apex could have done little to raise their hopes. The ground ahead was strewn with the bodies of New Zealanders and Gurkhas killed during the previous day's unsuccessful attack. Fifty years later, Bassett recorded his account of their hazardous journey:

> We'd no sooner got under way than . . . I remember Brigadier Johnson [*sic*] saying 'Keep low, keep low'. Well, now I realise why he said that because the fire was coming from our left. If I'd kept down in the slope I'd have been happy. Instead of that I ran into all sorts of trouble and we had to carry this line really in short rushes.
>
> I had a man wounded and I got about three-quarters of the way across, mostly under rifle fire and machine-gun fire and a bit of shrapnel – I think the shrapnel was the worst of the lot – and we ran into a squadron of Mounted Rifles [*sic*] . . . They commandeered my phone and held me up for about half an hour. In the meantime, the Brigade had sent another line on practically the

same route as these Mounted Rifles [this was the party led by Spr. Dignan]. They arrived without a scratch.

Anyway, being the senior NCO, I sent the man in charge across to the hill and he got to the foot of the hill and ran out of wire. So we caught up with him eventually and then I sent him up the hill, with his name taken, and I got a man named Birkett [Spr. William Arthur Birkett MM], who had been working with me on the line, and he and I stayed behind to straighten up the lines which were laying higgledy-piggledy all over the place. And then about half an hour later, I didn't time exactly, this chap, who'd brought the second line over, came and reported to me that the line had gone.

Bassett sent the man back to Brigade HQ with an urgent message from the Wellingtons, who were struggling to hold on, while he remained on the exposed slopes to superintend the inevitable line repairs. He recalled:

We were there practically until the morning of August 10th on these lines. Well, what we should have done really was to run out new lines but we didn't have [any] . . . All day on the 8th we were working on these lines, mending breaks, and on the 9th we did a bit of mending, but we were really tired. We were really worn out.

One of the signallers who'd been allotted to look after the telephone on the Chunuk Bair was badly wounded. We got that news, and then on the night of the 9th we laid a new telephone wire across to the Wiltshires, who had relieved our boys, and then we brought this wounded boy in. We couldn't get a stretcher and we had to bring him in on a blanket – four of us – and he had been wounded badly from the waist downwards . . . He had been out there a day and a night.

Writing about the action in a letter home dated 23 August, Spr. Dignan was full of praise for Bassett's leadership. He wrote:

Our wire gave out about 100 yd down the hill from Wgton HQ so I took a message up and reported and then when I got back Bassett . . . arrived with his party and some more wire so we made a duplicate [line] and Birkett and I took the line on to Wgton HQ . . . They stopped the Turks and then the Turks started massing somewhere and just then the phone went bung. Colonel Malone [OC Wellingtons] had an important message to go through about this massing so I took it leaving Birkett to take the phone. I sent the operators up while Bassett repaired the line.

. . . Meanwhile, the two operators [Whittaker and Edwards] had gone up and Bassett and Birkett came back on the spot where the Ak Mtd Rifles [*sic*] had been and mended the wire under fire and stayed out till early next morning . . . Total result of all this is that Bassett, Birkett, Whittaker, Edwards, McDermott and I had our names taken by the . . . Brigade Major. The six was eventually reduced to three with special for Bass as he was mentioned before [Bassett had been cited for bravery on 2 May].

As the battle ebbed and flowed, Bassett and his team were kept busy repairing numerous line breaks on the exposed slopes of Rhododendron Spur. He personally mended three on the 9th alone. These missions were always performed in the open and invariably under fire of varying degrees of intensity. Often, they occurred in the midst of Turkish counter-attacks less than 100 yd away. Yet miraculously, Bassett, whose only weapons were a revolver picked up from a dead Gurkha and a bayonet 'which touched the ground because I was so small', came through unscathed. 'I was so short that the bullets passed over me', he once jocularly remarked. In fact, he had been incredibly lucky. One bullet had gone through his tunic collar without touching him and another had torn off his right-hand pocket.

Sadly, his repeated acts of gallantry were, like those performed by the Wellingtons on the crest of Chunuk Bair, all in vain. On 10 August a mass attack finally overwhelmed the defenders. Hamilton's bold gamble had failed. Bassett survived the carnage of Rhododendron Spur, but shortly afterwards he fell ill and was evacuated from the peninsula on 13 August. It was while convalescing in hospital in Leicester that he learned, much to his surprise, of his Victoria Cross.

His citation, published on 15 October 1915, stated:

For most conspicuous bravery and devotion to duty on the Chunuk Bair Ridge, in the Gallipoli Peninsula, on 7th August, 1915 [sic]. After the New Zealand Infantry Brigade had attacked and established itself on the ridge, Corporal Bassett, in full daylight and under a continuous fire and heavy fire, succeeded in laying a telephone wire from the old position to the new one on Chunuk Bair. He has subsequently been brought to notice for further excellent and most gallant work connected with the repair of telephone lines by day and night under heavy fire.

Bassett's first reaction to the news was that a mistake had been made. Indeed, there had been one. The date in the citation, which was later inscribed on his Cross, should have read 8–9 August, or even 8–10 August. But that was the only error. Bassett later admitted: 'There was nobody more staggered than I was when I saw my name.' Those who had witnessed his numerous acts of bravery viewed things differently. Maj. Fred Waite, the New Zealanders' Official Historian, considered that 'no VC on the Peninsula was more consistently earned'. He added: 'This was not for one brilliant act of bravery, but for a full week of ceaseless devotion.'

Cyril Royston Guyton Bassett, the first New Zealander to win the Victoria Cross in the First World War, was born at Mount Eden, Auckland on 3 January 1892, the only son of Frederick Charles and Harriett Adelle Bassett. The family lived in Burleigh Street, and Cyril was educated at Grafton public school, Auckland Grammar and Auckland Technical College. He joined the National Bank of New Zealand in Auckland at the age of sixteen and, apart from military service in two world wars, was employed by the bank all his working life.

His military career began shortly before the First World War when he volunteered for the Auckland College Rifles. Despite his small stature, which very nearly barred him from the unit, he rose to the rank of lance-corporal. On 10 August 1914, the 22-year-old bank clerk and part-time soldier enlisted in the New Zealand Expeditionary Force. Two months later, by then a sapper in the Divisional Signals unit of the NZ Engineers, he embarked for Egypt.

Bassett took part in the initial landing at Anzac, later remarking of his baptism of fire: 'The only thing that occupied my mind was "I wonder how I'm going to behave when I get under fire. I wonder if I'm going to maintain my honour and integrity. . . ."' He ended his first day in action in command of a signals section.

The following month, the newly promoted L/Cpl. Bassett was among three signallers recommended for gallantry awards for their part in carrying a telephone wire across fire-swept ground between Walker's Ridge and Pope Hill after an abortive attack. Years later, he described the difficulties facing signallers on the peninsula: 'We didn't have buried line. Most of the lines . . . were in the air and, if left on the ground, well, they were knocked about by the troops and we had considerable difficulty in maintaining lines. . . . We didn't have enough wire or enough telephones.' After being evacuated seriously ill, Cpl. Bassett spent nearly nine months recuperating in England. He rejoined his unit in France, in June 1916, shortly before the Somme offensive. Commissioned in

Bassett on the Western Front after being commissioned

September 1917, Bassett was recommended for the Military Cross for his actions on the Western Front, but the award was not granted. He was twice wounded, in October 1917 and the following March.

Lt. Bassett returned to his native Auckland in December 1918. Demobilized a month later, he resumed his banking career. At the same time he joined the Territorials, serving until 1929, when he was placed on the Retired List with the rank of lieutenant. His career in banking continued to flourish. He was appointed branch manager at Paeroa and then Auckland Town Hall, a post he continued to hold until his retirement in 1952.

During the Second World War he served in the National Military Reserve and, from January 1941, as a captain in the New Zealand Corps of Signals. He did not go overseas, but regular promotion followed until he was given command of the Northern Districts Signals. In December 1943 Lt. Col. Bassett's service career ended. He was just a few days short of his fifty-second birthday.

Cyril Bassett took an active role in community affairs. He served as a Justice of the Peace and was a prominent member of numerous services organizations, including the Gallipoli Association, the Sappers Association, the King Empire Veterans Club and the Navy League. A fit man well into old age, he listed his recreations as yachting, fishing, swimming and gardening. Married to Ruth (née Grant), he had two daughters, and lived in retirement at 74, Stanley Point Road, Stanley Point. It was there, on 9 January 1983, that the last-surviving Gallipoli VC died.

A modest man, he always felt uneasy about being awarded the Commonwealth's highest gallantry award. He once said: 'When I got the medal I was disappointed to find I was the only New Zealander to get one at Gallipoli, because hundreds of Victoria Crosses should have been awarded there.' He added: 'All my mates ever got were wooden crosses.'

P.H. HANSEN

Hill 70 (Scimitar Hill), Sulva Bay, 9 August 1915

Capt. P. Hansen

Shells burst in the sea as the weary survivors of the 6th Lincolns sought refuge on the crowded shores of Suvla Bay. Released from their ordeal at the front, they watched the ships, from tiny North Sea trawlers to huge grey battleships, continue their work apparently unconcerned. From the cover of some rocks, a young NCO took advantage of the lull to write home. A year earlier, L/Cpl. A.H. Breese had been delivering mail in Lincoln. Now, in the second week of August 1915, he had plenty to write home about:

Last Monday, August 9th, we set out to attack the Turks, who were holding a hill beyond the one we captured on the 7th. Our Battalion was in the firing line, and after advancing some distance we discovered that we had fallen into a trap. We did not retreat, however, and our men are still holding the position. By the way, one of the Turkish shells has managed to hit a trawler and we have just watched it sink . . . After the battle on the 9th our Adjutant called for volunteers to rescue wounded from the fire, which had broken out between us and the Turks. The poor chaps were being roasted alive. Myself and two others went along with the Adjutant and rescued as many as we could. Next morning I learned that I was going to be recommended to our General. I do not know any more; probably you will hear before me . . .

The adjutant to whom Breese referred was Capt. Percy Hansen and the incident outlined in his letter would result in Hansen receiving the first Victoria Cross of the Suvla operations.

Hansen's background was somewhat unusual. Born in South Africa to wealthy Danish parents, he had been brought up in England, educated at Eton and Sandhurst, and, despite his Scandinavian roots, was thoroughly English in manner. Indeed, as a young subaltern his reputation for sartorial elegance earned him the sobriquet 'Piccadilly Percy'. Like many young officers excited by the prospect of action, he had talked openly of his ambition of winning the VC.

The 6th (Service) Battalion, the Lincolnshire Regiment, raised at Grantham during the first month of the war, landed at B Beach, Suvla Bay on the night of 6/7 August. Part of the 33rd Brigade of the 11th Division, they formed the divisional reserve. In the early hours of 7 August the Lincolns marched across the dry Salt Lake to storm Hill 53 (soon to be more popularly known as Chocolate Hill), the nearest of two mounds which led to a range of hills rising towards the strategically important Anafarta Spur.

Sketch map showing the location of the Sulva Bay VC actions

In one of the few positive and wholly successful actions performed on the first day, Chocolate Hill was captured. However, it was a triumph to be followed by the kind of squandered opportunity which would characterize and eventually undermine the Suvla venture. After taking the hill, Capt. Hansen, who was temporarily in command of the battalion, went forward with an officer of the 6th Borders to reconnoitre the Turkish positions. They advanced as far as Ismail Oglu Tepe, the southern slopes of the 2-mile-long Anafarta Spur, without encountering any opposition. Permission was requested to move forward and take the hill while the way was clear, but the Lincolns, full of fight from their early success, were ordered instead to withdraw to Lala Baba, on the fringes of the Salt Lake. It was a decision destined to have fatal consequences not only for many of the Lincolns but for the expedition as a whole.

After a day of stultifying inactivity on the 8th, the 33rd Brigade was instructed to carry out an attack in the direction of the Anafarta Spur at dawn the next day. Little opposition was anticipated and the attacking battalions, consisting of the 6th Lincolns, 6th Borders and 7th South Staffordshires, were assured that the high ground from Scimitar Hill (Hill 70), on the northern slopes of the spur, would be secured beforehand. In fact, the troops occupying the crest of the smooth rise, with its curving strip of sandstone shaped like a scimitar, were withdrawn hours before the attack without word being passed to the 33rd Brigade. It was a recipe for disaster soon to be fully realized. Hardly had the Lincolns begun their advance on Ismail Oglu Tepe, when heavy rifle-fire broke out from the north-east. At the same time, Turkish artillery began shelling Chocolate Hill. Far from finding their left flank protected, the 6th Lincolns, commanded by Lt. Col. M.P. Phelps, came under heavy fire from Turks dug in on the crest of Scimitar Hill. The Lincolns had been on the move for two hours and already it was clear their original goal was out of reach. Phelps later wrote:

> The battalion reached this point [Hill 70] which I had been told was held by one of our regiments [West Yorkshires], which information I had passed on to company commanders. When firing started I immediately went to the leading companies, who pushed on, taking up a position along the forward head of the hill. I there heard that the West Yorkshires [more likely the 6th East Yorkshires] had retired from the hill and D Company was forced to turn half left to meet an attack from the enemy on the flank. Casualties began at once . . . I found the line held, but under very accurate and close, if not heavy, fire, both from the front . . . and the high ground beyond. I then went to the left flank, where the men were quite steady and shooting hard. There were many casualties . . . I then fixed on a central point as Battalion Headquarters. I and my Adjutant [Capt. Hansen] were there at intervals during the entire action and sent messages from there. A few reinforcements now began to arrive, a company or less at a time, and went into the firing line. I then sent a report to Headquarters asking for more reinforcements and ammunition.

Phelps left his HQ to check on the position held by a party of the South Staffordshire. He noted:

> The trenches were full of dead and wounded, and I believe this corner was hardly held all day, as no one cared to go through the brush. As I returned, there was a rush of men to the rear, belonging to other battalions sent as reinforcements, which I, helped by Captain Hansen and Captain Duck, managed to stop, sending all these men back to the firing line. There were several of these rushes [seven or eight], all of which we managed to stop, taking the men back to the firing line. All the time shrapnel was bursting among the men from the right front, this added to the casualties. Fire came directly from the rear and pitched amongst the men. There is no doubt that this came from our own guns.
>
> During this time three small fires started, but died down. A further fire started now, however, and got a good hold of the scrub, driving back the men in the firing line and making it impossible to see. Unfortunately, there were far too many wounded to bring away. At 12.15 p.m. I reluctantly gave the order to withdraw, taking as many wounded as we could. There were then only 23 men left on the hill, mostly men of the battalion. I retired on a trench about

300 yards in rear and took over a section of the defence, which we immediately consolidated.

Our losses were 12 officers killed, wounded and missing, 391 rank and file, out of 17 officers and 561 rank and file who originally started out, leaving the battalion 5 officers and 174 rank and file strong.

The full horror of the confused battle which ended with Scimitar Hill obscured by a mass of flames and choking smoke can scarcely be appreciated by so dispassionate an account. Some of the messages, scribbled out by Captain Hansen in the heat of battle, however, paint a more graphic picture of the desperate nature of the fighting:

7am. Cannot hold out much longer without support . . . having a very bad time.

7.55. More ammunition urgently required. It is impossible to move forward from here. Casualties extremely heavy . . .

8.30. Ground on left flank is now on fire. Part of last reinforcements gone right to rear . . . Heavy casualties.

9.50. Don't think men will stand very much more . . . D Coy reduced to 15–20 rifles.

10.25. Our own artillery is now shrapnelling us. Two rounds have just fallen within 50 yards of Bn Hqrs.

12.15pm. Smoke and heat became so bad we were forced to retire about 200 yards [sic]. We are now reorganising. Regret to report that several wounded are being burned alive.

It was at this point that Capt. Hansen, who had been in the thick of things from the outset, decided to act. Scorning the safety of the support trenches at the foot of the blazing hill, he led a volunteer party of three men, consisting of L/Cpl. Breese, a signaller, L/Cpl. Goffin and L/Cpl. Clifton, back up the slopes and into the pall of smoke. According to Col. Phelps, they advanced 400 yd through the burning scrub and succeeded in rescuing six wounded men despite 'exploding ammunition and crossfire from the Turks'. Two days after the battle, Phelps wrote to Brig. Gen. R.P. Maxwell (GOC 33rd Brigade):

I wish to bring to the notice of the General Officer Commanding, the behaviour of Captain and Adj P H Hansen during the action of the 9th inst. He behaved with conspicuous coolness during the whole action, writing messages and taking them to various places under a heavy fire. He stopped on his own initiative several retirements of reinforcements and helped me stop several more [seven or eight in number] under a heavy fire . . . With a few

An artist's impression of Hansen's VC action

volunteers, went out to the front under fire and brought in several wounded, who would undoubtedly otherwise have been burnt alive. His conduct has invariably been excellent.

The battle of 9 August, or Black Monday as it became known to the troops at Suvla, was a disaster, redeemed only in part by the selfless gallantry of a few individuals like Percy Hansen. After watching the swaying fortunes of the 33rd Brigade on Scimitar Hill, soon to be rechristened Burnt Hill, Sir Ian Hamilton was close to despair. He wrote: 'My heart has grown tough amidst the struggles of the Peninsula, but the misery of this scene well nigh broke it.'

The 6th Lincolns were rested before playing a supporting role in the last great effort to seize the heights overlooking Suvla Bay, the same heights which had been theirs for the taking on 7 August. After the failure of the great assault on 21 August they took their turn in garrisoning the trenches at Suvla until the December evacuation put an end to the stalemate. Before then, however, Percy Hansen had added another exploit to his deeds on Scimitar Hill. The 33rd Brigade War Diary for September noted that Capt. Hansen carried out a daring reconnaissance which involved swimming round the seaward flank of the Turkish lines on the north of the bay. Sgt. H.J. Gibbons, of the 6th Lincolns, wrote of his solo mission on 9 September: 'The Adjt reconnoitred round behind the Turkish lines, found position of a Battery and Snipers. Coming back swam full into a Turk whom he shot, and got back safely with the exception of a few bruises.' The next day Gibbons noted: 'Adjutant went round with a Destroyer to point out position of guns he had discovered. He has also been appointed DAQMG so shall lose him I'm sorry to record.' In fact, Hansen did not leave. Col. Phelps went sick, suffering from a bout of dysentery, and Hansen assumed command of the battalion. His command, however, lasted only a fortnight before he too fell ill.

Capt. Hansen was evacuated to Egypt, where he learned of his VC award. The citation, published on 1 October, however, made no mention of his involvement in stemming the tide of panic-stricken reinforcements. It read:

For conspicuous bravery on the 9th August 1915 at Yilghin Burnu, Gallipoli Peninsula.

   After the second capture of the 'Green Knoll' his battalion was forced to retire, leaving some wounded behind, owing to the intense heat from the scrub which had been set on fire.

   When the retirement was effected, Captain Hansen, with three or four volunteers, on his own initiative, dashed forward several times some 300 or 400 yards over open ground into the scrub under a terrific fire, and succeeded in rescuing from inevitable death by burning no less than six wounded men.

L/Cpl. Breese, L/Cpl. Goffin and L/Cpl. Clifton (who later died of wounds) were all awarded the Distinguished Conduct Medal for 'conspicuous bravery and devotion to duty'.

Before the month was out, Hansen had added a Military Cross to his VC. The citation, published on 29 October, stated:

He made a reconnaissance of the coast, stripping himself and carrying only a revolver and a blanket for disguise. He swam and scrambled over rocks, which severely cut and bruised him, and obtained some valuable information and located a gun which was causing much damage. The undertaking was hazardous. On one occasion he met a patrol of twelve Turks, who did not see him, and later a single Turk whom he killed. He returned to our lines in a state of great exhaustion.

In November, Hansen arrived in England to continue his convalescence at the Royal Free Hospital, London. He received his Victoria Cross and Military Cross from George V at Buckingham Palace the following month at an investiture attended by four Australian Gallipoli VCs, F.H. Tubb, H.V.H. Throssell, W.J. Symons and J. Hamilton. Interviewed by journalists about his gallantry at Scimitar Hill, Hansen said candidly: 'They cut us up, but in turn we cut up four to five thousand of the enemy.' Of his own part in the action, he said: 'I was in the biggest funk of my life, and I hardly knew what was happening.'

Percy Howard Hansen was born on 26 October 1890 into a successful Danish trading family. His father, Viggo Julius Hansen, came from Naestved, some 60 miles south-west of Copenhagen, and his mother, Elsa (née Been), belonged to a wealthy shop owning family. Viggo Hansen ventured to South Africa and started his own grocery business, returning to Denmark to marry Elsa. The couple settled in South Africa and trade flourished with stores in Port Elizabeth and Johannesburg. Percy was born in Dresden, during one of the family's frequent trips to the European spas. The birth certificate issued by the Royal Saxon Registry Office described his father as a Privatmann, gentleman of private means. Percy's brother, Edgar Howard, was born in 1893, and it appears that the family moved to London around 1901–02 with the intention of bringing up both boys as English gentlemen. Percy attended a preparatory school called Hazelwood, in Limpsfield, Surrey, where his contemporaries included another future VC recipient, Geoffrey St George Shillington Cather. He went on to another school at Oxted before entering Eton on 20 September 1904, aged thirteen. His parents' address was given as 39 Hyde Park Gate, London SW.

Academically undistinguished, Percy left Eton for Sandhurst on 29 July 1908.

Around this time, or possibly earlier, Viggo Hansen was naturalised British, giving the rest of his family the same rights. The family also adopted the surname Howard Hansen, although it appears this was not widely used. Percy Howard Hansen was duly gazetted second lieutenant in the Lincolnshire Regiment on 11 March 1911.

In sharp contrast to his scholastic achievements, Hansen's military career was marked by considerable success. Promoted lieutenant on 3 August 1912, he was appointed adjutant and temporary captain in the 6th Lincolnshires on 4 September 1914. Five months later, on 2 February 1915, while the battalion was undergoing training at Grantham, he was given his captaincy.

Following his distinguished service in Gallipoli, Hansen was given a number of Staff appointments. He served as a brigade-major at Halton Park camp from June to September 1916 and then proceeded to France in December as a general staff officer (second grade). In this role, he added to his Gallipoli honours a French Croix de Guerre and the Distinguished Service Order (*London Gazette*, 16 September 1918). The citation read:

For conspicuous gallantry and devotion to duty. He volunteered to carry out a reconnaissance, and brought back valuable information obtained under heavy artillery and machine-gun fire, which had been unprocurable from other sources. Throughout he did fine work.

Capt. P. Hansen

195

Lt. Col. Hansen VC, DSO, MC, shortly before the Second World War

At the war's end, the much-decorated Hansen was posted as general staff officer (still second grade) to the Tactical School, Camberley. On 1 January 1919 he was gazetted brevet major and three months later he joined a distinguished band of officers, including Viscount Gort VC, DSO, MVO, MC, Bernard Freyberg VC, CMG, DSO and George Pearkes VC, DSO, MC, on the first post-war Staff College course. All four graduated and Hansen's first appointment was as brigade major with the 8th Infantry Brigade, Southern Command, a post he took up on 9 February 1920. He served in a similar capacity with the 12th Infantry Brigade before being appointed a GSO (second grade) in the 55th (West Lancashire) Division (TA) on 10 February 1925. A series of Staff posts

The Hansen family grave, Copenhagen

followed, including one in Jamaica, before Hansen was selected to command the 2nd Battalion, Lincolnshire Regiment. Immediately war was declared, however, Lt. Col. Hansen reverted back to his Staff role, taking up his mobilization appointment as AA and QMG to the 55th Division. Promoted brigadier in 1941, he commanded the Belfast area in 1942–3 before being made head of the Civil Affairs unit for Norway under SHAEF. Given his Scandinavian roots, it was a peculiarly appropriate appointment and brought him fresh honours in the form of the Legion of Merit, from the United States, and the Norwegian Royal Order of St Olav.

Brig. Percy Hansen, who reported on the nation's Victory Day March for a national newspaper, retired from the Army in 1946. Married to Marie Rose (née Emsell), he had one daughter, named Kinsa. Little is known of his life in retirement. He once listed his recreations as travel, lecturing and cinematography. In 1950 he resurfaced in a public capacity when he joined a guard of honour in Copenhagen to mark the visit of Winston Churchill. Shortly afterwards he suffered an attack of pneumonia. Complications set in and on 12 February 1951 Percy Howard Hansen, one of only two Gallipoli VC winners to win a second gallantry award for service on the peninsula, died.

W.T. FORSHAW

The Vineyard, Helles sector, 7–9 August 1915

Lt. W. Forshaw

It had been a quiet day on the Helles front; ominously so, in the opinion of 25-year-old William Forshaw, a subaltern serving with the 9th Manchesters. A schoolteacher by profession, the young Territorial officer had been on the peninsula for barely a fortnight. Yet already the spirit of optimism was beginning to fade. As far as 2nd Lt. Forshaw was concerned the portents did not appear good. Writing to his former headmaster on 21 May, he confided:

> I think I can safely say that it is a much stiffer proposition than was first anticipated. This country was made for defence – every inch of it – and the enemy are exceedingly well led. They are making the most of their natural advantages. Man for man, or even regimentally, they cannot compare with us, but their generals are good. . . . They are giving nothing away.

Over the succeeding weeks, the experience of the British forces at Helles would bear out his words. Three large-scale attacks, launched on 4 June, 28 June and 12 July, advanced the Allied lines by the merest of margins at a cost in lives which was impossible to sustain without far greater reinforcements. Trenches criss-crossed the southern neck of the peninsula, turning the Turkish position into a veritable stronghold. Such was the stalemate at Helles by the first week in August, the southern sector had become a virtual sideshow. Attention had swung north to Suvla Bay for the opening of a new front and a fresh effort to outflank the Turks.

It was in an attempt to ensure the success of the northern operations that the 42nd East Lancashire Division, which included among its units the 9th Manchesters, undertook the last major British offensive to be mounted south of Achi Baba. What was conceived as a diversionary attack, designed to draw Turkish reserves away from the main thrust, began at 3.50 p.m. on 6 August, some seven hours before transports began disgorging men and materials on to the darkened beaches of Suvla Bay. The Helles feint, launched by the reconstructed 88th Brigade of the 29th Division and continued by the 125th and 127th Brigades of the 42nd East Lancashire Division, was directed at a small kink in the Turkish lines straddling the two forks of the Kirte Dere. According to the optimistic and frighteningly simplistic plan, the assault battalions would slice through the northern face of the salient, capturing the frontline trench known as H13, leaving the Lancastrians to follow up the next day with an attack on the southern half of the Turkish lines, where they bisected a small vineyard to the west of the Krithia road.

The Turks, however, had long suspected a British attack at this point and were well prepared. When the woefully inadequate British bombardment subsided, they were ready and waiting for the assault. In the furious battle which followed, the leading waves were all but annihilated. A few parties bludgeoned their way into the Turkish trenches only to be slaughtered or compelled to retreat. In the confusion, orders for further attacks were given and then countermanded. Of the 3,000 British engaged, approximately 2,000 had become casualties and the 88th Brigade had almost ceased to exist as a fighting entity. The frontline trenches were clogged with wounded and shocked survivors. It had been a day of unmitigated disaster.

Yet despite the failure of the northern assault and the realization that the Turkish defences had been fatally under-estimated, the attack on the southern portion of the salient was not cancelled. The two-brigade attack, launched at 9.40 a.m. on 7 August, was made on a frontage of 800 yd with the objective of capturing and securing the main Turkish support line, F13–H11b. To reach it, the men of the 42nd East Lancashire Division would have to struggle through a labyrinth of trenches in one of the most intricately fortified sectors of the Turkish lines. It was scarcely a surprise, in view of the events of the preceding day, that the attack was bloodily repulsed at every point, save for the small vineyard on the right of the salient. Here fragments of the 6th and 7th Lancashire Fusiliers clung to their hard-won gains. By midday this pocket of resistance, a salient within a salient, was all the 42nd Division had to show for its endeavours. Military logic dictated a withdrawal from what appeared an untenable position. However, it was held not for reasons of strategic importance but on a point of principle. The Vineyard had become a symbol of stubborn pride.

During the afternoon, the remnants of the Lancashire Fusiliers were bolstered by the arrival of two platoons from A Company, the 9th Manchesters, otherwise known as 'Ashton's Own'. They were led by the same William Forshaw, who ten weeks earlier had so perceptively judged the Turkish powers of resistance. Now his own resolve would be put to the test.

Since arriving on the peninsula, the 9th Manchesters had escaped the worst of the fighting and their losses were correspondingly light. Forshaw had been promoted from quartermaster to the command of A Company, with the temporary rank of captain, shortly before the battle in which the 9th were held in reserve. His second in command was 2nd Lt. C.E. Cooke. For them, and for most of their men, the advance into the Vineyard represented a violent introduction to trench warfare.

Passing over the newly captured ground, they were guided to the north-western corner of the position, at the vital junction of the former Turkish trench, G12. Both sides knew it to be the key to the precarious British incursion. All that separated Briton from Turk at this point were hastily constructed barricades. To hold his post Forshaw had approximately twenty men armed with rifles and a plentiful supply of jam-tin bombs. Forshaw put the number of bombs at around 800 and, in the absence of machine-guns, saw in them his best chance of salvation. He later recalled:

> We decided that we would hold on to the position whatever it cost us, for we knew what it meant to us. If we had lost it the whole of the trench would have fallen into the hands of the enemy. I had half of the men with me, and the other half I placed along the trench with a subaltern [2nd Lt. Cooke].

Three Turkish-held saps converged on Forshaw's post, and it was from these that the Turks hurled themselves in a series of frenzied assaults beginning on the night of 7 August and continuing until the morning of 9 August. The close-quarter fighting was of almost medieval savagery. Seventy years later, Godfrey Clay, a member of Forshaw's force, remembered: 'We hadn't been in above half an hour when the Turks got out over the top and came at us . . . We kept them out . . . How I don't know. Mostly with rifle fire . . . I got a bullet through my hair that day.' Another of the defenders, Sgt. Harry Grantham, who had earned a DCM a month earlier, stated: 'We could see the Turks coming on at us, great big fellows they were, and we dropped our bombs right amidst them.' Forshaw was the life and soul of the defence. Wherever the fighting was most intense he was to be found, hurling bombs and shouting encouragement to his men. According to Sgt. Grantham:

> He fairly revelled in it. He kept joking and cheering us on and was smoking cigarettes all the while. He used his cigarettes to light the fuses of the bombs, instead of striking matches. 'Keep it up, boys', he kept saying. We did, although a lot of our lads were killed and injured by the Turkish fire bombs [sic].

Forshaw later explained: 'I was far too busy to think of myself or even to think of anything. We just went at it without a pause while the Turks were attacking, and in the slack intervals I put more fuses into bombs.'

An artist's impression of Forshaw's VC action

In a brief lull in the fighting on the first night, Forshaw was surprised to see a young Turkish officer peering over the parapet with his hands above his head. 'He seemed perfectly dazed and we took him prisoner', said Forshaw. During the next day, Forshaw's dwindling force beat off further attacks in which Cpl. S. Bayley and L/Cpl. T. Pickford figured prominently. After twenty-four hours of near continuous fighting without sleep or food and water, they were finally relieved by a detachment drawn from other battalions in the Division. As most of his men marched out of the Vineyard, Forshaw, together with Cpl. Bayley, volunteered to remain, and it was during their second night in the position that the Turks mounted their most determined counter-attack. Three times they threw themselves forward. Twice they were halted before reaching the parapet, but on one occasion they burst in. As they clambered over the barricade and dropped into the darkened trench they were met, almost inevitably, by Forshaw. He recalled:

Three of these big, dark-skinned warriors appeared. Immediately one made a move for a corporal who was digging a hole from which to fire during the night. I saw the Turk make for him with his long bayonet and I straight away put a bullet through him from my useful Colt revolver. My weapon was a very fine friend to me during those thrilling minutes. A second Turk came for me with his bayonet fixed, evidently with the object of covering his pal, who was making for the box of our bombs, but I managed to put them both out of action. They never came over the parapet again; but, realising as they did what the position meant, they kept up a fusilade during the whole night.

The crisis had passed, but the relentless pressure of the past two days' action had taken their toll on even Forshaw's powers of resistance. At 9.00 a.m. on 9 August he was relieved by 2nd Lt. Cooke and made his way back to battalion HQ. According to the unit war diary, he was 'quite done up and covered with bomb fumes. He had been hit by a shrapnel case and had been fighting for two days and nights without ceasing.' His courageous and energetic defence of the most exposed post made a deep impact on his comrades. The 9th Manchesters' war diary recorded:

He had shown extraordinary bravery and had by his personal example been the cause of the Vineyard trenches G12 being retained by us . . . The Brigadier-General of the 126th Brigade personally congratulated the commanding officer on the gallant behaviour of Lieut Forshaw, Second Lieut Cooke and the two platoons under them.

For some days after the action, Forshaw was unable to speak; the combination of shouting and smoking cigarettes had left him voiceless. Sick from the stench of bomb fumes and suffering from shock, he was nevertheless incredulous at his survival. 'I cannot imagine how I escaped with only a bruise', he later said. 'It was miraculous.' A few weeks after the battle, he stated:

> It was like a big game. I knew it was risky, of course, but in the excitement one loses all sense of personal danger. You get frightfully excited, and I think it was the excitement that held me up. You see men knocked out, dead and dying, all around you, but it doesn't trouble you in the least, except when you see good men and chums hit you feel determined to have revenge. That was why I volunteered to keep on after being relieved.

That the fighting left psychological scars, however, was clearly evident. Cpl. Bayley, who had fought alongside Forshaw during the two-day battle, wrote to his sister on 16 August:

> Myself and a few men and the captain held a trench which was almost impossible to hold, but we stuck it like glue, in spite of the Turks attacking us with bombs . . . Our captain has been recommended for the VC and I hope he gets it, because he was determined to hold the trench till the last man was finished. But we did not lose many. Our captain has not got over it yet, but it is only his nerves that are shattered a bit . . .

Forshaw was evacuated to Cairo 'suffering from shock', and from there he cabled his parents: 'Not wounded. Nearly fit again.' While convalescing news reached him on 9 September that he had been awarded the Victoria Cross. The citation read:

> For most conspicuous bravery and determination on the Gallipoli Peninsula from 7th to 9th August, 1915.
> When holding the north-west corner of the 'Vineyard' he was attacked and heavily bombed by Turks, who advanced time after time by three trenches which converged at this point; but he held his own, not only directing his men and encouraging them by exposing himself with the utmost disregard to danger, but personally throwing bombs continuously for 41 hours.
> When his detachment was relieved after 24 hours he volunteered to continue the direction of operations.
> Three times during the night of 8th–9th August he was again heavily attacked, and once the Turks got over the barricade, but after shooting three with his revolver he led his men forward, and captured it.
> When he rejoined his battalion he was choked and sickened by bomb fumes, badly bruised by a fragment of shrapnel, and could hardly lift his arm from continuous bomb throwing.

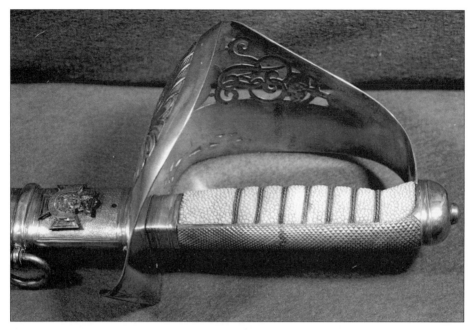

The sword presented to Forshaw. Note the VC representation

It was due to his personal example, magnificent courage and endurance that this very important corner was held.

It was the first VC to go to a member of the 42nd Division and letters of congratulation poured in. As well as Forshaw's award, there were decorations for other members of his gallant company. 2nd Lt. Cooke received a Military Cross and Cpl. Bayley and L/Cpl. Pickford were given DCMs.

Forshaw was invalided home on extended sick leave on 26 September. The following month he was given a hero's welcome. Fêted by press and public as the 'Cigarette VC' on account of the cigarettes he had used to light bomb fuses throughout the Vineyard fighting, he received little peace. His home town of Barrow-in-Furness presented him with a sword of honour at a civic reception, and the proud burghers of Ashton-under-Lyne, home of the 9th Manchesters, made him a Freeman. On 18 October came the biggest ceremony of all, the investiture of his Victoria Cross at Buckingham Palace. Through it all, he bore himself with great dignity, even though he was far from fully recovered. Back home, he confided: 'Shells have affected my eyes to some extent, and my nerves are somewhat out of order. I cannot concentrate my thoughts properly.'

William Thomas Forshaw was born on 20 April 1890, the eldest of two sons to Thomas Forshaw, of Fairfield Lane, Barrow-in-Furness. His father was head foreman at Vickers Shipyard.

Educated at Dalton Road Wesleyan School, Holker Street Boys School and Barrow's Higher Grade School, he left home at eighteen to train as a teacher at Westminster College. After completing the course, he returned home to study for his intermediate exam. He helped pay his way by taking evening classes at his old senior school and Barrow Technical School, where his students included six Turks stationed in the town while a ship was being built for their government.

In the years leading to the outbreak of war, Forshaw taught at the Dallas Road School, Lancaster, and the North Manchester (prep) Grammar School. He was a fine athlete, played football and rugby, and later became an accomplished golfer and tennis player.

His connection with Ashton grew out of a friendship with a fellow teacher. A fine bass singer, he joined the Ashton Operatic Society, and also enlisted in the Ashton Territorial Battalion of the Manchester Regiment. Commissioned second lieutenant in May 1914, Forshaw was promoted lieutenant on the outbreak of war.

The beginning of hostilities interrupted his studies; he had been due to take his final exam in September. Instead, he found himself sailing for Egypt with the 42nd East Lancashire Division, where for the remainder of 1914 and the early part of 1915, the Lancashire Territorials continued their training. Forshaw evidently enjoyed himself during the battalion's spell on the banks of the Suez Canal. At the Divisional sports day he won the 220 yd sprint, and he recorded:

The life there was a holiday for most of the officers and men, but I was acting as quartermaster and had a very busy time trying to get supplies over the canal by means of a hand-worked ferry boat, which averaged an hour and a half per trip. Still, the weather was perfect, and when one could steal an hour off there was some excellent bathing.

Following his services at Gallipoli, Forshaw's promotion to captain was confirmed. A year later, Capt. Forshaw VC married a nurse in Ashton-under-Lyne.

Transferring to the 76th Punjabis, Indian Army in 1917, Forshaw took part in four frontier campaigns before retiring from the Army in November 1922. Teaching jobs, however, were hard to come by, even for a schoolmaster with a VC. Forshaw therefore decided to take a two-year appointment in the RAF Educational Service, in Egypt.

After leaving the RAF, he returned to England in 1925. He settled at Rushmere St Andrew, near Ipswich, and then Martlesham Hall. At each place he started a preparatory school for boys, but bankrupted himself in the process. Compelled to take a teaching job in an Ipswich council school, he drifted from job to job before deciding to pursue a new career.

Joining Gaumont British, Forshaw went on to specialize in the company's Industrial Film Production Department. His interest in film and photography dated back to before the First World War. As a subaltern in Egypt and on the peninsula, he was noted as an enthusiastic photographer, several of his off-duty pictures appearing in the Ashton newspapers. After the war he branched out into writing and produced a number of commercial films.

During the Second World War he was a major in the 11th City of London (Dagenham) Battalion of the Home Guard, later serving as a staff officer. In 1941 he and his wife moved to Holyport, in Berkshire as evacuees. It was there, at his home, Foxearth Cottage, that he died on 26 May 1943. He had apparently suffered a heart attack while cutting a hedge in his garden.

Unusually, for an officer recipient of the Victoria Cross, Forshaw was buried in an unmarked grave at Touchen-End, near Maidenhead. Four decades later an initiative was launched, involving his old regiment, to place a memorial stone on the cemetery wall in honour of the 'Cigarette VC'.

D.R. LAUDER

The Vineyard, Helles sector, 13 August 1915

Pte. D. Lauder

When Capt. William Forshaw stumbled exhausted into the 9th Manchesters HQ on the morning of 9 August, his bomb-throwing arm hanging limp by his side, it appeared as if his epic defence had finally secured the Vineyard. The most hard-pressed battalions of the 42nd Division were relieved and by the end of the day the 126th Brigade, which included Forshaw's battalion, were clearing the newly won ground and improving the defences. Sporadic fighting continued over the next three days, but Turkish efforts appeared half-hearted.

They had not, however, given up. In the late evening of 12 August they began a heavy bombardment of the lightly held forward trenches. As the frontline quaked, the CO of the 9th Manchesters sent his orderly forward to find out the situation. Pte. Reginald Potts succeeded in reaching Capt. Kenshaw at the same moment the Turks launched their infantry assault. Potts recounted:

Captain Kenshaw sent me back with word that the Turks were attacking very strongly through the Vineyard and that reinforcements were wanted urgently. Shells were bursting in all directions, and the stretcher bearers were busy carrying ammunition to the firing line, where the Ashton boys, fighting shoulder to shoulder, were keeping the Turks back.

The Turkish tide, however, eventually swamped the Manchesters, forcing them back from the positions won at such a high cost in Lancashire lives. As night turned to day on 13 August the fighting swayed back and forth across this small, disfigured patch of sun-baked ground. Private Potts, of the 9th Manchesters, recalled:

An order came down the line for bomb throwers to go into the sap that extended from one firing line towards the Turkish trenches . . . I volunteered for the job, and went with Lieutenant Cooke [the same officer who had accompanied Captain Forshaw into the Vineyard on 7 August]. The others in the bomb-throwing place were mostly Burnley lads. I don't know how I stuck it at all. I never dreamed I should come out alive. Lieutenant Cooke did splendidly, and if anyone deserved the Victoria Cross, he did. He kept the bombs going right merrily, and fought like a trump. It was awful to see the other chaps being knocked out, and to think every moment that it was your turn next. We kept it up for 20 hours, until relieved by a Scottish Division.

There was to be no VC for 2nd Lt. Cooke, although he would, as we have seen, later receive a Military Cross for his part in the battle. The second stage of the fight for the Vineyard would, however, be marked by another outstanding act of individual heroism, on this occasion performed by a soldier belonging to the 52nd Lowland Division, who were sent to relieve the Lancastrians. The Scots had suffered heavy losses in the futile frontal assaults of 28 June and 12 July, and were held in reserve for the August offensive. But the increasingly desperate plight of the weary Lancastrian battalions had made necessary their return to action.

By 11.30 a.m. on 13 August the 1/4th Royal Scots Fusiliers, a Territorial unit largely recruited from Ayrshire, had begun replacing the worn-out remnants of the 9th Manchesters. They immediately took over the firing line and posted a small number of men in the support trenches.

An advance party, consisting of bombers from the 1/4th Royal Scots Fusiliers and the 5th King's Own Scottish Borderers, occupied a communication trench running along a ditch on the north-western rim of the Vineyard, not far from the post in which Capt. Forshaw had conducted his gallant defence. The Scots had been sent ahead of the main body to find out the lie of the land, but no sooner had they arrived when they were embroiled in stemming a Turkish thrust along the communication trench from the direction of the G12 line. The trench was still being barricaded to form a bombing block and, in the words of the 52nd Divisional History, 'a furious struggle ensued', in the course of which Lt. William Maxwell, bombing officer of the 5th KOSBs, was killed together with a number of men from both battalions. The Turks, however, were stung by the ferocity of the defence and fell back in disorder. A small bombing party, led by Capt. J. Howard Johnston, of the 1/4th RSF, followed up, driving the fleeing Turks into a cul-de-sac. Speedily bombed out of that position, they were forced to run the gauntlet of machine-gun and rifle fire across the open. Few reached the G12 line. During the respite won by the bombers, the barricade was completed and half of the Vineyard secured.

By late afternoon the battle was almost over. The mixed party of bombers, numbering less than a dozen men, continued to hurl bombs at the Turks in order to prevent any interference with the work on a permanent barricade. One of the bombers was 21-year-old Pte. David Ross Lauder. To amuse himself Lauder, together with his comrades, most of whom were novices in the art of bomb-throwing, kept a tally of the bombs thrown over the lip of the sap. Lauder's own score was into its second hundred when accidental disaster threatened to wreak havoc among the small party. Lauder later recalled:

> I threw a bomb that fell short. I saw it slip down the parapet and roll towards the bombing party. A three second fuse does not allow you very long for thinking. I recognised the fault as mine and the only course that seemed open to me was to minimise the explosion as much as possible. So I put my right foot on it. The explosion was terrific and the concussion was awful. My foot was clean blown away, but, thank goodness, my comrades were saved.

Although grievously injured, Lauder was still conscious when he was carried back to the 1/4th RSF fire trench where he received emergency medical attention. Sgt. E. Stalker, of the 5th KOSBs, one of the bombers who brought him out of the sap, remembered his courage twenty-five years later: 'He sure was a game lad, and I would very much like to congratulate him again. I say "again", because I have often done so in my thoughts, and thanked him for saving some of my men and myself from death or, at least, a severe peppering.' Lauder's self-sacrificial courage was still fresh in the mind of Capt. J. Bruce (1/4th RSF) when he wrote to his family. He described the incident as the pluckiest thing he had seen in Gallipoli. Official recognition, however, was slow in coming.

After initial treatment on the peninsula, Lauder was evacuated to hospital in Malta. Later, when sufficiently recovered, he was transferred to England. Eventually, he was fitted with an artificial leg, just below the right knee. By January 1917 he was able to walk quite freely with only the slightest halt in his stride. Discharged from the Army, he lived with his wife and young child at 674 Gallowgate, Glasgow, and took a job in a munitions factory at Parkhead.

Lauder had received the Serbian Medal for Bravery as a reward for his action, but it was not until 13 January 1917 that the *London Gazette* carried news of his own nation's reward for outstanding valour. The citation for his Victoria Cross stated:

> For most conspicuous bravery when with a bombing party retaking a sap.
> Private Lauder threw a bomb, which failed to clear the parapet and fell amongst the bombing party. There was no time to smother the bomb, and Private Lauder at once put his foot on it, thereby localising the explosion. His foot was blown off, but the remainder of the party through this act of sacrifice escaped unhurt.

Lauder shortly after his VC was announced

In keeping with VC citations from this period, the date and location of the action were withheld. No reason was given, either at the time or subsequently, for the delay in recognizing his undoubted bravery. Later the same year, David Lauder travelled to London to receive his VC from George V at Buckingham Palace. Dressed in civilian clothes, he was stopped by a policeman on duty outside the palace gates. Years later Lauder delighted in recalling their conversation: 'Now then, don't tell me you're a VC', said the incredulous constable, to which Lauder replied by showing him his official invitation from the War Office. 'Who would have thought it', said the policeman. 'A little chap like you; but you must have a big heart, my lad.'

David Ross Lauder, the first member of the Royal Scots Fusiliers to win the VC in the First World War, was born in East Glentire, Airdrie, on 21 January 1894. His early years were spent in Dalry. He worked as a carter in the town and, in his spare time, trained with the local Territorials as a member of the 1/4th Royal Scots Fusiliers. In February 1913 he married Dorina Cavanagh McGuigan, and that same year they celebrated the birth of their first son, Angus.

Shortly after his call-up at the outbreak of war, Lauder's wife left Dalry and settled in Glasgow, near to her sisters.

After a period of training in Britain, the 52nd Division was sent to Gallipoli in the spring of 1915, arriving on the peninsula during the first week of June. The division's passage to Gallipoli had been fraught with difficulty and misfortune. En route to the embarkation port, a troop train carrying members of the division had crashed, killing 210 men and injuring a further 224. The 1/4th Royal Scots Fusiliers escaped another near catastrophe by the narrowest of margins when the SS *Reindeer*, in which they were being transported from Mudros to Helles, collided with the SS *Immingham*. The *Immingham*, which was returning empty, sank immediately, but the *Reindeer*, although badly holed, limped back to Mudros. In the face of this potentially harrowing experience, the Scots had behaved remarkably well. According to the Official Historian, 'the troops upheld the best traditions of the Service and no loss of life was incurred'.

The 1/4th Royal Scots Fusiliers were not involved in the division's first major operation, the ill-fated action of 28 June. But they were given a fearful mauling in the operations around Achi Baba Nullah on 12 July. In less than an hour on that scorching morning the battalion lost all but one of their officers and nearly half their rank and file were killed or wounded. The charge, in which the Fusiliers carried three lines of Turkish trenches, was said to have made a deep impression on David Lauder, who lost so many of his friends from pre-war days.

After being discharged from the Army, Lauder settled down to civilian life in Glasgow with his growing family. Between 1916 and 1924 the Lauders

Lauder in later life

had four more children, two sons and two daughters. He joined the GPO as a telephone operator, rising to become supervisor at the Pitt Street Exchange.

Lauder divorced his first wife and was remarried in 1925 to Rachel Bates. They had five children, although two were to die in infancy.

Throughout his life, he continued to suffer from the effects of his terrible injury. His daughter, Violet Lauder, told the author: 'He still had pieces of shrapnel in his leg and in one of his hands right until he died.' His war wounds did not, however, prevent Lauder from performing a peacetime act of gallantry in April 1937 when he was a passenger aboard a tramcar which jumped the rails and collided with a bus in Glasgow's Hope Street. Despite being dazed and cut, Lauder helped the more seriously injured out of the wreckage before reporting for work!

When the Second World War broke out, Lauder spent his nights working as a telephone switchboard operator and his days as a part-time air raid warden in Dalmarnock Ward. It is believed he also served for a time in the Home Guard.

He retired from his job with the GPO in 1960, but continued to work part-time as a nightwatchman for a local bakery. 'He was always very active', his daughter Violet recalled. Throughout those years he kept in close contact with his former regiment and fellow holders of the Victoria Cross in Glasgow.

David Ross Lauder died at his home, 39 Corran Street, Cranhill, Glasgow, on 4 June 1972. Four days later, a piper from the Royal Highland Fusiliers, successors to the Royal Scots Fusiliers, played a lament at his funeral. Included among a large turnout were a number of senior army officers, old comrades, friends and relatives. In 1979 David Lauder's medals, including his VC and Serbian Medal for Bravery, were sold for £10,000. They appeared again at auction in 1994, where they fetched £17,000.

The Lauder VC medal group

F.W.O. POTTS

Hill 70 (Scimitar Hill), Sulva Bay, 21–3 August 1915

Tpr. F. Potts

In the early evening of 21 August, as night began to creep across the glowering hills of Suvla, Sir Ian Hamilton turned his back on the pall of confusion enveloping the battlefield. 'By 6.30 p.m.', he wrote, 'it had become too dark to see anything. The dust mingling with the strange mist, and also with the smoke of shrapnel and of the hugest and most awful blazing bush fire formed an impenetrable curtain'. Although he could not have known it, the flames lighting up the darkening sky represented the dying embers of a campaign and a career in which hope had once burned so bright. Amid the choking smoke, the closing act in a tragedy of immense proportions was being played out with grim relentlessness.

The best-laid plans of General de Lisle and his staff had gone hopelessly awry. By nightfall it was over. The greatest battle fought on the peninsula in terms of numbers of men engaged had become the most costly and least successful. Intended as an attempt to capture the W Hills, Scimitar Hill and 112 Metre Hill, objectives which should have been attainable within the first twenty-four hours of the Suvla Bay operations, the battle of 21 August involved three British divisions, the 11th, the veteran 29th and the newly arrived 2nd Mounted Division. The latter consisted of Yeomanry units regarded by some as the cream of the nation's rural volunteers.

The operation had been carefully timed to begin at 3.00 p.m. to take advantage of the setting sun. By that hour it would be at the backs of the advancing British, lighting up the Turkish positions and shining directly in the eyes of the defenders. But a quirk of nature intervened to derail de Lisle's plans. 'Soon after midday', the Official Historian wrote, 'the sun disappeared into banks of unseasonable cloud, and a veil of haze rose up from the Suvla plain to hide the Turkish positions'.

By the time the dismounted Yeomanry arrived on the scene, after a march of parade ground precision across the dry Salt Lake, the haze had thickened to a smog. Assigned the task of exploiting the success of the 29th Division, the inexperienced commanders of the 2nd Mounted Division faced the daunting task of capturing positions they could scarcely see against an enemy already buoyed by their success. The depressing scene was described by the Official Historian: 'The mist was growing thicker, scrub fires were raging, and pillars of smoke were blotting out the view. Streams of wounded were struggling back to cover. The din of battle was deafening; and daylight would only last another hour.'

Despite the confusion, the 2nd (South Midland) Yeomanry Brigade launched its attack on Scimitar Hill shortly after 6.00 p.m. Briefly, it seemed as if their elan combined with their good fortune in approaching the hill up the less heavily defended northern and central slopes would be crowned by success. They stormed the crest, but were beaten back by enfilading fire. In the chaos of the abandonment of the summit, many seriously wounded men were left on the hill; trapped in no man's land by a furious cross-fire and burning scrub.

Among those consigned to what seemed a gruesome death on the slopes of Scimitar Hill was Tpr. Fred Potts, a 22-year-old member of the 1/1st Berkshire Yeomanry which, together with the Bucks Hussars and the Dorset Yeomanry, formed the 2nd Brigade.

The Berkshires had been on the peninsula only three days, and the attack was their first operation. A more testing baptism of fire seems hard to imagine. Led by Maj. E.S. Gooch, the unit had gone into action with 9 officers and 314 men. By nightfall, only 4 officers and 150 men remained. Potts, a member of B Squadron, came through the march across the Salt Lake unscathed to reach the foot of Scimitar Hill, officially styled Hill 70 but more familiarly known to the troops as Burnt Hill. Advancing in short spurts, their presence partially masked by the tall scrub, the Berkshires made good progress at first. Pausing beneath the summit, Potts and his comrades were ordered to 'fix bayonets', and then an officer led them in the final rush, shouting: 'Come on, lads! Give 'em beans!'

In a letter written to his sister from a hospital ship shortly after the battle, Potts recounted his experiences:

We had already captured a Turkish trench, and when the order was given to charge over we went.

About 20 yards from the other side I received a wound in the thigh. It completely knocked me off my feet and I had to lie there. Presently, another of our chaps crawled to where I was. He was shot in the groin. There we lay all that night suffering from thirst, but it was much worse the next day. It seemed [as] though we should go mad for want of a drink.

When the second night came we decided to move if possible. This was no light job, as firing had been going on all round us – one bullet actually grazed my ear. However, we managed it somehow.

Then we were able to get some water from the water bottles of the men who had been killed. Rather a painful job taking it, but one of necessity.

Soon after we moved away the Turks visited the place, and by the terrible screams and groans we judged that they were killing off the poor chaps who still had a spark of life in them. We found a hiding place for the remainder of the night and next day. We dared not show ourselves during the day for fear of snipers, and oh, the thirst! I crawled from one body to another getting water. It was like wine, although it was nearly boiling.

At nightfall we decided that anything was better than to die of thirst, so we endeavoured to crawl to where we could find the British lines.

The other chap could hardly move and after a few yards had to give up, so I laid him on a shovel and dragged him down the hill bit by bit for about three-quarters of a mile.

Before we started I prayed as I have never prayed before for strength, help and guidance. I felt confident we should win through.

On reaching the bottom of the hill we came to a wood. Here I left the other chap to find a way through. I had not gone more than 20 yards when I received the command to halt. By good luck I had struck a British trench.

I soon told my tale, and it was not long before they found stretchers for both of us and took us into their trenches, where we were treated with every kindness.

From here we were conveyed to a Field Ambulance dressing station and had some hot tea. Oh it was grand! We were then put on an ambulance cart and sent to the Welsh casualty clearing station and thence on board this boat.

The man who Potts had saved was Tpr. Arthur Wilfred Andrews, a fellow Reading volunteer from the 1/1st Berkshire Yeomanry. Andrews was badly wounded and in terrible pain. What Potts failed to mention in his letter was that a third wounded man had been killed by their side. Nor did he tell of how during their final descent, Andrews, realizing the strain on his comrade, had urged Potts to leave him and seek safety alone. Only later did Potts recount the full story of the final drama, in an account first published in the *London Magazine* of 1916. In it, Potts related:

Tpr. A. Andrews, centre, the man whose life Potts saved

He [Andrews] sat on the shovel as best he could – he was not fastened to it – with his legs crossed, the wounded leg over the sound one,

An artist's impression of Potts's VC action

and he put his hands back and clasped my wrists as I sat on the ground behind and hauled away at the handle.

Several times he came off, or the shovel fetched away, and I soon saw that it would be impossible to get him away in this fashion.

When we began to move, the Turks opened fire on us; but I hardly cared now about the risk of being shot, and for the first time since I had been wounded I stood up and dragged desperately at the shovel, with Andrews on it. I managed to get over half a dozen yards, then I was forced to lie down and rest. Andrews needed a rest just as badly as I did, for he was utterly shaken and suffered greatly . . .

Potts, his face smeared with blood from his wounded ear and his leg roughly bandaged, presented a remarkable sight to the men of the 6th Royal Inniskilling Fusiliers. Andrews was brought in, and when the full story emerged the officers of the Inniskillings were determined Potts' unselfish courage should be recognized. On 28 August Maj. W.P.B. Fraser wrote:

I have pleasure in bringing to notice an act of conspicuous bravery and devotion by Pte W. Potts [*sic*] of the Berks Yeomanry, Mounted Division, who, though himself severely wounded in the thigh and buttocks in the attack on Hill 70 on the 21st August, 1915, after lying out over 48 hours under the Turkish trenches, succeeded in fixing a shovel to the equipment of his comrade Pte Arthur Andrews of the same Corps, who was severely wounded in the groin, and dragging him back across 600 yards of ground to within a short distance of our line at about 9.30 p.m. on the 23rd inst. Pte Potts remained beside his comrade during the 48 hours, though he could himself have reached our trenches during that period. Witnesses:– Captain R.H. Scott. No. 11290, Sgt W. Brown, No. 12854 L/Cpl E. Crawlec. All 6th R Innis. Fus, 31 Inf Brig.

Maj.-Gen. W.E. Peyton (GOC, 2nd Mounted Division) was in no doubt that Potts' 'exceptionally gallant conduct and devotion' qualified him for the highest award. He wrote: 'I consider that this is a case in which this man should be awarded the Victoria Cross, and strongly recommend that his case be forwarded to GHQ for favourable consideration'.

On 1 October the *London Gazette* announced the award of the VC to No. 1300 Pte. Frederick Potts, although the *Gazette* erroneously christened him Alfred. The citation read:

For most conspicuous bravery and devotion to a wounded comrade in the Gallipoli Peninsula. Although himself severely wounded in the thigh in the attack on Hill 70, on the 21st August, 1915, he remained out over forty-eight hours under the Turkish trenches with a private of his regiment who was severely wounded and unable to move, although he could himself have returned to safety. Finally, he fixed a shovel to the equipment of his wounded comrade, and using this as a sledge, he dragged him back over 600 yards to our line, though fired at by the Turks on the way. He reached our trenches at about 9.30 p.m. on the 23rd August.

Potts with members of his family after the announcement of his VC.

News of the award reached Potts while he was recovering from his wounds at the Orchard Convalescent Hospital in Dartford. At his home in Reading, his sister told a journalist: 'You know Fred will simply hate seeing all this in the papers. I feel awfully sorry for him to go through it all. As for a public demonstration, I am sure he would sooner charge up Hill 70, with all its terrors!'

On 9 October the young hero, fêted as the first Yeoman to win the VC in the war, was discharged from hospital and arrived unexpectedly at his parents' home, 54 Edgehill Street, Reading. It was the signal for the celebrations to begin, and events to mark his award were still going on two months later when he was summoned to Buckingham Palace to receive his Cross from George V.

His selfless gallantry had captured the imagination of the public. 'The hero with the shovel', as the Press dubbed him, was given a great reception by his home town. The mayor of Reading presented him with an illuminated address, offering civic congratulations set in a silver casket decorated with golden shovels. Among the many gifts showered upon him were a desk from the Berkshire Territorial Force Association, a gold watch and chain from his employers at the Pulsometer Engineering Company, a tea service from his workmates, a clock from the University College, Reading, and £25 of War Bonds from a prominent local citizen, who had promised it as a reward to the first Berkshire Yeoman to win the VC.

Frederick William Owen Potts was born on 18 December 1892, the son of Mr and Mrs Thomas Potts. Educated at the Central School and Wokingham Road Higher Elementary School, he was a regular church-goer and later became a member of the St Giles' Branch of the Church of England Men's Society. After leaving school, he spent three years as an evening student at the University College, Reading, studying machine construction, mathematics and mechanics. He worked as a fitter at the Pulsometer Engineering Company in the town, and lived with his parents.

In 1912 Potts, then aged nineteen, joined the Berkshire Yeomanry. The unit was mobilized on 5 August 1914 and spent the first eight months of the war training in Berkshire and Norfolk before embarking for Egypt in April 1915. During August the 2nd Mounted Brigade was ordered to Gallipoli to serve as infantry. On the 14th the 1/1st Berkshire Yeomanry, having been ordered to leave behind their swords, bandoliers and spurs, embarked at Alexandria, aboard the SS *Michegan*. At Mudros the unit transferred to the SS *Hythe* and landed at Suvla on 18 August. Three days later, in the attack on Scimitar Hill, the Berkshires suffered almost 50 per cent casualties.

So severe was Potts' thigh wound that he did not return to active service with his unit. Promoted lance-corporal, he was released from the Army on 'compassionate grounds' before the end of the war.

Potts (back row, fourth from left) before going overseas with members of his squadron of the
Berkshire Yeomanry

On 15 December 1915, six days after receiving his VC and at the height of his
fame, he married Ruth Wellstead, at St Giles' Church, Reading. The couple were
to have two daughters. At first they lived at his parents' home, where Potts
launched his own credit drapery venture. He eventually became a master tailor
and later ran a business from Alpine Street, Reading.

A man of right-wing sentiments, he was adopted as an anti-Socialist candidate
for Katesgrove Ward in the Reading Town Council elections of 1929, but was
defeated by 851 votes.

Throughout his life, Potts retained his links with ex-servicemen's associations.
He was a member of the Royal British Legion, and he attended the VC Garden
Party of 1920 as well as the Remembrance Day parade in London nine years
later in which 300 VC recipients participated.

During the Second World War, Potts, by then a prominent freemason and a
ruri-deaconal representative for St Giles' Church, joined the Home Guard and
was commissioned as a lieutenant.

Much of his work during this period was geared towards the services,
particularly the RAF, and most of his spare time was spent on Home Guard

duties. The twin pressures took their toll and, in 1943, with his health failing, he entered Greenlands Nursing Home. There, on 3 November 1943, Fred Potts VC died.

Three days later, his coffin, draped with the Union Jack, was borne from his house at 4 College Road to St Bartholomew's Church, for a funeral service prior to cremation at Reading crematorium. The escort was provided by members of the Home Guard in which Potts had served, and the service was attended by representatives of the Berkshire Yeomanry, the Special Constabulary and the Aldermaston Lodge of Freemasons. Also among the mourners on that autumn day was Arthur Andrews, the man Potts had risked his own life to save. Andrews, whose wounds sustained on Scimitar Hill kept him in hospital until 1917, out-lived his rescuer by a further thirty-seven years, dying aged eighty-nine in 1980.

Twelve years later, to mark the centenary of Potts' birth, a memorial was unveiled at Brock Barracks, Reading, as a tribute to the only Berkshire Yeoman to win the Victoria Cross.

H.V.H. THROSSELL

Hill 60 (Kaiajik Aghala), 29 August 1915

2nd Lt. H. Throssell

Gen. Sir A. Godley's visit to the 10th Australian Light Horse on the afternoon of 28 August was a short one. As the men sheltered in their bivouac at Damakjelik, the commander of the NZ Brigade, charged with the task of capturing Hill 60, briefed the unit's officers. The 10th, he explained, were to seize a trench on the summit. 'I know you will get it', he said. 'It's the holding that's the difficulty.'

But his tone was rather too jaunty for a man whose repeated efforts to capture the 66-yd rise had already cost the lives of thousands and turned a few acres of scrubland into an open cemetery. 'Is it only one trench you want us to take?' asked one of the assembled officers with a note of thinly disguised sarcasm. 'Only one', came the quiet reply.

The young Light Horseman with the dry sense of humour was 2nd Lt. 'Jim' Throssell. In the coming operation he was to lead the second wave into the captured trench and defend it against the inevitable counter-attacks.

Throssell had been on the peninsula for three weeks. In that time he had already survived one ill-starred operation; the infamous assault on the Nek where, four days after joining his unit, he had led a troop over the top after seeing three waves mown down. Almost half of the 300 men of the 10th, engaged in the battle of 7 August, were killed or wounded. Throssell, after sheltering in dead ground in no man's land, was able to crawl back unharmed. His brother Ric was not so fortunate. He was among the seriously wounded. Since then, sickness and casualties had thinned the 10th's ranks still further. By 28 August, they could only muster 180 men.

Known as Kaiajik Aghala (the Sheepfold of the Little Rock) to the Turks, Hill 60 was little more than a pimple on the broad, flat expanse of the Azmak Dere plain. Its importance lay not only in its commanding view of the parched landscape, but in its location at the junction of the Anzac Corps and the British positions at Suvla. This small rise, bristling with 3-ft-high scrub and an unknown number of Turkish trenches, had been one of the objectives for the ill-fated offensive launched on 21 August. But like the British assault on the neighbouring W Hills, the Anzac efforts at Hill 60 had ended in failure. A second attempt the following day was similarly defeated. But the Anzac commanders refused to give in. Five days later, the New Zealanders succeeded in capturing two trenches, unimaginatively styled Nos 2 and 3 trenches. They were situated on the southern slopes, just below the upper ring of Turkish trenches believed to encircle the crest of the hill. In a confused night action, the 9th Australian Light Horse extended the New Zealanders' gains, only to be ejected by a fierce counter-attack.

By 28 August Anzacs and Turks were sharing the same trenches on the southern rim of the hill, separated only by sandbag barriers. However, despite their proximity, the location of all the Turkish positions was still uncertain. Much of the day was spent strengthening the defences and clearing up. The hill was littered with the corpses of Gurkhas, Australians, Connaught Rangers, New Zealanders and Turks. The bodies were removed wherever possible, but many could not be reached. The grotesque sights and the sickly smell of rotting bodies were among the most hideous features of the close-quarter fighting on Hill 60.

In the late afternoon the officers who would lead the next assault made a reconnaissance of the position. It was approaching dusk when Capt. Phil Fry, the commander of the first wave, and Throssell were guided along a path which crossed a ditch exposed to Turkish fire. Throssell later recalled: 'We just doubled up and ran for our lives, treading on dead and wounded men. It was awful, but we had to find out what was before us'.

The view from Nos 2 and 3 trenches, however, was far from clear, and there were calls for the attack to be postponed. These were turned down for fear of allowing the Turks more time to strengthen their position. Around midnight 180 men of the 10th Light Horse, split into two squadrons, were led across the Azmak Dere and into the forward trenches. On their way up, each second NCO and man was given a sandbag containing ten cast-iron spherical bombs. Every man carried an additional two sandbags in their equipment to ensure there were sufficient to build barriers once the position was captured.

Their objective, a 150-yd stretch of trench, lay about 80 yd across open ground known to be covered by a Turkish machine-gun emplacement. An officer and four men were given the job of silencing this post with bombs ten minutes before the main assault. Then, the first wave would charge across the open, with bomb and bayonet, followed by the second wave, who were bringing with them picks and shovels to consolidate the position.

The plan went like clockwork. The machine-gun was destroyed and Fry's men surged across a moon-lit no man's land and into the trench before the Turks knew what had befallen them. Shortly afterwards, Throssell arrived with the second wave. The operation had lasted but a few minutes, and work began immediately on erecting a barricade near a bend in the captured trench. While his men set about their task, Throssell stood guard. As the Turks began to feel their way forward, he shot down five in rapid succession. The remainder withdrew a safe distance and then resorted to throwing bombs in the general direction of the working party. It was the beginning of one of the fiercest bomb-fights to take place on the peninsula. Throssell's advance party fought it out with the Turks, using not merely their own supply of bombs but a number of longer-fused Turkish ones which landed on the floor of their trench. Prominent among them were Corporals S.H. Ferrier and H.M. McNee, and Troopers F. McMahon and W.J. Henderson. In citing their gallantry, Throssell recorded: 'Whenever a Turkish bomb landed in the trench these men immediately picked it up and threw it out again, frequently succeeding in lobbing it back among the Turks. I saw this act, not once but dozens of times . . .'

At about 1.30 a.m., the Turks succeeded in placing a biscuit tin packed with explosive at the foot of the barricade, wrecking it. Throssell and his party, however, retreated to a second, unfinished barrier about 10 yd back and from there repulsed the first Turkish counter-attack with bombs and rifle fire. A second attack, fifteen minutes later, was also beaten off, but only after some Turks had reached the parapet of the captured trench. During this attack Capt. Fry was killed, and command devolved upon Throssell.

The bombing duel continued until 3.00 a.m., when the Turks rushed the barricades again. Throssell, assisted by Lt. 'Tom' Kidd, known in the 10th as 'Bomb-proof Kidd', led the Australians in defeating the attack. An hour later, the Turks launched their most powerful attack of all. Throssell later recalled:

It was in the very early morning – between 4 o'clock and 4.30 – that our worst trial came. The expected counter-attack came then, and we were hopelessly outnumbered. We had started out with only 160 men [*sic*] and many had fallen, while the Turks seemed to be in unlimited numbers. We who held the section of the trench on the extreme right next to the Turks had to get our men in

An artist's impression of Throssell's VC action

the next section to take down half of their sandbag barricade so that our men in the next section could hop over and give up the section when things got too hot. Twice we had to do this, giving up five yards of trench each time and replacing the sandbag barricade. Early in the counter-attack I got a bullet through the left shoulder. Not until long after did I know that a bullet had gone through my neck; it felt just like a blow. We could see the bayonets above the Turks' trenches just as thick as they could stick.

Then they crawled out of their trenches and came straight at us. In the dim light we could see them against the skyline. I passed the word to our fellows, and when the first of the Turks got within 10 yards we cheered and shouted, and, standing up in the trenches, started firing as fast as we could. There was no thought of cover. We just blazed away until the rifles grew red-hot and the chocks jammed, and then we picked up the rifles the wounded or killed men had left. Twenty yards was about our longest range, and I have no idea how many rounds we fired; I think I must have fired about a couple of hundred, and when we were wondering how long we could stand against such numbers, the Turks turned and fled.

In a few minutes they came at us again, and the same thing was repeated. We had no machine-guns, and had to fire away with our rifles as quickly as we could. After the second repulse they changed their tactics and came at us again from front, rear, and flank as well, getting behind us – between our trench and that occupied by the New Zealanders.

Someone must have said something about retiring, though I did not hear it, and all round there were angry cries of, 'Who said retire?' The hubbub was awful. Every man was determined to stick to the trench, and along with the firing they were yelling and shouting like demons. The noise must have deceived the Turks as to our numbers, for they were all round us within ten yards, and if they had come on we should have been overwhelmed. Just at the critical moment, as it was getting daylight, a machine-gun came across from the New Zealand line, and was quickly placed in position. It settled the Turks' third and final charge – and the trench was ours.

The relentless Turkish pressure had, however, taken a heavy toll of the defenders. Of Throssell's closest allies, Tpr. Frank McMahon was killed and most of the others wounded. Tpr. Tom Renton suffered a serious leg wound and Cpl. McNee had one hand shattered by a bomb blast. Most seriously injured of all was Cpl. Syd Ferrier, who was said to have thrown 500 bombs during the night-long struggle. According to his unit history: 'His arm was blown off by an exploding enemy missile, but he continued hurling his bombs, until, faint and exhausted, he collapsed in the trench . . .' Together with Throssell, he was evacuated from the peninsula but died on board a hospital ship a week later.

Throssell, who had ignored advice to seek medical aid, was eventually ordered out of the captured position at 7.00 a.m. Capt. Horace Robertson later recounted:

> I gave him a cigarette, and ordered him to the dressing station. He took the cigarette, but could do nothing with it. The wounds in his shoulders and arms had stiffened, and his hands could not reach his mouth. He wore no jacket, but had badges on the shoulder straps of his shirt. The shirt was full of holes from pieces of bomb, and one of the 'Australias' was twisted and broken, and had been driven into his shoulder. I put the cigarette in his mouth and lighted it for him. Then he left, but he returned after his wounds were dressed, and I realised that the concussion of bursting bombs had made him light-headed, so I rather roughly ordered him out again, and said he was not to return.

Throssell heaped praise on his gallant comrades for the successful defence. His own diary entry was a model of brevity: 'Fine bayonet charge – Major Scott in command of Regt. Capt Fry killed – suffered about 90 casualties – Regt only mustered 160 bayonets for the charge. Wounded. Left by hospital ship *Devonnah.*' Of his own role, there was nothing. But the CO of the 10th could not ignore such a display of inspirational leadership. In his report to brigade HQ, he wrote: 'This officer fought magnificently and I cannot speak too highly of the splendid work he did encouraging the men and by his personal example keeping their spirits up although badly wounded himself at the time.'

As Throssell departed the scene of his triumph, the Allied commanders hailed the success of the operation. That night, Sir Ian Hamilton noted: 'This evening we were all in good form owing to the news from Anzac. Knoll 60, now ours throughout, commands the Biyuk Anafarta valley with view and fire – a big tactical scoop.' Such celebrations, however, were premature. In reality, the trenches won at such a heavy cost in Australian, New Zealand, British and Gurkha lives were not on the summit of Hill 60 at all, but just beneath it. Beyond them lay another line of Turkish trenches every bit as formidable. In time, the trench Throssell and his men had fought so hard to hold would be christened Ivy Lane and become part of the Allied frontline. But the crest of Hill 60, upon which so many hopes rested, remained in Turkish hands to the bitter end.

Suffering from deafness caused by the exploding bombs, Throssell was evacuated to England where surgeons succeeded in restoring his hearing. In his weakened state, however, he contracted meningitis which very nearly killed him. He was still recovering in Wandsworth Hospital when his brother Ric told him he had been awarded the Victoria Cross. The citation in the *London Gazette* of 15 October 1915 stated:

For most conspicuous bravery and devotion to duty during operations on the Kaiakij Aghda (Hill 60), in the Gallipoli Peninsula, on 29th and 30th August, 1915 [*sic*]. Although severely wounded in several places during a counter-attack, he refused to leave his post or to obtain medical assistance till all danger was passed, when he had his wounds dressed and returned to the firing line until ordered out of action by the medical officer. By his personal courage and example he kept up the spirits of his party, and was largely instrumental in saving the situation at a critical period.

Two months later, Throssell, his head swathed in a woollen scarf, was well enough to attend a Buckingham Palace investiture where he received his Cross from King George V. For their part in the action at Hill 60, Cpl. McNee, Tprs. Henderson and Renton were awarded DCMs.

Hugo Vivian Hope Throssell was born on 27 October 1884 at Northam, Western Australia, the youngest son of thirteen brothers and sisters to George and Annie Throssell. His father was a self-made man. One of three brothers who arrived at the Swan River Settlement from Ireland in 1850, he rose to become the Hon. George Throssell, commissioner for Crown Lands in the Western Australian Government and, briefly, its second premier. A successful landowner and shop owner, he was mayor of Northam for nine years.

Like his brothers, Hugo Throssell, known as 'Jim' in the family, was educated at Prince Alfred College, in Adelaide. There he displayed much greater prowess on the sports field than in the classroom. Later, his headmaster remembered him as a boy with a 'buoyant nature, generous to a fault, always ready to see fair play, especially when the rights of smaller boys were involved'.

Returning to Northam, he took a job in the office of his elder brother Lionel's store and flour mill business. He did not last long there. In late 1909, 'Jim' moved to Ashburton Downs, in the north-western corner of Australia, where he worked as a stockman. A year later, in partnership with his brother Ric, he took over a 1000-acre property at Cowcowing, a gift from their father. They were farming there when war broke out. Selling off their team, the Throssell brothers hid their farm equipment and rode 60 miles to Northam to enlist. It was 29 September 1914, and they were both posted to the 10th Australian Light Horse. On his enlistment papers, 'Jim' stated he had been a sergeant in the Prince Alfred College Cadets and listed six years' service with 18th Light Horse. Promotion followed rapidly. He was made sergeant a week later and commissioned second lieutenant on 3 February 1915.

When his unit embarked for Egypt, 'Jim' Throssell was left behind in command of C Squadron. Two weeks later, he sailed aboard HMAT *Itonus* together with his squadron and fifty men of the 2nd Reinforcements.

The 10th Light Horse took no part in the original landings at Gallipoli, but the unit volunteered to serve as infantry to fill gaps caused by the heavy casualties. To his chagrin, Throssell was left in charge of 150 men and 560 horses. The unit had been on the peninsula for almost three months before Throssell arrived at the head of eighty-one reinforcements on 4 August. They were just in time to take part in the diversionary attack on the Turkish positions at the Nek, 'that fool charge' as he later called it.

After the August fighting, Throssell was evacuated to begin his long struggle against ill health brought on by his wounds. In April 1916 he was invalided to Australia, where he received a 'hero's welcome'. He took part in a number of recruiting drives, before returning to his unit which was then serving in Palestine. He rejoined the 10th Light Horse on 17 March 1917, shortly before the Battle of Gaza.

Throssell (third from left) still recovering from meningitis, attending the VC investiture with W. Symons, F. Tubb, and J. Hamilton, December 1915

During the fighting, Throssell was badly wounded in the thigh and foot. His brother Ric was killed and Throssell spent the night scouring the battlefield in vain for his body. The loss of his brother left deep psychological scars. His son later wrote:

The war became a savage reality where even victory was a tragedy, the price of which was pain and death. The strange joy of battle that sustained him at the Nek and Hill 60 and inspired the men who fought with him died after the Gaza action. There were no more 'great charges' in his diary: no inspiring anecdotes.

After recovering from his wounds in Egypt, Throssell went back to his unit. Promoted captain shortly afterwards, he commanded the guard of honour from the 10th Light Horse at the triumphant parade through Jerusalem in December 1917. His war, however, was almost over. The following year his health, undermined by wounds, climate and sickness, failed again. After a spell with a training unit, he returned to Australia. He left the Army on 13 February 1919. A fortnight earlier, on 28 January, at the Collins Street Registry Office, in Melbourne, 'Jim' Throssell had married the Australian writer Katharine Susannah Prichard. The couple had met in England while he was recovering from his wounds sustained at Gallipoli. They had one son, named Ric after his brother, who later served as Director of the Commonwealth Foundation.

The Throssells settled on a small farm at Greenmount, near Perth, and soon became embroiled in controversy. Throssell joined his wife, a founder member of the Australian Communist Party, in supporting striking workers and the unemployed. In July 1919 he rode at the head of a victory parade through the streets of his home town of Northam. Addressing the crowds, the hero of the Light Horse described how 'war had made him a Socialist'. It was greeted in silence.

Appointed a member of the Soldier Settlers' Board, he also worked briefly in the Department of Agriculture in Western Australia. During the 1920s he moved into real estate but as the decade wore on his money-making ventures ran into trouble. The slump, coupled with an unsuccessful attempt to wipe out his debts, brought him to the brink of financial ruin. Believing that he could better clear his debts and provide for his family by securing for them a war service pension, Throssell committed suicide by shooting himself as he sat on the verandah of his Lazy Hit Ranch. It was 19 November 1933 and he was forty-nine years old.

In his last will and testament, he wrote: 'I have never recovered from my 1914–18 experiences. . . .' It was officially recorded that he had 'died by a bullet wound in the head self-inflicted while his mind was deranged due to war wounds'.

'Jim' Throssell, the only Light Horseman to win the VC in the First World War, was buried in Karrakatta cemetery, Perth, with full military honours.

Today two streets, one in Greenmount and the other in Melbourne, bear his name. He is also commemorated on a plaque in Greenmount, where he settled after the war. The Victoria Cross, which he had considered pawning to ease his financial difficulties, was donated to the People for Nuclear Disarmament by his son in 1984. Later his medals were purchased by the Returned Services League of Australia and presented to the Australian War Memorial, Canberra.

R. BELL DAVIES

Near Ferejik Junction, Bulgaria, 19 November 1915

*Sqdn. Cdr. R. Bell Davies, RNAS
Eastchurch, 1912–13*

The role of air power in the Dardanelles Campaign was restricted to the margins of naval and land-based operatives, making it little more than a sideshow within a sideshow.

British involvement in aerial operations centred on the motley collection of aircraft which were officially designated No. 3 Squadron, Royal Naval Air Service, under the command of the enigmatic Sqn. Cdr. Charles Samson DSO. Samson was already a popular hero, having won acclaim as the leader of an intrepid band of airmen during the battle for Belgium in the first weeks of the war. An independently minded leader, he proved a great innovator, operating armoured cars against the German invaders. His new command consisted of twenty-two aircraft, of various types, only five of which were considered of any practical use. The squadron's primary role was to carry out aerial reconnaissance and artillery spotting. But the adventurous Samson was always seeking out opportunities of carrying the war to the Turks. Apart from occasional brushes with the small force of German and Turkish aircraft, Samson's pilots flew numerous bombing sorties. On one occasion, Samson bombed a motor car said to be carrying Kemal Pasha, narrowly missing him, and in another sortie, his second in command, Sqn. Cdr. Richard Bell Davies DSO, was credited with a direct hit on an aircraft hangar at the German airfield near Chanak.

Sqn. Cdr. Davies' involvement in the Dardanelles Campaign began before the landings when he undertook a number of reconnaissance missions over Cape Helles. On the morning of 25 April he acted as aerial spotter for HMS *Prince George*, which was supporting the French landings at Kum Kale.

By July, the squadron had assembled at Imbros, near to Sir Ian Hamilton's HQ. Attention was then focussed on the impending operations at Suvla Bay. With Samson having gone away on leave, Davies was in temporary command. It was a difficult and stressful period with huge demands being made on the small force of airmen. Davies, however, came through the test remarkably well. Samson wrote of him: 'He had nearly done as much as I; but he looked and was unchanged. He only

No. 3 Wing en route to Gallipoli. Bell Davies is in the front row, second from right.

weighed about nine stone, and looked as if a puff of wind would blow him over. Looks deceived, though; it would take a 100 lb bomb to knock him out'.

The squadron's strength was boosted by the arrival of some Nieuport Scouts, of which Samson and Davies each claimed one. In October, while flying his Nieuport on a bombing sortie against Turkish transports, Davies narrowly escaped death when his engine cut out, forcing him to come down in the sea 5 miles off Imbros. A trawler came to his rescue and, having taken him on board, began towing the semi-submerged biplane towards shore. After ten minutes, however, the aircraft sank, prompting the trawler skipper to remark to Davies: 'Bain't nobody else in the machine, Mister, be there?'

Bulgaria's entry into the war widened the conflict and presented No. 3 Squadron with fresh targets. Samson won approval for bombing attacks designed to disrupt communications between Turkey and her new ally. Their first mission was against a railway bridge spanning the River Maritza near the Bulgarian border. The target, which provided one of the main links between Bulgaria and Constantinople, lay 200 miles across the Gulf of Saros, on the Thrace mainland, near Adrianople. Sqn. Cdr. Samson struck the first blow. On 8 November he dropped two 100 lb bombs from a specially converted Maurice Farman which shook the bridge's supports so badly that it was out of action for four days. Two days later, Davies repeated the operation, piloting the same machine, complete with an additional fuel tank. The four-hour-long mission was not without incident. In his flying log, Davies recorded:

> Followed road to Burges bridge, passed through rain then clear. Considerable transport on roads . . . Dropped two 100 lb bombs at bridge. Both just missed right. Ht 2,000 feet. Machine hit by rifle fire in wings. Returning throttle wire broke when off Gallipoli. Had to land on switch.

Bad weather so delayed Davies' return that Samson had given him up for lost. He was in the process of writing to his next-of-kin when the Maurice Farman arrived back at Imbros. On inspection it was found that four bullets had struck the aircraft near to the nascelle. Davies' bombs had fallen on the railway line at Uzun Kepri station, close to the bridge. Over the next few days Samson maintained the pressure with a series of sorties against the bridge and Army camps dotted along their flightpath. Then, on 13 November, he switched his attentions towards the Bulgarian side of the border.

In what was almost certainly the first British air attack launched against their new enemy, squadron commanders Samson and Davies, both flying Nieuports, raided Ferejik Junction, a rail station just inside Bulgarian territory near the Maritza River. Davies was the first to attack. His log noted: 'Dropped 3 20 lb bombs at Stn at Ferejik straddled line. Heavy clouds and rain.' Samson, who arrived just as Davies completed his attack, saw one bomb hit the railway track outside the station. Both aircraft came under heavy rifle and machine-gun fire but escaped unscathed. The return flight, however, proved uncomfortable as they ploughed through a heavy rainstorm. The Maritza Bridge defences having been considerably strengthened, Samson continued his attacks on Ferejik Junction. Two more raids were carried out over the next five days, and they culminated in the squadron's biggest operation, in which all five available aircraft were to be employed against the Bulgarian railhead.

The squadron's three previous visits had already torn up track and ripped the roof off of one of the station buildings. But for the next attack each aircraft was to have a specific target. At supper on the eve of the raid, Samson passed round his order book. He would lead the mission in his Nieuport, with Davies in the other Nieuport, Flt. Sub-Lt. Gilbert Smylie, a 6-ft-tall, newly arrived pilot, and Flt. Lt. Barnato, piloting two Henri Farmans, and Flt. Lt. Heriot and his observer Capt. Edwards in the Maurice Farman. Davies, who had not flown since the first attack on Ferejik, was less than pleased with his CO. He later recalled:

> I was deeply engaged with the operation of building winter quarters and was rather annoyed to find he had put me down to fly one of the Nieuports, carrying

20 lb bombs, to Ferrijik [sic] Junction. I did not think those little bombs could do much harm, and I wanted to press on with supervising the building work.

Whether he voiced his disapproval is not clear. If he did it was to no avail. Shortly after 10.00 a.m. on 19 November Davies took off in a Nieuport 12, No. 3172, a two-seater converted to a single seat by the simple expedient of covering the second cockpit. Slung beneath the fuselage were six of the 20 lb Hales bombs which he considered almost useless.

The flight out was uneventful. Arriving over Ferejik in company with Samson and Smylie, Davies carried out his attack and was turning for home when he spotted Smylie's Henri Farman on the ground. In making his low-level bomb run, Smylie had been caught by heavy ground fire. With his engine stopped, he glided to a safe landing in one of the dry watercourses which cut through the Maritza marshes, within a mile of the railway station. Smylie clambered out of the aircraft unharmed and immediately saw a party of Bulgarians making towards him. Preferring the prospect of a Turkish prison camp to a Bulgarian one, he set fire to his aircraft and headed across the marshes towards Turkish territory. He had not ventured far, however, when, much to his surprise, he saw one of the squadron's Nieuports descending. It was Davies. Having circled low over the marshes in search of a possible landing site, he decided to set his aircraft down in one of the dry watercourses and pick up Smylie. It was a manoeuvre fraught with danger. Aside from the proximity of the Bulgarians, the ground, baked firm by the sun, was extremely rough and the high landing speed of the Nieuport meant there was a risk of the aircraft crashing. As an experienced aviator, Davies would have been well aware of the hazards but he chose to ignore them. Many years later, he modestly wrote:

It never occurred to me that we were likely to be interfered with by enemy troops. The marshes were wide and rough with tall banks of reeds and scrub. What did worry me was the possibility of finding two men to rescue, for I knew that some of our military observers had been detailed to take part in the operation as bomb aimer [in fact, Capt. Edwards was the only one] . . . I could only carry one passenger . . .

As I circled down I could see the Farman burning. I flew low round it looking for Smylie and received an almighty shock when the plane suddenly blew up. I had no idea there was a bomb still on board and, in case there were any more, I hastily climbed away. Then I saw Smylie emerge from a little hollow in which he had been lying and wave.

Having realized that the Nieuport was preparing to land close to his burning aircraft, Smylie had deliberately exploded a bomb still slung beneath his Farman

An artist's impression of Davies' VC action

in order to prevent it detonating as his would-be rescuer touched down. Going as close to the aircraft as he dare, Smylie fired at the bomb's fuse with his revolver and succeeded in hitting it at the third attempt.

Shortly afterwards, Davies made a safe, if bumpy, landing close to the downed pilot. While he took care to keep his engine running, Smylie turned the Nieuport by its wing-tip. Then, with Smylie steadying the aircraft, Davies taxied back across the river bed to allow himself the best possible take-off run. Smylie then had to climb in, which was no easy matter. An engine cowl covered the space where the passenger seat had been. Davies recorded: 'He had to climb over me, slide under the cowl and crouch on all fours between the rudder bar and the engine bearers with his head bumping on the oil tank. He managed somehow to stow himself away looking most uncomfortable.'

All this time, the Bulgarians were closing in on their quarry. A hail of fire was directed at the Nieuport as it sped across the dry river course. Davies, however, controlled his take-off to perfection. Forty-five minutes later, at 12.20 p.m., Davies touched down at Imbros, complete with his unscheduled passenger. Long overdue, Davies had been given up for lost and Samson later admitted to having retired to his office 'feeling more depressed than I have felt for years'. The emergence of Smylie was greeted with astonishment by the squadron's aircrew. But Davies, in Samson's words, was 'absolutely unperturbed'. Davies' entry in his flying log was a model of understatement:

> Dropped 3 20 lb bombs at Stn at Ferejik. Comdr and Smylie in compy. One bomb burst on line. Returning saw Smylie's machine burning in marshes. Landed and picked him up. Ground firm and fairly level. Kept engine. He got under cowl. Returned, machine climbing well. Time 10.5–12.20.

Samson was struck by the gallantry of both rescuer and the man he rescued. He noted how Smylie, having risked his life to detonate the bomb hung up under his own aircraft, had taken off his flying coat and coolly scribbled a message, which he left for the Bulgarians, stating: 'Please return my coat, which I have had to leave, to No. 3 Wing.'

Both Davies and Smylie were recommended for the Victoria Cross. Samson also put Davies' name forward for early promotion. Smylie's award was down-graded to a Distinguished Service Cross. But there could be no question of Davies' selfless courage and outstanding skill, and on New Year's Day in 1916 the *London Gazette* duly announced the award of a VC to Sqn. Cdr. Richard Bell Davies DSO. The citation accompanying both Davies' VC and Smylie's DSC stated:

> On the 19th November, these two officers carried out an air attack on Ferrijik Junction [*sic*]. Flight-Lieutenant Smylie's machine was received by very heavy

fire and brought down. The pilot planed down over the Station, releasing all his bombs except one, which failed to drop, simultaneously at the station from a very low altitude. Thence he continued his descent into the marsh.

On alighting he saw the one unexploded bomb, and set fire to his machine, knowing that the bomb would ensure its destruction. He then proceeded towards Turkish territory.

At this moment he perceived Squadron-Commander Davies descending and fearing that he would come down near the burning machine and thus risk destruction from the bomb, Flight Sub-Lieutenant Smylie ran back and from a short distance exploded the bomb by means of a pistol bullet. Squadron-Commander Davies descended at a safe distance from the burning machine, took up Sub-Lieutenant Smylie, in spite of the near approach of a party of the enemy, and returned to the aerodrome, a feat of airmanship that can seldom have been equalled for skill and gallantry.

Davies arrived back in England shortly after the announcement of his VC, following the British abandonment of the peninsula. Promoted wing commander, he went on leave before taking up his new appointment as district commander of RNAS stations in northern England. Three months later, on 15 April, he went to Buckingham Palace to receive his Cross from George V.

Richard Bell Davies, one of the pioneers of naval aviation, was born on 19 May 1886, at 3 Topstone Road, Kensington, the son of William Bell Davies and his wife Mary Emma (née Beale). Both his father, a successful civil engineer, and his mother died before he was six years old. The young orphan was brought up by his mother's brother, Dr Edwin Beale, a throat and chest specialist at the Victoria Park and Great Northern hospitals.

Educated at Bradfield College, Davies enlisted in the Royal Navy on 20 April 1901 as a cadet on HMS *Britannia*, Dartmouth. It was the sight of aerial pioneer Claude Grahame-White's flight at the fleet's summer manoeuvres of 1910 that helped shape the rest of his life. That autumn he accepted an offer of flying lessons to naval officers. But by the time he arrived, the privately owned aircraft had been taken over by the Admiralty. Fearing he would not be selected for training, Davies undertook a course of private instruction. Under the tutelage of Grahame-White, he qualified during his Easter leave. His flying certificate was British Empire No. 90.

Davies had to wait until 1913 to fulfil his ambition of joining the Navy's fledgling air service. It was while at the Naval Flying School at Eastchurch that he first came into contact with Acting Cdr. Samson, then the base commander. Davies swiftly made an impression and his rapid progress was marked by his appointment as first lieutenant at Eastchurch shortly after qualifying as a 'flying officer'. By the close of 1913 Davies was a squadron commander in the Royal Flying Corps, Naval Wing. Following a brief spell in Somaliland, where he reported on the viability of using aircraft to quell the 'Mad Mullah', Davies returned to Eastchurch, arriving shortly before the outbreak of war.

Davies became a member of Samson's mobile squadron, later officially styled No. 3 Squadron, RNAS. The unit flew out to Ostend at the end of August and there followed a nomadic existence during which their exploits made Samson one of the war's first heroes. Forced by the speed of the German advance to repeatedly move their landing fields, the squadron's pilots carried out a variety of missions, from reconnaissances to attacks on military installations. Davies was fully engaged in these operations. On 20 December he carried out a solo bombing raid against a suspected airship shed at Brussels. A month later, together with Flt. Lt. R.E.C. Peirse, he took part in a gallant sortie against the German submarine base at Zeebrugge, which resulted in both pilots being admitted to the Distinguished Service Order. Their joint citation stated:

These officers have repeatedly attacked the German submarine stations at Ostend and Zeebrugge, being subjected on each occasion to heavy and accurate fire, their machines being frequently hit. In particular, on 23rd January, they each discharged eight bombs in an attack upon submarines alongside the Mole at Zeebrugge, flying down to close range. At the outset of this fight, Lieutenant Davies was severely wounded by a bullet in the thigh, but nevertheless he accomplished his task, handling his machine for an hour with great skill in spite of pain and loss of blood.

By the time the awards were gazetted, on 10 April, Davies was fully recovered and stationed on the island of Tenedos in preparation for the operations at Gallipoli. Following the failure of the campaign, Davies was appointed, in early 1916, to the reformed 3 Wing, RNAS. From its base in France, the unit, which was to form the nucleus of Britain's first strategic bombing force, launched a series of raids against German industrial targets. As the wing's chief of flying operations, Davies directed and flew on a number of these missions.

Promoted senior flying officer of the Grand Fleet the following year, he took command of air operations from the seaplane carrier HMS *Campania*. Davies was heavily involved in the development of the Navy's first aircraft carriers and in July 1918 he helped plan the audacious raid by seaborne Sopwith Camels on the airship sheds at Tondern. In recognition of his involvement in the development of the early aircraft carriers, which included carrying out a number of dangerous, experimental flights, Davies was awarded an Air Force Cross. His

Cdr. R. Bell Davies, head of Naval Air Section, 1920–4

war services were further recognized by the French, who made him a Chevalier of the Legion of Honour and awarded him the Croix de Guerre avec Palme.

Davies was appointed lieutenant colonel in the Royal Air Force on the formation of the new service in April 1918. But in May 1919 he returned to the Navy. Promoted commander, he was head of the Naval Air Section from August 1920 to February 1924.

On 29 September 1920 he married Mary Montgomery, only daughter of Maj.-Gen. Sir Kerr Montgomery KCMG, CB, DSO. They had one daughter, and a son who followed him into the Navy.

After his four-year term in command of the Naval Air Section, Davies returned to general service as executive officer of HMS *Royal Sovereign*. For the next thirteen years he balanced air service with sea-going commands, rising to the rank of flag captain and chief staff officer to the rear-admiral commanding the First Cruiser Squadron. He was promoted commodore of the RN Barracks, Devonport, before becoming the first rear-admiral, Naval Air Stations in 1937.

Davies retired in 1941 with the rank of vice-admiral, but shortly afterwards returned to active service as a convoy commodore. Given command of HMS *Dasher*, an escort carrier under construction, Davies was recalled to the Admiralty before the vessel became operational. In 1943, however, Davies was given a new command; the *Pretoria Castle*, a Union Castle liner which was in the process of being converted to an aircraft carrier. After the work was completed, the ship was used for aircraft landing experiments and, much to Davies' disappointment, her only active employment was as a convoy escort between Scapa Flow and Iceland. In 1944 Davies retired for the second and last time. His final honour was to be appointed a Companion of the Bath. His last twenty years were spent in peaceful retirement. Shortly before his death in Haslar Naval Hospital, on 26 February 1966, he completed his memoirs, which were posthumously published as *Sailor in the Air*. His account, reflecting his genuine modesty, made no mention of his Victoria Cross award.

In a remarkable career, Richard Bell Davies played a leading and influential role in the development of the naval air arm from its pioneering days at Eastchurch through to its dominant status in maritime strategy. Yet it might be said that his finest epitaph came from the pen of his former chief and friend, Charles Samson. Writing of Davies in 1930, he declared:

> He was a splendid fellow . . . No one could have had a more loyal second-in-command than I had, and to a large extent the happiness of the Squadron was due to his tact and popularity, a man without any conceit or selfishness, a brilliant pilot, and a doughty man of war if ever there was one.

A.V. SMITH

Fusilier Bluff, Helles sector, 23 December 1915

2nd Lt. A.V. Smith

In the days leading up to Christmas 1915 Allied morale on the peninsula was at its lowest ebb. Celebration at the successful evacuations of the garrisons at Suvla Bay and Anzac Cove had given way to disillusionment. No amount of praise for the withdrawal of men and material from beneath the very noses of the Turks could disguise the abject failure of the operations at Gallipoli. To the weary troops occupying the Helles sector, the Allies' last remaining toehold, the future appeared bleak. Worn down by the appalling climate and unsettling rumours of an imminent withdrawal, they faced the wretched prospect of facing an enemy greatly reinforced and with its morale significantly raised by the Allies' admission of defeat in the northern sectors.

To counteract the obvious Turkish advantages, Lt. Gen. Sir F.J. Davies (GOC, VIII Corps) ordered his divisional commanders to maintain an active and aggressive defence. The Turks were to be driven out of their positions by trench mortars, catapults and grenades, and the British line pushed forward by sapping, mining and by the capture of key points. It was with this purpose in mind, and amid an atmosphere of uncertainty about the fate of the Helles garrison, that 2nd Lt. Victor Smith led a bombing party from the 1/5th East Lancashires into an advanced post at Fusilier Bluff, in the northernmost corner of the British lines, on 22 December.

The previous fortnight had been a busy one for the 24-year-old East Lancashire territorial officer. While politicians and generals argued over how best to extricate the troops from what they perceived to be the Gallipolian quagmire, Smith, a pre-war Blackpool police inspector, was doing his best to carry out his Corps commander's orders.

On the night of 10–11 December he carried out a solo patrol in front of his battalion's positions on Fusilier Bluff. What he later described as 'a little reconnaissance I carried out on my own over the top one night', involved crawling across the pitted ground separating the opposing lines and creeping along the Turkish parapet, taking care to duck beneath the numerous snipers' loopholes. Returning safely, he brought with him valuable information about the Turkish defences. The mission resulted in an official commendation from Maj.-Gen. W. Douglas (GOC, 42nd East Lancashire Division), who praised him for his 'gallant action'.

Smith barely had time to send the general's congratulatory card to his parents before his unit was engaged again. With the evacuation of the Anzac and Suvla Bay garrisons nearing its miraculous conclusion, the 1/5th East Lancashires were ordered to carry out one of a number of small-scale attacks along the Helles front, with the intention of diverting Turkish attention away from events in the north. In the early afternoon of 19 December, mines were exploded opposite Fusilier Bluff. Parties of the 9th and 10th Manchesters, supported by bombers from the 1/5th East Lancashires and the West Lancashire RE Company, immediately rushed across the open. Some of the men reached to within a few feet of the Turkish positions, but finding that no crater had been formed they were forced to withdraw. Reports of the operation make no mention of 2nd Lt.

Smith, but as brigade bombing officer, a post he had held since October, it is highly probable he was involved. Sgt. Ingham Ridehalgh, his bombing sergeant during the campaign, later testified to his officer's courageous and forceful leadership. He was, said Ridehalgh, always to the front, always the first to start bombing. In short, he asserted Smith to be the bravest man he had seen on the peninsula.

Three days after the unsuccessful assault, Smith prepared for another bombing 'stunt' at the bluff. He fondly imagined it would be his last spell in the line before his unit was relieved. In a letter to his parents in which he reassured them about his health, he wrote: 'All being well on Christmas Day we shall not be in the trenches.' His task on 22 December was to make life as uncomfortable as possible for the Turkish troops opposite the Lancastrians' position by showering them with bombs. It was, by any

2nd Lt. A.V. Smith (right) in the trenches at Gallipoli

standards, a routine operation, though not without its own hazards. Smith, however, was well versed in such missions. On one occasion his bombers were said to have thrown upwards of 700 bombs in a single night in an attempt to destroy Turkish fire screens and so-called 'bird-cages', wire mesh covers designed to protect troops against grenades and raiding parties. As was customary, the bombing was to be carried out at night, presumably to incur maximum psychological damage as well as physical destruction.

It had been a quiet day at Fusilier Bluff on 22 December. Although the weather was cold, the rain which had been making life in the trenches so uncomfortable for friend and foe alike had abated. The recent downpours, however, had left the trenches muddy and slippery, a factor which would play a profound part in the subsequent action. Smith's party, including one other officer, were in position before midnight. It would appear that the Turks were the first to start bombing, although it is unclear whether the Lancastrian bombers were sent in as a retaliatory measure or that their mission had been simply pre-empted. Precise details of the bombing operation are not recorded. It is not known how many grenades were thrown, nor is the duration of the bomb fight recorded anywhere. Smith, as usual, was leading by example. Countless bombs were hurled, almost in the manner of a training exercise. But then tragedy struck. As he prepared to throw a bomb over the parapet, Smith slipped and fell and in that moment the bomb rolled from his hand on to the floor of the trench. As an experienced bombing officer, he knew he had less than five seconds to react. Shouting a warning in the darkened bay, he instinctively made to run towards the cover of a nearby traverse. But as he did so, he noticed that some men had been unable to reach safety. In that moment, he made up his mind. He turned and threw himself on the bomb moments before it exploded, killing him instantly.

According to the terse entry in the war diary of the 1/5th East Lancashires, Smith's act of supreme self-sacrifice occurred at 12.30 a.m. on 23 December. At 4.00 p.m. that same day, he was buried at the head of Y Ravine in what the battalion chaplain described as a 'beautiful soldiers' cemetery near the summit of the more southerly hillside that bounds the ravine known as Y ravine, which slopes downwards to Y Beach and the Aegean Sea'. On the cross above his grave was the simple inscription: 'He gave his life to save others'.

From beginning to tragic end, Smith's act of gallantry had lasted but a few seconds. Yet the indelible impression it made on those who had witnessed it and, as news spread, the whole Allied garrison was both deep and heartfelt. It was as if the desperate courage of this young officer, so near the end of the fighting, had come to symbolize the sacrifice shown by countless others throughout the doomed campaign. References to his action featured repeatedly in soldiers' letters home. Most of them had only heard tell of the incident. Company Sgt. Maj. A.

Green, of the 9th Manchesters, was one of the few able to write from personal experience. To his wife, he wrote:

> If you said your prayers for me . . . they were answered, for on the night of the 22nd I was on duty in the trench ten yards away from the Turks who were bombing us awful. When I arrived at 12 o'clock two officers had come to throw bombs back at the Turks. There would be 15 or 16 of us in the trench, when a bomb fell from one of the officer's hands. I stood directly behind them, and one of them, whose name was Lieut Smith . . . saw that we could not all get away, and he threw himself deliberately on the bomb to save us either from death or at least being crippled for life. He was killed instantly and only two others were slightly wounded. He gave his life for us. I have had some narrow squeaks, but none worse than that, as it would have cleared out the lot of us.

There were many others to testify to 2nd Lt. Smith's last act. Writing to Smith's parents, Lt. Col. W.M. Acton (CO, 1/5th East Lancashires) declared: 'It is a short story, but the military history of any nation can tell of no finer deed, and to lose him in this way must leave his parents the proudest in the universe.' Another fellow officer wrote: 'He died to save the lives of others – the bravest most magnificent sacrifice I have ever heard of. . . .' He went on to explain: 'A fatigue party was coming along, and to save them Victor threw his body on the bomb and was riddled by the explosion. If he doesn't get the VC, then no one should have it.'

It was a sentiment shared by everyone, from humble private to exalted general. Brig. Gen. A.W. Tufnell, who had taken command of the 126th Brigade a fortnight after Smith's death, attempted to rationalize the action. Writing to Smith's parents, he said:

> Possibly, he may have thought that he could still extinguish it; possibly he had no time to consider whether there was such a possibility; more likely he deliberately forfeited his life to save others from death and injury. Whatever his thoughts and decision may have been, his act was one of bravery such as I personally have never heard surpassed . . . His name has gone forward with strong recommendation for the award of the Victoria Cross.

Reports of the official moves to honour the young officer appeared in the Press in his parents' home town of Burnley, where his father was chief constable. Tributes from soldiers and civilians alike poured in. The homage was led by the king himself. A letter from the Keeper of the Privy Purse stated:

> His Majesty has read with feelings of admiration the record of Lieutenant Smith's noble conduct and splendid self-sacrifice, and cannot but feel the

Smith's grave at Gallipoli

manifestations of admiration on the part of all classes of the community will in some degree lighten your burden and prove a lasting solace in years to come.

With the benefit of hindsight, it is impossible to escape the conclusion that the posthumous award of the Victoria Cross to 2nd Lt. Smith was anything other than a foregone conclusion. The citation stated:

For most conspicuous bravery. He was in the act of throwing a grenade when it slipped from his hand and fell to the bottom of the trench, close to several of our officers and men. He immediately shouted a warning, and himself jumped clear into safety; but, seeing that the officers and men were unable to get into cover, and knowing well that the grenade was due to explode, he returned without hesitation and flung himself on it. He was instantly killed by the explosion. His magnificent act of self-sacrifice undoubtedly saved many lives.

Four days later, Gen. V. d'Urbal (GOC, Xth French Army Corps) broke with convention and published a general order to his troops citing 2nd Lt. Smith's gallant action. It concluded: 'The General commanding the Xth Army considers this act of sacrifice performed by one of our brave Allies is well worthy of being brought to the notice of all'.

Alfred Victor Smith was born in Guildford, Surrey, on 22 July 1891, the only son of William Henry Smith and Louisa, née Green. His father had served seven years in the 11th Hussars, taking part in the Gordon Relief Expedition of 1884–5, before joining the Police Force, in which he rose to the rank of chief constable of St Albans, in Hertfordshire. Victor Smith (his first christian name appears to have been rarely used) was educated at Hatfield Road School, St Albans. He possessed a fine singing voice and was a chorister and tenor soloist at St Albans Cathedral before the family moved to Burnley, Lancashire in 1905, on his father's appointment as chief constable of the northern town. Continuing his education at Burnley Grammar School, Victor became a Sunday School worker. He left school aged eighteen and spent eighteen months working at the town's new Labour Bureau before deciding to join the police.

Victor Smith became a member of the Blackpool force, whose chief constable was a friend of his father. Promotion quickly followed. From acting-inspector, he became an inspector, working in the weights and measures department. Miss Winifred Pringle, daughter of Blackpool's chief constable, recalled: 'Victor was a fresh-faced, good-living young man. He was a kindly chap and so full of fun, and popular with the men.' She remembered him working in the weights and measures office:

> I can see him now with his sleeves rolled up and laughing. He used to ladle out molten lead and splash it onto the stone-flagged floor and it made funny shapes. He did it to amuse me and the other children. My father said that Victor was very bright and would certainly have had a fine police career.

His noted singing voice made him a popular performer in local operatic societies and concerts. He was also a keen swimmer and gymnast and, with other policemen, a member of the seaside resort's fire brigade and life-saving squad. During a royal visit to Blackpool, the young police inspector, noted for his 'exceptional smartness and ability', served as his chief constable's orderly. His future success seemed assured. Then came the war.

Victor Smith was one of the first to volunteer for active service. On 10 October 1914 he was gazetted as second lieutenant to the 2/5th East Lancashire Regiment. He served at the Burnley depot and at Southport before volunteering, with four more officers, to join a reinforcements draft for the 1/5th East Lancashires, then in Egypt. He arrived in Port Said on 11 April 1915, and after a course in Cairo he joined the battalion on 4 May. Four days later, the unit sailed as part of the 42nd East Lancashire Division for Gallipoli, going ashore at Cape Helles on 13 May. Together with several other officers from the newly arrived division, Smith was attached to a unit of the 29th Division as a means of gaining combat experience and filling gaps. During his early days on the peninsula, he saw fighting with the Royal Munster Fusiliers and the King's Own Scottish Borderers.

At the end of July he was evacuated to Alexandria, suffering from a bout of dysentery. A spell of convalescence followed in Cyprus before he sailed for Mudros, where he underwent a course in bombing, a form of warfare still new to many of the troops on the peninsula. Gaining first-class passes, he was appointed brigade bombing officer, a post which took him back to his unit at Cape Helles. There, his popularity and optimism in the face of great adversity helped lift

A memorial to A.V. Smith

morale. Years afterwards, one veteran would remember him leading them in a 'sing-song' on Gully Beach after coming out of the line.

Throughout the fighting and the harsh autumn weather, Smith's own morale appears never to have flagged. At a time when most men's thoughts were turning to evacuation, he was to be found risking his life on patrols and bombing operations. It was little wonder that he was held in such awe by his men. Ingham Ridehalgh, his bombing sergeant and himself a veteran of Omdurman, said of him: 'I, or any of the men, would have followed "Vic" anywhere. He was like one of us, and a better officer I never saw.'

The telegram announcing Victor Smith's death arrived at his parents' home in Burnley less than two hours after his postcard wishing them a happy Christmas. Almost a year to the day after their son's final gallant gesture, William and Louisa Smith went to Buckingham Palace to receive the Victoria Cross. A few days before, a portrait of the young VC winner by the artist John Cooke was unveiled amid much civic pomp in Burnley. Today the painting is still displayed in the Towneley Hall Museum, together with his VC and Croix de Guerre, posthumously awarded by the President of France. Other memorials to the Gallipoli Campaign's last VC can be found in St Albans Cathedral, St Catherine's Church, Burnley, and St John's Parish Church, Blackpool. The magnificent bronze tablet on the wall of St John's Church features a likeness of Victor Smith, between impressions of his two gallantry awards, with the inscription, which serves as a fitting epitaph:

> In Remembrance
> Of a gallant soldier one in
> heart and ever loyal to duty
> A VICTOR SMITH VC
> Lieutenant 5th Batt East Lancashire
> Regiment, Inspector of the Blackpool
> Police, this memorial is dedicated
> Less than 25 years but crowned with
> the love than which no Man hath greater
> in the words of his commanding officer
> HE GAVE HIS LIFE TO SAVE OTHERS
> at
> Fusilier Bluff Gallipoli Peninsula
> December 23rd, 1915
> By throwing himself upon a live
> grenade and was awarded the
> Victoria Cross and the Croix de Guerre
> for this magnificent act of self
> sacrifice which saved many lives.

SOURCES

The sources used in the preparation of this book include the following:

The Lummis VC files at the National Army Museum, London
The Victoria Cross files at the Imperial War Museum, London
The Public Record Office, Kew, Surrey
Regimental Museums and Archives
The London Gazette 1914–20 (HMSO)

E.G. Robinson
Dardanelles Details, Naval Review 24, Capt. B.H. Smith, 1936
Dardanelles Dilemma, E.K. Chatterton, Rich & Cowan, 1935
Britain's Sea Soldiers, A History of the Royal Marines, 1914–1919, Gen. Sir H.E. Blumberg
Operations in the Dardanelles, Reports on Minesweeping, (PRO)
The Times

C. Bromley, R.R. Willis, A.J. Richards, F.E. Stubbs, J.E. Grimshaw and W. Keneally
The Landing of the 89th Infantry Brigade, H.M. Farmar, Sackville Press, n.d.
With the 29th Division in Gallipoli, Revd O. Creighton, Longmans, Green & Co., 1916
The History of the Lancashire Fusiliers, 1914–1918, J.C. Latter, Gale & Polden, 1949
The Lancashire Fusiliers' Annual
Gallipoli Gazette
Lancashire HQ, Royal Regt of Fusiliers
'The Landing in Gallipoli', Maj. R.R. Willis VC, *Gallipoli Gazette*, July 1934
Memoir and documents relating to Sgt. A.J. Richards VC (IWM)
War Diary, 1st Bn Lancashire Fusiliers (PRO)
Wigan Observer
Wigan Examiner
Hull Times
The *Daily Mail*
St Paul's School, Barnes

E. Unwin, G.L. Drewry, W. St A. Malleson, A.W. St C. Tisdall, W.C. Williams and G.McK. Samson
Case of Sub-Lt. A.W. St Clair Tisdall, RNVR (PRO)
Verses, Letters and Remembrances of Arthur Walderne St Clair Tisdall VC, Sub-Lieutenant RNVR, Sidgwick & Jackson, 1916.
At Antwerp and the Dardanelles, Revd H.C. Foster, Mills & Boon, 1918
Capt. E. Unwin VC, letters (Capt. H.C. Lockyer collection, IWM)

Eye-witness accounts of Unwin VC action (PRO)
H. St A. Malleson
J. McWilliam (daughter of W. St A. Malleson VC)
J.P. Macintyre
The First World War Letters of Lieut G.L. Drewry VC (IWM)
The Immortal Gamble, A.T. Stewart and Revd C.J.E. Peshall, A & C Black Ltd, 1917
Chepstow Museum
Carnoustie Library
Asbourne Telegraph
South Wales Argus
The Times

C.H.M. Doughty-Wylie and G.N. Walford
Doughty-Wylie Papers, The Regimental Museum, Royal Welch Fusiliers
Regimental Records of the Royal Welch Fusiliers, Vol. 4, D. Ward, 1928
Lt. Col. G.B. Stoney DSO, (ms, letters, IWM)
The Landing at V Beach, Gallipoli, Lt. Col. H.E. Tizard (ts, IWM)
L.O. Doughty-Wylie (letters, diary, IWM)
Dictionary of National Biography, 1912–1921
Harrow School archives
Gallipoli 1915, P. Liddle, Brasseys, 1985

W. Cosgrove
War Diary, 1st Bn Royal Munster Fusiliers (PRO)
The Irish at the Front, M. MacDonagh, Hodder & Stoughton, 1916
Cork Examiner
Cork Holly Bough
The Rangoon Gazette

W.R. Parker
Case of Lance-Corporal W.R. Parker, RMLI (PRO)
The Royal Marines Victoria Crosses, M.G. Little, Royal Marines Museum, n.d.
Britain's Sea Soldiers, A History of the Royal Marines, 1914–1919, Gen. Sir H.E. Blumberg, Swiss & Company, 1929
Royal Marines Museum
V.C. de Ville (daughter)
Nottingham Evening Post
Nottinghamshire Guardian

E.C. Boyle
Report of Proceedings of Submarine E14, April 27–May 18, 1915 (RN Submarine Museum)
Diary of Ldg Seaman J.T. Haskins, DSM (IWM)
Passage of the Dardanelles by E14, E.G. Stanley, DSC (RN Submarine Museum)
By Guess and By God, W.G. Carr, Hutchinson, 1930

SOURCES

M.E. Nasmith
Some Recollections of Submarine Work in the Sea of Marmora in 1915, M.E. Nasmith (IWM)
Report of Proceedings of Submarine E11, May 19–June 7, 1915 (IWM)
Dardanelles Patrol, P. Shankland and A. Hunter, Collins, 1964

A. Jacka
Jacka, VC, I. Grant, Macmillan in association with the Australian War Memorial, 1989
Australian Dictionary of Biography
The History of the 14th Battalion, AIF, N. Wanliss, Arrow Printery, 1929
Jacka's Mob, E.J. Rule, Angus & Robertson, 1933

G.R.D. Moor
War Diary, 2nd Bn, The Hampshire Regt (PRO)
RHQ, Royal Hampshire Regt
History of the Royal Hampshire Regt, Vol II, C.T. Atkinson, Gale & Polden, 1950
Regimental Journal
Playing With Strife, Lt. Gen. Sir Philip Neame VC, KBE, CB, DSO, Harrap, 1947
North Devon Journal
Braunton Museum
The Cheltenham Society

H. James
Regimental HQ, Worcestershire and Sherwood Foresters Regt
The Worcestershire Regiment in the Great War, Capt. H. FitzM. Stacke, G.T. Cheshire &
Sons, n.d.
War Diary, 4th Bn Worcestershire Regt (PRO)
Letters to the Official Historian (PRO)
The Firm (Regimental Journal)
The Royal Scots 1914–1919, Maj. J. Ewing, Oliver & Boyd, 1925
Birmingham Post
Birmingham Mail
Birmingham Gazette
A.H. James (correspondence)

G.R. O'Sullivan, J. Somers
Regimental Office, Royal Irish Rangers
The Royal Inniskilling Fusiliers in the World War, Sir Frank Fox, Constable, 1928
War Diary, 1st Bn Royal Inniskilling Fusiliers (PRO)
Letters to the Official Historian (PRO)
Wimbledon College
The Guardian, Cloughjordan
The Tipperary Star
The Anglo-Celt Cavan

P.H. Hansen
Eton College
Royal Lincolnshire Regt. Museum

News of the World
Public Record Office
History of the Lincolnshire Regt, 1914–1919, Maj.-Gen. C.R. Simpson, Medici Society,
1931
Diary and papers of Sgt. H.J. Gibbons (IWM)
The Lincolnshire Chronicle

W.T. Forshaw
War Diary, 1/9th Bn Manchester Regt. (PRO)
The 42nd (East Lancashire) Division 1914–1918, F. Gibbon, Country Life Library, 1920
Museum of the Manchesters, Ashton-under-Lyne
Tameside Local Studies Library, Stalybridge
Furness Museum, Barrow-in-Furness
The Barrovian
The Morning Post
The Ashton Reporter

D.R. Lauder
RHQ, The Royal Highland Fusiliers
War Diary, 1/4th Bn, Royal Scots Fusiliers (PRO)
History of the Royal Scots Fusiliers 1678–1918, John Buchan, Thos Nelson & Sons, 1925
T.R. Lauder, V. Lauder
The 52nd (Lowland) Division 1914–1918, Lt. Col. R.R. Thompson, MC, MacLehose,
Jackson & Co., 1923
Glasgow Herald
Glasgow Evening News
Sunday Mail

**F.H. Tubb, A.J. Shout, W.J. Symons, W. Dunstan, A.S. Burton, L.M. Keysor and
J. Hamilton**
Diary of Frederick H. Tubb VC (via H. Murray Hamilton)
The Seventh Battalion, AIF, A. Dean and E.W. Gutteridge, 1933
Capt. A.J. Shout VC, brief memoir (via A. Staunton), Ferguson & Osborn, n.d.
The First Battalion, 1914–1919, B.V. Stacey, F.J. Kindon, H.V. Chedgley, 1931
Randwick to Hargicourt, History of the Third Battalion, AIF, E. Wren, R.G. McDonald,
1935
No Brains At All, K. Dunstan, Viking, 1990
Australian Dictionary of Biography
Ballarat Courier
Bendigo Advertiser
Canberra Times
Euroa Gazette
The Age
Melbourne Herald
Melbourne Argus
Melbourne Sun

SOURCES

Reveille
Mufti

C.R.G. Bassett
Taped interview with C.R.G. Bassett VC (Liddle Collection, Leeds University)
Where the Prize is Highest, G. Bryant, Collins, 1972
New Zealand VC Winners, J. Sanders
The New Zealanders at Gallipoli, F. Waite, Whitcombe & Tombs, 1921
Gallipoli: The New Zealand Story, C.J. Pugsley, 1984
New Zealand Herald

F.W.O. Potts
The Gallipolian
The London Magazine
I Was There, Vol. 1, 1914–16, Amalgamated Press, 1938
The Reading Standard
The Reading Observer
The Berkshire Yeomanry Museum
History of the Berkshire Yeomanry (unpub)

H.V.H. Throssell
My Father's Son, R. Throssell, Mandarin, 1990
Westralian Cavalry in the War, A.C.N. Olden, Alexander McCubbin, n.d.
Australian Dictionary of Biography
The West Australian

R. Bell Davies
Flying Logbook of R. Bell Davies VC, DSO (Fleet Air Arm Museum)
Sailor in the Air, Vice-Admiral R. Bell Davies VC, CB, DSO, AFC, Peter Davies, 1967
Fights and Flights, Air Commodore C.R. Samson CMG, DSO, AFC, Ernest Benn, 1930
For Valour: The Air VCs, C. Bowyer, Grub Street Aviation Classics, 1992
RNAS Wing War Diary (PRO)

A.V. Smith
The 42nd East Lancashire Division 1914–1918, F. Gibbon, Country Life Library, 1920
War Diary, 1/5th Bn East Lancashire Regt (PRO)
Towneley Hall Art Gallery and Museum, Burnley
Burnley Express and Advertiser
Burnley News
Blackpool Times
West Lancashire Evening Gazette
Hertfordshire and the War, n.d.

BIBLIOGRAPHY

Ashmead-Bartlett, E. *The Uncensored Dardanelles*, Hutchinsons, 1928

Aspinall-Oglander, C.F. *Military Operations Gallipoli*, Vols 1 and 2, Heinemann, 1929 and 1932

Bancroft, J.W. *Devotion to Duty*, Aim High, 1990

Bean, C.E.W. *Official History of Australia in the War: The Story of Anzac*, Vols 1 and 2, (Third edition, 1934), Angus & Robertson

Boyle, W.H.D. *Gallant Deeds*, Gieves, 1919

Brodie, C.G. *Forlorn Hope*, Frederick Books, 1915, 1956

Compton-Hall, R. *Submarines and the War at Sea 1914–1918*, Macmillan, 1991

Crook, M.J. *The Evolution of the Victoria Cross*, Midas Books, 1975

Gillam, J. *Gallipoli Diary* (reprint), Strong Oak Press with Tom Donovan Publishing, 1989

Halpern, P.G. *The Keyes Papers 1914–1918*, Vol. 1, Navy Records Society, 1972

Hamilton, Sir Ian. *Gallipoli Diary*, Vols 1 and 2, 1920, Arnold

James, R. Rhodes. *Gallipoli*, Batsford, 1965

Jameson, W. *Submariners V.C.* Davies, 1962

Jerrold, D. *The Royal Naval Division*, Hutchinsons, 1923

Liddle, P. *Men of Gallipoli*, Allen Lane, 1976

Lisle, Sir B. de. *Reminiscences of Sport and War*, Eyre & Spottiswoode,1939

Mackenzie, C. *Gallipoli Memories*, Cassell, 1929

Nevinson, H.W. *The Dardanelles Campaign*, Nisbet, 1918

Steel, N. *The Battlefields of Gallipoli Then and Now*, Leo Cooper, 1990

Stoker, H.G. *Straws in the Wind*, Herbert Jenkins, 1925

This England Register of the Victoria Cross, 1981

Usborne, C.V. *Smoke on the Horizon*, Hodder & Stoughton, 1933

Walker, R.W. *To What End Did They Die*, R.W. Walker Publishing, 1985

Wester Wemyss, Lady. *The Life and Letters of Lord Wester Wemyss, Admiral of the Fleet*, Eyre & Spottiswoode, 1935

Wester Wemyss, Lord. *The Navy in the Dardanelles Campaign*, Hodder & Stoughton, 1924

Wigmore, L., and Harding, B. *They Dared Mightily*, Australian War Memorial, 1963

Williams, W.A. *The VCs of Wales and the Welsh Regiments*, Bridge Books, 1984

Winton, J. *The Victoria Cross at Sea*, Michael Joseph, 1979

INDEX